Introduction to the Devout Life

Introduction to the Devout Life

BY

St. Francis de Sales

KALPAZ

ISBN: 978-93-5128-503-8

First Published in 1891
Indian Reprint in 2017

Published by

Kalpaz Publications
C-30, Satyawati Nagar,
Delhi – 110052
E-mail: kalpaz@hotmail.com
Website: kalpazpublications.com
Ph.: +91-9212142040

Cataloging in Publication Data—DK
Courtesy: D.K. Agencies (P) Ltd. <docinfo@dkagencies.com>

Francis, *de Sales, Saint,* 1567-1622., author.
[Introduction à la vie dévote. English]
Introduction to the devout life / by St. Francis de Sales.
pages cm
Translated from French.
"First published in 1891"—Title page verso.
ISBN 9789351285038

1. Meditations. I. Title.

BX2179.F8I54 2017 DDC 248.482 23

Sketch of the Life of St. Francis of Sales

ST. FRANCIS OF SALES was the eldest son of Francis, Count of Sales, the head of an ancient and noble family, seated at the Chateau of Sales, near Annecy, in Savoy; he was born at the family seat, Aug. 21, 1567. His mother, Frances of Sionas, a woman of exemplary holiness, took the greatest pains to bring up her son in innocence and the knowledge and love of God. She often repeated to him those words of Queen Blanche to her son St. Louis, "I had rather see you dead than hear that you had committed one mortal sin"—words which he quotes in the Devout Life. Her prayers and pains were abundantly rewarded; for the boy grew up of a sweet and good disposition, handsome in person, of great intelligence, and from his earliest years upwards remarkable for his purity of life and earnest devotion. He was educated at the neighbouring College of Annecy till twelve years of age, and was then sent to the University of Paris, where his principal teacher was the celebrated Maldonatus; at eighteen he went, for the special study of law, to Padua, where he was the favourite pupil of the famous Guy Pancirola; at twenty he finished his university career with a considerable reputation, and travelled for some time. His father had great hopes of the future of so promising a son; and by the time of his return home, had obtained for him of his Sovereign, the Duke of Savoy, the important post of Counsellor of the Parliament of Chambery, and had also arranged a marriage for him with a young lady whose beauty, rank, fortune, and goodness, made her a most desirable match.

Francis had, however, resolved upon entering the service of God in the ministry of the Church, and his father, with some natural disappointment and hesitation, consented to give up to God the son who, he had fondly hoped, would worthily support the family honours and be a guardian to a numerous family of brothers and sisters.

The Count desired that Francis should still accept the office which had been obtained for him, which was quite compatible, according to the custom of the times, with his clerical character, but he resolutely refused, desiring to give himself entirely to the proper work of the ministry. His cousin, Louis of Sales, Canon of Annecy, had, however, in the meantime, obtained for him the Provostship of the Church of Annecy, in which the Episcopal see was then fixed, since the Calvinists had driven the Bishops out of Geneva. This office, with some difficulty, the young deacon was induced to accept.

The Bishop immediately employed him in preaching; he showed great zeal in the work, and his ability and the fervour of his preaching stirred up the Catholics and made many conversions from among the Calvinists, who were numerous in the diocese.

In 1594, Duke Charles Emmanuel of Savoy recovered the sovereignty of the Duchy of Chablais and other districts about the Lake of Geneva, of which the Canton of Berne had dispossessed his family sixty years before. The Duke was desirous that steps should be taken to recover the inhabitants to the Catholic Church, and commended the work to the Bishop. Francis volunteered for this duty, which, owing to the bigoted fierceness of the people, was one of personal danger, and his cousin, Canon Louis, accompanied him. When they reached the frontier of the district they dismissed their horses and servants, and the two entered upon their mission in apostolic simplicity, as well as with apostolic zeal. For four years he laboured with great diligence, amidst violent opposition and in frequent danger, and with little success; but then his labours began to bear fruit, which rapidly increased until 40,000 or 50,000 of the people, it is said, were converted; and at length, in 1598, the Catholic religion was publicly reinstated throughout the district. The Calvinists ascribed principally to his meekness the wonderful conversions which he made among them. He had several conferences with Theodore Beza; and his biographers claim that Francis had good hopes of winning that great light of the Reformed religion back to the Catholic pale, which death, however, frustrated. The wisdom and success with which he had accomplished this great work made him famous beyond the bounds of his own country.

The Bishop of Geneva now sought to have Francis appointed as his coadjutor in the see. On his nomination, he went to Rome to ask for the papal benediction, and was received with great distinction.

In 1599, a war which Savoy had waged with France, terminated in the cession of the Bailiwick of Gex to the French monarchy, and St. Francis was sent by the Duke to arrange with Henry IV. for the interests of the Catholic religion in the ceded territory. He was received with the highest respect at the French Court. His sermons made a great impression, and here too he made some illustrious converts from among the Huguenots. The impression we have already gathered as to the cause of his power over opponents is confirmed by the saying of Cardinal Perron, who was a famous controversialist: "I can confute the Calvinists," he said, "but to persuade and convert them you must carry them to the coadjutor of Geneva." The King tried in vain to induce him, by the offer of the first vacant bishopric, to settle in France. On a subsequent occasion he offered to nominate him for the Cardinalate, an honour which he also declined. While returning home he heard of the death of the Bishop of Geneva, and his own consequent succession to the see. He at once retired to the Chateau of Sales, and prepared himself, by a twenty days' retreat, for his consecration. His subsequent life and labours, as represented by his biographers, were those of an ideal bishop. "In his house every thing was done as regularly as in a monastery. They rose, they attended prayer, they went to Divine Service, they sat down to meals, they took recreation, they retired, at fixed hours. His table was frugal, he dressed in woollen only, abstaining from silk and costly attire. The furniture and arrangement of his house, though dignified, were perfectly plain. He rose every day at four o'clock, and observed an exact economy of time. Every day he said mass; he said office on his knees. He fasted every Friday and Saturday. On Sundays and festivals he attended the Cathedral. He was always present at the feasts of devotion kept in any of the churches of the town. Every year he made a retreat of ten days. The alms he gave were wonderful, considering the limited means of his see. In his diocese he set himself to reform morals, he ordered his clergy to catechize on Sundays and holidays throughout the year, and on every day during Lent. He inquired strictly into the real fitness of candidates for ordination; he reformed several monasteries; established machinery for the higher branches of a liberal education at the Cathedral city. He diligently visited his diocese, going on foot to the remote villages among the mountains, and taking delight in preaching to the poor."

He was famous not only as an Evangelist and as a Bishop but also as a Director of Souls. The gentleness and sweetness of his character attracted penitents to pour their sins and sorrows into his ear; his purity and love and zeal inspired them with holy resolutions of amendment; and his works prove that he possessed great skill as well as tenderness and zeal in dealing with the soul.

In 1610 he founded the Congregation of the Visitation of the Blessed Virgin, Madame de Chantal being the first Mother. He had observed that many women desired to live a religious live who were prevented by advanced years or bodily infirmity or weakness of constitution from encountering the austerities of other religious orders. He founded this congregation to receive such persons, and the principles on which he founded it are specially interesting in the present revival among us of the Religious Life. His design was to unite the comtemplative and active elements of the Religious Life in proportions so nicely adjusted that they might aid one another. In place of outward austerities, of which aged and infirm people were incapable, he inculcated the practice of interior mortifications. The dress was of the same fashion as people wore in the world, only black in colour and without ornament. The sisters were to go about visiting the sick. The houses were to be endowed, but individual poverty carefully observed. The order was to have no general; but the individual houses were to be under the government of the bishop of the diocese in which they were situated. Afterwards the Saint was led to remodel his congregation into a cloistered order with a habit and rule, retaining the other principles of his original plan. The order spread into various countries, and became numerous and famous, so that at the date of his canonization in 1645, after it had been established only forty-five years, it numbered 130 houses. He died in 1622, at the age of fifty-six, in the twentieth year of his episcopacy.

St. Francis wrote a book on the Love of God, Sermons, Letters, Preparation for the Mass, and Instructions to Confessors, but his best known work is the Introduction to the Devout Life. He himself relates in the Preface what was the origin of the work. That he thought it but a slight performance is only another illustration of the truth that what a man does best he often does easiest, and does not appreciate its value because it has cost him no effort. But it, at once, obtained a wide circulation, and has ever since been held in the highest esteem. It may, perhaps, be put on a level with the Imitation of Christ, and the Spiritual Combat.

In adapting a new translation of it to the use of members of the English Church, the Editor has laid down for himself the principle of making as few omissions and alterations as possible. He has sometimes, perhaps, in pursuing this principle, gone to the very edge of what is permissible in the English Church, and beyond what he himself would recommend; but it seemed desirable rather to leave it to the discretion of the reader to make some reservation in accepting a passage here and there than to leave him continually in doubt whether he had or had not before him the authentic work of the great Author. It is suprising how few omissions and alterations it has been found necessary, on this principle, to make. Two whole chapters have been omitted, one for doctrinal reasons, the other because it relates to subjects which it seems undesirable to retain in a work intended for indiscriminate circulation,[1] and a few other passages are also omitted, in which the reader is desired to invoke the Saints, or to seek the intercession of the Blessed Virgin. The alterations are chiefly the substitution of the term Holy Communion or Holy Eucharist for that of Mass where-ever it occurs.

1 They are Part I. chap. xvi. Of honouring and invoking the Saints and Angels. Part II. chap. xxxix. Of the honesty of the marriage bed.

A Dedicatory Prayer of the Author

O SWEET JESUS, my Lord, my Saviour, and my God, behold me prostrate before the Majesty, devoting and consecrating this work to Thy glory ; give life to its words by Thy blessing, so that the souls for which I have made it may receive from it the sacred inspirations which I desire for them ; and particularly that of imploring for me Thy infinite mercy, to the end that, while I show others the way of devotion in this world, I may not myself be eternally rejected and confounded in the other; but that, with them, I may for ever sing, for a canticle of triumph, the words which, with my whole heart, I pronounce, in testimony of my fidelity, amidst the chances of this mortal life : *Live Jesus, live Jesus ; yea, Lord Jesus, live and reign in our hearts for ever and ever. Amen.*

The Author's Preface

My Dear Reader, I beg you to read this Preface for your satisfaction and for mine

GLYCERA, the flower girl, knew so well how to diversify the combination and arrangement of her flowers, as with the same flowers to make a great variety of nosegays. So that when the painter Pausias tried to emulate her skill he failed, for he could not vary his painting so many ways as Glycera did her nosegays. Thus the Holy Ghost disposes and arranges, with so much variety, the instructions of devotion which He gives us by the tongues and pens of His servants, that, although the doctrines are always the same, the treatises which are made out of them are very different, according to the different ways in which they are put together. I certainly neither can, nor wish, nor ought to write, in this Introduction, anything but what has been already published by those who have written before me on this subject. The flowers which I offer you are the same as theirs; but the nosegay which I have made of them differs from theirs, because it is made up in a different way.

Almost all who have hitherto treated of devotion

have had in view the instruction of persons wholly retired from the world, or at least have taught a kind of devotion leading to this absolute retirement. My intention is to instruct such as live in towns, or families, or at court, and who, by their condition, are obliged to lead, as to externals, the ordinary life. Such persons often will not even consider the question of undertaking the devout life, under pretext of its supposed impossibility in their circumstances, for in their opinion as no beast dares to taste the seed of the herb *Palma Christi*, so no man ought to aspire to the palm of Christian piety as long as he lives in the bustle of temporal affairs. Now I shall show them, that as the mother-of-pearl fish lives in the sea without taking in a drop of salt-water, and as there are near the Chelidonian islands springs of fresh water in the midst of the sea, and as the fire-flies fly in the flames without singeing their wings, so a strong and steadfast soul can live in the world without imbibing any worldly humour—can find springs of sweet piety in the middle of the salt-waters of the age—and fly amidst the flames of earthly lusts without burning the wings of the holy desires of the devout life. It is true that this is difficult, and therefore I could wish that many would endeavour to accomplish it with more ardour than has been hitherto done; and I, weak as I am, shall endeavour by this treatise to contribute some help to those who, with a generous heart, shall undertake so worthy an enterprise.

Yet it is not altogether by my own choice or inclination that this Introduction is made public. A soul full of honour and virtue, having sometime ago received from God grace to desire to lead the devout life, requested my special aid for that purpose, and I, having many ties of duty towards her, and having long remarked in her a great disposition for this undertaking, applied myself very earnestly to instruct her well; and having led her through all the exercises suitable to her design and her condition of life, I left with her written notes to which she might have recourse when she found it needful. She subsequently communicated these writings to a famous, learned, and devout religious, who, judging that others might derive profit from them, earnestly exhorted me to make them public. It was not difficult for him to persuade me, because his friendship had great influence over my will, and his judgment great weight with mine.

In order, however, that the whole might be more useful and agreeable, I have revised it and put it into some sort of order, adding several directions and instructions in furtherance of my design. But I have done all this with scarcely any leisure, for which reason you will find nothing here like an exact treatise, but only a collection of well-intended directions, which I have delivered, or at least have desired to so do, in plain and intelligible language. And as to ornaments of style, I have not even cared to think about them, having too many other things to do.

I address my words to PHILOTHEA, because, desiring to accommodate to the general use of many souls what I originally wrote for one, it is convenient to make use of a name common to all who aspire to devotion, for PHILOTHEA means one who loves God. Regarding then throughout a soul which by the desire of devotion aspires to the love of God, I have divided this Introduction into five parts. In the first I endeavour, by certain exhortations and exercises, to convert the simple desire of Philothea into a settled resolution; this she makes in the end, after her general confession, by a firm protestation; and it is followed by the Holy Communion, in which, giving herself to her SAVIOUR and receiving HIM, she enters happily into His holy love. This done, to lead her onward, I show her two great means of uniting herself more and more to His Divine Majesty,—the use of the Sacraments, by which this good God comes to us, and prayer by which He draws us to Him; and with this I occupy the second part. In the third part, I point out to her how she ought to exercise herself in certain virtues which tend to her further advancement, dwelling on certain particular directions which she would not easily find elsewhere, or think of for herself. In the fourth part, I discover to her certain snares of her enemies, and show her how to avoid them, and proceed on her way. And finally, in the fifth part, I cause her to go apart for a while in order to refresh herself, to take breath, and to recruit her strength, in order that she may be able afterwards the more successfully to make progress, and press forward in the devout life.

This is a capricious age, and I foresee very well that some will say that it only belongs to religious and people who profess devotion to give such special directions concerning piety; that it requires more leisure than a Bishop can have, who is burdened with so heavy a diocese as mine; and that it will too much divert a mind which ought to be engaged in matters of importance. But, my dear reader, I say to you, with the great St. Denis, that it belongs especially to Bishops to lead souls to perfection, since their order is supreme among men as that of the seraphim among the angels, so that their leisure could not be better employed than in this work. The ancient Bishops and Fathers of the Church were at the least as devoted to their charges as we are; but that did not prevent them, as appears from their letters, from undertaking the care of the special direction of certain souls who applied to them for their aid. And in this they imitated the Apostles, who, though occupied with the whole harvest of the world, yet gathered some remarkable ears with a special and individual affection. Who does not know that Timothy, Titus, Onesimus, St. Thecla, and Appia, were the dear children of the great St. Paul; as St. Mark and St. Petronilla were of St. Peter—for St. Petronilla, as Baronius and Galonius learnedly prove, was not the carnal but only the spiritual daughter of St. Peter; and did not St. John, too, write one of his canonical epistles to the devout Lady Electa?

It is a labour, I confess, to guide individual souls, but a labour which brings its own reward, like that of the husbandmen in harvest and vintage, who are never better satisfied than when they have most to do. It is a labour which refreshes and revives the heart by the sweetness it brings to those who are engaged in it, as the cinnamon does in Arabia Felix to those who are laden with it. The tigress, they say, when she finds one of her cubs, which the hunter leaves in the road to occupy her while he carries off the rest of her litter, loads herself with it be it ever so big, and is none the heavier but rather lighter in the race she runs to put it safe in her den, natural love lightening her burden. How much more willingly does a paternal heart take charge of a soul which he has met with desiring to attain to holy perfection; carrying it in his bosom, as a mother carries her little child, without feeling the beloved burden. But, doubtless, it must be a paternal heart; and therefore it is that the Apostles and Apostolic men called their disciples not only their children, but, still more tenderly, their little children.

For the rest, my dear reader, it is true that I write of the devout life without being myself devout, but certainly not without the desire to become so; and it is this desire which gives me courage to undertake to instruct you. For as a famous learned man said: A good way to learn is to study, a better way is to hear, but the best way is to teach. "It often happens," said St. Augustine, writing to his devout Florentina, "that the ministration of giving makes us worthy to receive, and the ministration of teaching lays the foundation of learning."

Alexander caused the beautiful Campaspe, who was so dear to him, to be painted by the matchless Apelles. Apelles, compelled to gaze upon Campaspe, as fast as he drew her features in his picture imprinted the love of them on his heart, and became so enamoured, that Alexander, discovering it, and pitying him, gave her to him in marriage, depriving himself, for his sake, of her whom he most loved in the world. "In which," says Pliny, "he showed the greatness of his soul, as much as by some great victory."

Now, I am of opinion, my reader and friend, that because I am a Bishop God wills that I should paint upon the hearts of His people, not only common virtues, but also His dear and well-beloved devotion. And I undertake it willingly, not only out of obedience and sense of duty, but also in the hope that while impressing it upon the minds of others, my own may perchance become holily enamoured of it, and that His Divine Majesty, seeing me thus in love with it, may give it to me in an eternal marriage. The fair and chaste Rebecca, watering Isaac's camels, was chosen to be his wife, and received from him ear-rings and bracelets of gold. And so I promise myself, by the infinite goodness of my God, that for conducting His dear sheep to the wholesome waters of devotion, He will make my soul His spouse, putting into my ears the golden words of His holy love, and on my arms the strength to put them into practice, in which lies the essence of true devotion; and this I beseech His Divine Majesty to vouchsafe to give me, and to all the children of His Church, to which Church I desire ever to submit my writings, my actions, my words, my desires, my thoughts.

ANNECY. This day of St. Magdalen 1608.

Contents

PART THE SECOND

CONTAINING INSTRUCTIONS FOR ELEVATING THE SOUL TO GOD BY PRAYER AND THE SACRAMENTS

PART THE THIRD

CONTAINING CERTAIN COUNSELS CONCERNING THE PRACTICE OF THE VIRTUES

PART THE FOURTH

CONTAINING NECESSARY COUNSELS AGAINST THE MORE ORDINARY TEMPTATIONS

PART THE FIFTH

CONTAINING EXERCISES AND INSTRUCTIONS FOR RENEWING THE SOUL AND CONFIRMING HER IN DEVOTION

INTRODUCTION

TO

The Devout Life

Introduction to the Devout Life

PART THE FIRST

CONTAINING THE COUNSELS AND EXERCISES NECESSARY FOR CONDUCTING THE SOUL FROM ITS FIRST DESIRE FOR THE DEVOUT LIFE TO A FULL RESOLUTION TO EMBRACE IT

CHAPTER I

Description of True Devotion

YOU aspire to devotion, dearest Philothea, because, being a Christian, you know that it is a virtue very pleasing to the Divine Majesty. But inasmuch as the little faults which one falls into at the beginning of any work increase greatly as it progresses, and at last are almost irreparable, it is necessary, before everything else, that you should know what the virtue of devotion is. For since there is only one true kind of devotion, while there are many false and vain, if you do not know which is the true, you may deceive yourself, and waste your time in following some kind of devotion which is useless and superstitious. Aurelius painted all the faces of the personages in his pictures with the features of the women whom he loved; and so every one paints devotion according to his own desires and fancies. One who is given to fasting, esteems himself very devout provided he fasts, although his heart is full of rancour; and while he scruples to dip the tip of his tongue in wine, or even in water, out of temperance, he does not hesitate to plunge it into his neighbour's blood by slander and calumny. Another esteems himself devout because he says a great number of prayers every day, though afterwards his tongue indulges in all sorts of disagreeable, domineering, injurious speeches among his servants and neighbours. A third readily opens his purse to give alms to the poor, but will not open his heart to give forgiveness to his enemies; while another will forgive his enemies, but will never pay his creditors till the law makes him. All these people are commonly taken for devout people, but really they are nothing of the kind.

The servants of Saul sought David at his house. Michal put an image into his bed and covered it with David's clothes, and made them believe that it was David himself who was sick and asleep. Thus many people cover themselves with external practices which belong to devotion, and the world thinks that they are really devout and spiritual people, while in truth they are nothing but images and shadows of devotion. True and living devotion, O Philothea, presupposes the love of God, or rather it is nothing else than the true love of God; but not any kind of love; for inasmuch as the Divine love adorns our souls it is called grace, because it renders us pleasing to the Divine Majesty; inasmuch as it gives us strength to do good it is called charity; but when it has arrived at such a degree of perfection that it not only makes us do good, but makes us do it earnestly, frequently, with alacrity, then it is called devotion. Ostriches never fly; fowls fly heavily, low, and seldom; but eagles, doves, and swallows fly often, swiftly, and high; so sinners do not fly towards God, but all their goings are on the earth and for the earth; good people who have not yet attained to devotion fly towards God by good deeds, but seldom, slowly, and heavily; devout persons fly towards God often, promptly, and high. In short, devotion is nothing else but a certain spiritual lightness and vivacity, by means of which charity operates in us, or we by it, with alacrity and affection. And as it is the part of charity to make us perform all God's commandments generally and universally, it is the part of devotion to make us perform them promptly and diligently. Therefore he who does not observe all God's commands cannot be reckoned either good or devout; since, in order to be good, he must have charity, and to be devout he must have, over and above charity, a great vivacity and promptitude in charitable deeds. And since devotion consists in a certain eminent degree of charity, it not only makes us prompt, active, and diligent in the observation of all the commandments of God, but, over and above that, it provokes us to do promptly and with delight as many good works as we can, not only those which are commanded, but also those which are only of counsel or inspiration. For just as a man newly cured of some sickness walks as much as is needful, but slowly and heavily, so is it with the sinner healed of his sin; he walks as much as God commands him, but slowly and heavily, until he has attained devotion; and then, like a man perfectly whole, he not only walks, he runs, he leaps in the way of God's commandments; and still more, he enters upon and runs in the paths of heavenly counsels and inspirations. In short, charity and devotion do not differ from one another more than flame from fire, for charity is a spiritual fire, which, when intensely inflamed, is called devotion. So that devotion adds no thing to the fire of charity except the flame which renders charity prompt, active, and diligent, not only in the observation of God's commandments, but also in the practice of heavenly counsels and inspirations.

CHAPTER II

The Nature and Excellency of Devotion

1. THEY who discouraged the Israelites from going into the promised land, told them it was a country which devoured its inhabitants, meaning that the

air was so unwholesome, that it was impossible to live long there ; and that, on the other hand, the natives were such monsters, that they ate up other men like grasshoppers. So the world (my dear Philothea) defames holy devotion as much as it can ; representing devout persons with a vexed, sad, and gloomy countenance ; declaring that devotion engenders melancholy and unsociable humours. But as Joshua and Caleb protested that the promised land was not only good and beautiful, but also that the acquisition of it would be easy and pleasant, so the Holy Ghost, by the mouths of all the saints, and our Saviour by His own mouth, assures us that a devout life is easy, happy, and desirable.

2. The world sees that devout people fast, pray, suffer injuries, serve the sick, give to the poor, watch, control their anger, repress and stifle their passions, deprive themselves of sensual pleasures, and do other acts which in themselves are sharp and rigorous ; but the world does not see the inward cordial devotion which renders all these actions agreeable, pleasant, and easy. Consider the bees upon the thyme : they find there a very bitter juice ; yet in sucking it they turn it into honey, because such is their nature. O worldlings ! it is true, devout souls find much bitterness in these exercises of mortification, but, in performing them, they convert them into sweetness and delight. Fire, flames, racks, swords, seemed flowers and perfumes to the martyrs, because they were devout. If, then, devotion can give a sweetness to the cruelest torments, and to death itself, what can it not do for virtuous actions? Sugar sweetens green fruits, and tempers the crudity and unwholesomeness of those which are ripe. Devotion is the true spiritual sugar, which takes away bitterness from mortification, and hurtfulness from consolation ; it takes away discontent from the poor man, and solicitude from the rich ; desolation from the oppressed, and insolence from the exalted ; sadness from the solitary, and dissoluteness from the merry companion : it serves for fire in winter, and dew in summer ; it knows how to abound, and how to suffer

want; it renders alike profitable honour and contempt; it entertains pleasure and pain almost with the same cheerfulness; and fills our souls with a wonderful sweetness.

3. Contemplate Jacob's ladder, for it is the true representation of a devout life. The two sides, between which we ascend, and in which the rounds are fastened, represent prayer which asks the love of God, and the sacraments which confer it; the rounds are nothing but the different degrees of charity, by which we advance from virtue to virtue; either descending, by action, to the help and support of our neighbour, or ascending, by contemplation, to a loving union with God. Now look (I beseech you) upon those who are on this ladder: they are either men who have angelical hearts, or angels who have human bodies. They are not young, yet they seem so, because they are full of spiritual vigour and activity. They have wings to fly, and soar up to God in holy prayer; but they have feet also to walk with men, by a holy and friendly conversation. Their faces are beautiful and cheerful, because they receive all things with sweetness and content; their legs, arms, and heads are all uncovered, because their thoughts, affections, and actions, have no other design nor motive than to please God; the rest of their bodies is covered, but only with a beautiful and light robe, to show that they make use, indeed, of the world and worldly things, yet in a most pure and upright manner, only taking sparingly what is necessary for their condition. Such are devout persons. Believe me (dear Philothea), devotion is the pleasure of pleasures, and the queen of virtues. It is the perfection of charity. If charity be milk, devotion is the cream; if charity be a plant, devotion is its flower; if charity be a precious stone, devotion is its lustre; if charity be a precious balm, devotion is its odour; yes, the odour of sweetness which comforts men and rejoices angels.

Chapter III

That Devotion is suitable to all sorts of Vocations and Professions

1. IN the creation, God commanded the plants to bring forth their fruits, every one according to its kind ; even so He commands Christians, who are the living plants of the Church, to bring forth their fruits of devotion, every one according to his condition and vocation. Devotion ought to be practised differently by the gentleman, by the workman, by the servant, by the prince, by the widow, by the maiden, and by the married woman : and not only so, but the practice of devotion must be accommodated also to the capacity, the employment, and the obligations of each one in particular. For (I pray you, Philothea) would it be fitting for a bishop to desire to be as retired as a Carthusian ; and for married people not to lay by any more than Capuchins ; if the artizan should be all day in church, like a monk ; and the religious continually open to all manner of calls for the service of his neighbour, like a bishop ; would not such devotion be ridiculous, unreasonable, and insupportable? This fault, nevertheless, happens very often ; and the world, which does not discriminate or wish to discriminate between devotion and the indiscretion of those who pretend to be devout, blames and murmurs at devotion, while it ought only to blame these disorders.

2. No, Philothea, devotion, when it is true, injures nothing, but rather makes all things perfect : and when it runs counter to any one's lawful vocation, then without doubt it is false devotion. The bee, says Aristotle, gathers honey from flowers without hurting them, leaving them as whole and fresh as it found them ; but true devotion does better still, for not only it does not injure any sort of calling or of business, but, on the

contrary, it adorns and beautifies them.

3. All kinds of precious stones, cast into honey, become more brilliant thereby, each one according to its colour ; and all persons become more acceptable in their vocation, when they join devotion with it ; household cares are thereby rendered tranquil, the love of husband and wife more sincere, the service of the prince more faithful, and all kinds of business more easy and pleasant.

4. It is an error, and even a heresy, to endeavour to banish the devout life from the ranks of soldiers, the shops of tradesmen, the courts of princes, or the households of married people. It is true, Philothea, that devotion, purely contemplative, monastical, and religious, cannot be exercised in these vocations ; but besides these three sorts of devotion, there are divers others suitable for perfecting those who live in secular conditions. Abraham, Isaac, and Jacob, David, Job, Tobias, Sarah, Rebecca, and Judith, bear witness of this in the Old Testament ; and in the New, St. Joseph, Lydia, and St. Crispin, were perfectly devout in their shops. St. Anne, St. Martha, St. Monica, Aquilla, Priscilla, in their households ; Cornelius, St. Sebastian, St. Maurice, in the profession of arms ; Constantine, Helen, St. Louis, St, Amadeus, and St. Edward, on their holy thrones. It has even happened that many have lost perfection in solitude, which, notwithstanding, is so much to be desired for perfection ; and have preserved it in company, which seems so little favourable to perfection. Lot, says St. Gregory, who was so chaste in the city, defiled himself in solitude. Wheresoever we are, we may and ought to aspire to the perfect life.

Chapter IV

Of the necessity of a Guide for entering upon and making progress in Devotion

1. YOUNG Tobias[1] being commanded to go to Rages, answered, *I know not the way thither: go then* (replied his father), *and seek thee a man which may go with thee.* I say the same to you, my Philothea; would you in good earnest walk in the way of devotion, seek some good man who may go with you and guide you: this is the advice of advices. Though you search, says the devout Avila, you will never so assuredly find the will of God as by the way of this humble obedience, so much recommended and practised by all the ancient saints. The blessed mother Teresa, seeing that Lady Catherine of Cardona performed such great penances, desired much to imitate her therein, against the advice of her confessor, who forbade her. And when she was much tempted to disobey in that particular, God said to her, Daughter, thou art in a good and safe way: seest thou her penances? but I value more thy obedience. And hence she so highly esteemed this virtue, that besides the obedience due to her superiors, she vowed a particular one to a man of excellent perfection, obliging herself to follow his direction and guidance, by which she was infinitely comforted; like many devout souls before and after her, who, for the more entire resignation of themselves to God, have submitted their wills to that of His servants; which St. Catherine of Sienna highly applauds in her Dialogues. The devout princess, St. Elizabeth, submitted herself with an exemplary obedience to Conrad. And one of the advices given by the great St. Louis to his son, a little before his death, was this: Confess often, choose an able and upright confessor, who can instruct thee to do those things which are needful for thee.

[1] Tobit v. 2 4 (Vulgate).

2. "*A faithful friend*" (says the Holy Scripture) "*is a strong defence; he that hath found such an one hath found a treasure. A faithful friend is the medicine of life, and they that fear the Lord shall find him.*"[2] These divine words (as you may see) chiefly regard immortality, for which it is necessary, above all things, to have this faithful friend, who may guide our actions by his directions and counsels, and by this means save us from the ambushes and wiles of the Evil one. He will be to us a treasure of wisdom in our afflictions, sorrows, and falls; he will serve us for a cordial to refresh and comfort our hearts in spiritual diseases: he will preserve us from evil, and make what is good in us better: and when any infirmity shall befall us, he will hinder it from being mortal, for he will recover us.

3. But who shall find this friend? The wise man answers, "*They that fear the Lord:*" that is, the humble, who earnestly desire their spiritual advancement. Since then it concerns you so much, Philothea, to go with a good guide in this holy journey of devotion, beseech God with great fervency to grant you one according to His own heart; and doubt not, for He will send you an angel from heaven, as He did to young Tobias, rather than fail to give you a good and faithful one.

4. And he ought always to be an angel to you: that is to say, when you have found him, do not consider him simply as a man, and do not confide in him, or in his human knowledge, but in God, who will help you and speak to you, by means of this man, putting into his heart and his mouth whatsoever shall be requisite for your happiness: so you ought to listen to him as to an angel descended from heaven to conduct you thither. Deal with him with an open heart, in all sincerity and fidelity; manifesting clearly to him your good and your evil without pretence or dissimulation: and by this means your good shall be tried and more assured, and your evil shall be corrected and amended; you shall be relieved and strengthened by him in your afflictions, and moderated and regulated in your consolations. Place in him an entire confidence

2 Ecclus vi. 14-16.

mixed with a holy reverence, in such sort that the reverence may not diminish the confidence, nor the confidence destroy the reverence due to him. Confide in him with the respect of a daughter towards her father: respect him with the confidence of a son towards his mother. In a word, this friendship ought to be firm and sweet, altogether holy, sanctified, divine, and spiritual.

5. To this end, choose one amongst a thousand, saith Avila, but I say one amongst ten thousand; for there are fewer than one would imagine who are capable of this office. He must be full of charity, skill, and good sense. If any one of these three qualities be wanting in him, there is danger; and therefore I say again, ask him of God, and having obtained him, bless his Divine Majesty; remain constant, and seek no other, but rather go on with him simply, humbly, and confidently, for you will have a most happy journey.

Chapter V

That we must begin with the Purifying of the Soul

1. THE flowers *appear on the earth*[1] (says the sacred spouse), *the time of pruning is come.* What are the flowers of our hearts, O Philothea, but good desires? Now as soon as they appear, the hand must be put to the knife, to prune off from our consciences all dead and superfluous works. The alien maid, in order to be married to an Israelite, was required to put off the robe of her captivity, to pare her nails, and shave her hair; and the soul that aspires to the honour of being a spouse of the Son of God, ought to put off the old man, and put on the new, by forsaking sin, and then to pare and shave away all manner of hindrances which may divert her from the love of God. The beginning of our health is to be purged from offensive hu-

[1] Canticles ii. 12 (Vulgate).

mours. St. Paul in a moment was cleansed with perfect purgation; so was St. Catherine of Genoa, St. M. Magdalen, St. Pelagia, and some others: but this sort of purgation is wholly miraculous and extraordinary in grace, as is the resurrection of the dead in nature, so that we ought not to pretend to it. The ordinary purifying and healing (whether of the body or the mind) is only effected by little and little, by going on from one step to another, with time and pains.

2. The angels upon Jacob's ladder have wings, yet they fly not, but ascend and descend in order, from step to step. The soul which rises from sin to devotion, is compared to the dawning of the morning, which drives not away the darkness in an instant, but by degrees.[2] The slow cure, says the proverb, is the safe cure. The diseases of the soul, as well as those of the body, come post-haste on horseback, but go away on foot at a snail's pace. Courage and patience then, O Philothea, are necessary in this enterprise. Alas! how much are those souls to be pitied, who, seeing themselves subject to many imperfections, after being a little exercised in devotion, begin to be troubled, disquieted, and discouraged, suffering their hearts almost to yield to the temptation to forsake all, and return back? But on the other hand, is it not also exceedingly dangerous for those, who, by a contrary temptation, make themselves believe that they are cleansed from their imperfections the first day of their purgation, and esteeming themselves perfect, though scarce as yet initiated, take upon them to fly without wings.

3. O Philothea, in what danger are they of relapsing, through being taken too soon out of the physician's hands. Ah! "*It is in vain to rise before it is light*" (says the prophet), "*rise after you have rested;*"[3] and he himself practising this lesson, and having been already washed and purified yet desires to be cleansed again.

4. The exercise of the purgation of the soul, neither can nor ought to end but with our life; let us not then afflict ourselves because we have imperfections, for our perfection consists in resisting them;

[2] Prov. iv. 18.

[3] Ps. cxxvii. 2 (Vulgate).

and we cannot resist them without seeing them, nor vanquish them without encountering them. Our victory does not lie in not feeling them, but in not consenting to them. But to be disturbed by them is not to consent to them: nay, it is necessary, for the exercise of our humility, that we be sometimes wounded in this spiritual combat; but we are never conquered, except when we have lost either life or courage. Now imperfections or venial sins cannot deprive us of spiritual life, for that is not lost but by mortal sin. It only remains then that they should not make us lose courage. "*Deliver me, O Lord*" (said David) "*from fear and faint-heartedness.*" It is a happy condition of this war, that if we fight valiantly we are always conquerors.

Chapter VI

Of the First Purgation, which is that of Mortal Sin

1. THE first purgation which must be made, is that of sin; the means of making it is the rite of confession. Seek the most worthy confessor you can; take in hand some one of the little books which have been composed for helping consciences to make a good confession; read it carefully, and observe from point to point in what you have offended, beginning from the time you had the use of reason, to the present hour. If you distrust your memory, write down what you observe; and having so sought out and gathered together the sinful corruptions of your conscience, abhor and reject them with the greatest grief and contrition your heart can conceive, pondering well these four things: That by sin you have lost the grace of God; forfeited your part in heaven, incurred the perpetual pains of hell; and renounced the eternal love of God.

2. You see, Philothea, that I speak of a general confession of the whole life, which, I admit, indeed, not to be

always absolutely necessary, yet I consider withal that it will be exceeding profitable to you in this beginning, and therefore I earnestly advise it. It often happens that the ordinary confessions of those who live a common and vulgar life are full of great defects, for often they do not prepare themselves at all, or very little; they have not sufficient contrition; nay, it often happens that they confess with a tacit will of returning to sin, inasmuch as they are not willing to avoid the occasions of sinning, nor to make use of the means necessary to amendment of life; and in all these cases a general confession is requisite to secure the soul. But besides this, a general confession recalls us to the knowledge of ourselves. It stirs us up to a wholesome shame and sorrow for our past life; makes us admire the mercy of God, who has so long and so patiently awaited us: it quiets our hearts, refreshes our spirits, excites in us good resolutions, gives occasion to our spiritual father to give us advice suitable to our condition, and opens our hearts, that we may with more confidence express ourselves in our ensuing confessions. Therefore, when speaking of a general renewing of our heart, and of an entire conversion of our soul to God, by means of a devout life, I am right, it seems to me, Philothea, in recommending to you this general confession.

CHAPTER VII

Of the Second Purgation, which is that of the Affection to Sin

1. ALL the Israelites departed in reality out of the land of Egypt, but they did not all depart in affection; therefore, in the wilderness, many of them repined that they had not the onions and flesh pots of Egypt. So there are penitents, who forsake sin, in fact, but not in affection; that is, they purpose to sin no more,

but it is with a certain reluctance of heart to deny themselves and abstain from the miserable delights of sin. Their heart renounces sin, and departs from it, but for all that does not leave off looking back that way often, as Lot's wife did towards Sodom. They abstain from sin, as sick men do from melons, which they forbear, because the physician threatens them with death if they eat them ; but it is vexatious to them to refrain ; they talk of them and discuss whether they might not have them ; they will at least smell them ; and account those happy who may eat them. So these weak and faint-hearted penitents abstain from sin for a time, but they regret it ; they would willingly sin and not be damned ; they speak of sin with a kind of satisfaction and relish, and think those happy who commit it.

2. A man resolved on revenge will change his mind in confession : but soon after he will be found among his friends, taking pleasure in speaking of his quarrel and saying, Had it not been for the fear of God he would have done this or that ; and how difficult is God's law in this point of forgiving; and would to God he might be revenged. Ah! who sees not, that although this poor man be free from sin, he is encumbered with the love of sin : and though out of Egypt in effect, he is there yet in desire, longing after the garlic and onions he was wont to eat! Like a woman, who having abandoned her wanton amours, still likes to be admired and courted. Alas! how great danger such people are in !

3. O Philothea, since you desire to undertake a devout life, you must not only forsake sin itself, but also cleanse your heart from all affections towards sin. For, besides the danger of relapsing, these wretched passions will perpetually enfeeble and depress your spirit ; so that you will not be able to do good works, cheerfully, diligently, and frequently, in which, however, lies the very essence of devotion. Souls that have quitted sin itself, but still have these affections and pinings after sin, may, in my opinion, be compared to sickly girls, who are not ill, yet all their actions are distempered; they eat without relish, sleep without rest, laugh without delight. and

rather drag themselves along than walk. Just so these souls do good, but with so great spiritual weariness, that it takes away all the grace from their good works, which are few in number, and small in effect.

CHAPTER VIII

Of the Means to make this Second Purgation

1. NOW the first means for arriving at this second purgation, is a lively and strong apprehension of the great injury sin does us; which causes us to enter into a deep and fervent contrition. For as contrition, be it ever so little, so it be true, especially being joined to the virtue of the sacraments, cleanseth us sufficiently from sin, so, when it is great and fervent, it cleanseth us from all affections towards sin. A weak hatred makes us loathe and avoid the company of him we hate; but if it be mortal and violent hatred, we not only avoid and abhor him, but we dislike and cannot endure the conversation even of his friends and kindred; yea, we hate his very picture, and everything which belongs to him. So when the penitent hates his sin only with a light, though a true contrition, he resolves, indeed, to sin no more; but when he abhors it with a powerful and vigorous contrition, he then not only detests the sin, but all the affections, belongings, and approaches of sin.

2. We must then, Philothea, increase our contrition and repentance as much as possible, that it may extend to the least belonging of sin. St. Mary Magdalen, in her conversion, so utterly lost the taste for sin, and for the pleasure she had taken in it, that she never more thought of it. And David protested that he not only abhorred sin,[1] but also all the ways and paths of it. In this point consists the renewing of the soul, which the same prophet compares to the growing young of an eagle.[2]

[1] Ps. cxix. 104. [2] Ps. ciii. 5.

3. Now, to gain this apprehension and contrition, you must earnestly exercise yourself in these following meditations, which, being well practised, will, by the help of God's grace, root out of your heart all sin, with its principal affections. I have drawn them up entirely for this purpose. You will use them in order as I have placed them, taking only one for each day, and that, if it may be, in the morning, which is the most proper time for all spiritual exercises, and you will ruminate on it for the rest of the day. But if you are not yet accustomed to meditation, see that which will be said on the subject in the second part.

Chapter IX

FIRST MEDITATION

On our Creation

Preparation.

PLACE yourself in the presence of God.

Beseech Him to inspire you.

Considerations.

Consider that only so many years ago you were not in the world, and that your being was in truth a nothing. Where were we then, O my soul? The world had already lasted so many ages, and we had not been heard of.

God caused you to come forth out of this nothingness, to make you what you are; having no need at all of you, but merely of His own goodness.

Consider the being which God has given you, for it is the highest in the visible world, capable of eternal life, and of being perfectly united with His Divine Majesty.

Affections and Resolutions.

Humble yourself profoundly before God, saying from your heart with the Psalmist, "*O Lord, my substance is as nothing before*

Thee"[1] and how hadst Thou remembrance of me to create me? Alas, my soul, thou wert engulfed in that ancient nothingness, and hadst yet been there, had not God drawn thee thence: and what couldst thou have done in that nothingness?

Give thanks to God. O my great and good Creator, how am I indebted to Thee, since Thou hast vouchsafed to take me in my nothingness, to make me, by Thy mercy, what I am. What can I ever do to magnify worthily Thy holy name, and render thanks to Thine inestimable goodness?

Be confounded. But alas, my Creator, instead of uniting myself to Thee by love and service, I have been rebellious through my inordinate affections, erring and straying from Thee, to unite myself to sin; glorifying Thy goodness no more than if Thou hadst not been my Creator.

Abase yourself before God. O my soul, know that the Lord is thy God; it is He that hath made thee, and not thou thyself. O God, I am the work of Thy hands.

1 Psa. xxxix. 5 (Vulgate).

I will no more henceforth take pleasure in myself, since of myself I am nothing. Whereof hast thou to boast, O dust and ashes?[2] Yea, O nothing, whereof hast thou to exalt thyself?

To humble myself, therefore, I resolve to do—such and such things; to suffer—such and such disgraces; I will change my life, follow henceforth my Creator, and honour in myself that condition of being which He has given me, employing it entirely in obedience to His will, by such means as shall be taught me, and as I shall ask from my spiritual guide.

Conclusion.

Give thanks to God. "*Praise the Lord, O my soul, and all that is within me praise His holy name,*"[3] for His goodness has drawn me out of nothing, and His mercy has created me.

Offer. O my God, I offer to Thee, with all my heart, the being which Thou hast given me; I dedicate and consecrate it to Thee.

Pray. O God, strengthen me in these affections and resolutions. Our Father, &c.

2 Ecclus. x. 9.
3 Psa. ciii. 1.

After your prayer, walk awhile, and out of these considerations which you have made, gather a little nosegay of devotion, to smell at all the rest of the day.

CHAPTER X

SECOND MEDITATION

On the End for which we were Created

Preparation.

PLACE yourself before God.

Beseech Him to inspire you.

Considerations.

God did not place you in the world for any need He had of you, who are altogether unprofitable to Him, but only to exercise His goodness in you, in giving you His grace and glory. And to that end He has given you understanding to know Him, memory to be mindful of Him, will to love Him, imagination to represent to yourself His benefits, eyes to behold the wonder of His works, a tongue to praise Him; and so of the other faculties.

Being created, and put into the world for this end, all actions contrary to it are to be avoided and rejected; and those which conduce not to this end ought to be contemned as unprofitable and superfluous.

Consider the wretchedness of worldlings who never think of this, but live as though they believed themselves created for no other end than to build houses, plant trees, heap up riches, and spend their time in amusements.

Affections and Resolutions.

Confound yourself, reproaching your soul with her wretchedness, which heretofore was so great, that she seldom or never thought of all this. Alas! (you shall say) what did I think of, O God, when I never thought of Thee? What did I remember when I forgot Thee? What did I love, when I loved not Thee? Alas! I ought to have fed upon truth, and I have glutted myself with vanity, and have served the world, which was created only to serve me.

Detest your past life. I renounce you, O vain thoughts and unprofitable fancies; I abjure you, O frivolous and hateful remembrances; and you, O unfaithful and disloyal friendships, lewd and wretched slaveries, unprofitable gratifications, and irksome pleasures, I renounce you.

Return to God. And Thou, O my God, my Saviour, Thou shalt be from henceforth the sole object of my thoughts; never more will I apply my mind to thoughts displeasing to Thee. My memory shall be filled all the days of my life with the greatness of Thy goodness, so mercifully exercised on me; Thou shalt be the delight of my heart, and the sweetness of my affections.

Ah! henceforth I will abhor—such and such vanities and trifles, to which I have applied myself;—such and such unprofitable employments, in which I have squandered away my days;—such and such affections which have captivated my heart; and to this end I will use—such and such remedies.

Conclusion.

Thank God who made you for so excellent an end. Thou hast created me, O Lord, for Thyself, to the end that I may rejoice eternally in the greatness of Thy glory; when shall I be worthy of it? when shall I bless Thee as I ought?

Offer. I offer Thee, O my dear Creator, all these affections and resolutions, with all my heart and soul.

Pray. I beseech Thee, O God, to accept these my desires and vows, and to give Thy holy benediction to my soul, to the end that it may accomplish them, through the merits of the blood of Thy Son which He shed upon the cross. *Make your little nosegay of devotion as before.*

CHAPTER XI

THIRD MEDITATION

On the Benefits of God

Preparation.

PLACE yourself in the presence of God.

Beseech Him to inspire you.

Considerations.

Consider the bodily gifts which God has given you; what a body, what conveniences to maintain it, what health and lawful comforts for it; what friends and assistances. And consider all this in comparison with the lot of so many other persons, much more worthy than yourself, who are destitute of all these blessings; some defective in body, health and limbs; others subjected to reproaches, contempt, and dishonour; others weighed down with poverty; and God has not suffered you to be so miserable.

Consider your gifts of mind. How many are there in the world stupid, mad, foolish; and why are you not among them? God has favoured you. How many are there who have been brought up coarsely and in gross ignorance? And by God's providence you have been well nurtured and educated.

Consider your spiritual graces, O Philothea. You are a child of the Church. God has given you a knowledge of Himself even from your youth. How often has He given you His sacraments? How often inspirations, interior illuminations, and warnings for your amendment? How often has He pardoned you your faults? How often has he delivered you from occasions of sin to which you have been exposed? And have not your past years been so much time and opportunity to advance the good of your soul? Consider in detail how good and gracious God has been to you.

Affections and Resolutions.

Admire the goodness of God. O how good is my God towards me! O how good is He! How rich is Thy heart, O Lord, in mercy and plenteous in goodness! O my soul, let us rehearse for ever the mercies He has bestowed upon us.

Wonder at your own ingratitude. But what am I, O Lord, that Thou wert mindful of me! Ah, how great is my unworthiness! Alas, I have trodden Thy benefits under foot; I have dishonoured Thy graces, converting them into abuse and contempt of Thy sovereign goodness. I have opposed the depth of my ingratitude to the height of Thy grace and favour.

Stir yourself up to gratitude. Well, then, my heart, be now no more unfaithful, ungrateful, and disloyal to this great Benefactor. And how shall not my soul henceforth be wholly subject to God, who has wrought so many wonders and graces in me, and for me?

Ah! withdraw, then, your body, Philothea, from—such and such pleasures, and consecrate it to the service of God, who has done so much for it. Apply your soul to know and acknowledge Him by—such and such exercises as are requisite for that purpose. Employ diligently the means which are in the Church to save yourself, and love Almighty God. Yes, O my God, I will frequent Prayer and Sacraments; I will hear the Holy Word; I will do works of inspiration and counsel.

Conclusion.

Thank God for the knowledge He has now given you of your duty, and for all the benefits hitherto received.

Offer Him your heart, with all your resolutions.

Pray Him to enable you to practise them faithfully, through the merits of His Son's death. Our Father.

Make the spiritual nosegay as before.

CHAPTER XII

FOURTH MEDITATION

On Sin

Preparation.

PLACE yourself in the presence of God.

Beseech Him to inspire you.

Considerations.

Call to mind how long it is since you began to sin, and examine how much, since that beginning, sins have been multiplied in your heart; how every day you have increased them against God, against yourself, and against your neighbour, by word, by desire, and by thought.

Consider your evil inclinations, and how often you have followed them ; and by these two points you will see that your faults are more in number than the hairs of your head, yea more than the sand of the sea. Consider, in particular, the sin of ingratitude against God, which is a general sin, and extends itself over all the rest, making them infinitely more enormous. Consider, then, how many benefits God has bestowed on you, and how you have abused them all against the Giver. And, in particular, how many inspirations you have despised, how many motions of the Spirit you have rendered useless. And, above all, how many communions have you received, and where are the fruits of them? What is become of all these precious jewels, with which your dear Spouse adorned you? They have all been buried under your iniquities. With what preparation have you received them? Think on this ingratitude, that God having so run after you to save you, you have always fled from Him to lose yourself.

Affections and Resolutions.

Be confounded at your misery. O my God, how dare I appear before Thine eyes? Alas, I am but an imposthume of the world, and a sink of ingratitude and sin. Is it possible I have been so disloyal as not to have left any one of my senses, not any one of the powers of my soul, which I have not corrupted, violated, and defiled; and that not so much as one day of my life has passed in which I have not wrought such wicked deeds. Is this the return I should have made for the benefits of my Creator, and the precious blood of my Redeemer?

Ask pardon, and cast yourself at the feet of your Lord, like a prodigal son, like a Magdalene, or like a woman that has defiled her marriage-bed with all sorts of adulteries. O Lord, have mercy on this poor sinner! Alas, O Living Fountain of Compassion, have pity on this wretch.

Resolve to live better. No, O Lord, never more, with the help of Thy grace, never more will I abandon myself to sin. Alas, I have loved it but too much; now I detest it and embrace Thee, O Father of Mercy, I desire to live and die in Thee.

To blot out my past sins, I will accuse myself of them courageously, and will not leave one unbanished from my heart.

I will do all I can to root out all the plants of sin from my heart, and, in particular, of—such and such vices, which chiefly harass me.

To accomplish this, I will constantly embrace the means which shall be recommended to me, and think I have never done enough to repair such grievous offences.

Conclusion.

Thank God who has waited for your amendment until now, and has given you these right affections.

Offer Him up your heart for their accomplishment.

Pray Him to strengthen you. Our Father.

Make your spiritual nosegay.

Chapter XIII

FIFTH MEDITATION

On Death

Preparation.

PLACE yourself in the presence of God.

Beseech Him to inspire you by His grace.

Imagine yourself to be in extreme sickness, lying on your death-bed, without any hope of recovery.

Considerations.

Consider the uncertainty of the day of your death. O my soul, you must one day quit this body: when will it be? In winter or in summer? in town or country? by day or by night? Will it be suddenly, or with notice? by sickness or by accident? Shall you have leisure to confess? Shall you have the assistance of your Ghostly Father? Alas! of all this we know nothing: this only is certain that we shall die, and that always sooner than we expect.

Consider, that then the world will end so far as it concerns you; there will be no more of it for you; it will turn upside down before your eyes; for then the pleasures, the vanities, the worldly joys, and vain affections of our lives will seem to us like shadows and clouds. Ah, wretch! for what trifles and delusions have I offended God? You will see then that you have forsaken God for nothing. On the contrary, devotion and good works will then seem to you so sweet and delightful. O why did I not follow this fair and pleasant path? Then sins, which seemed very small, will appear great as mountains, and your devotion very small.

Consider the long languishing farewells your soul will then say to this lower world; she will say farewell to its riches, to its vanities, and vain companies; to its pleasures, to its pastimes, to its friends and neighbours; to relations, to children, to husband, to wife, in short, to every creature; and finally, to her own body, which she will leave pale, wan, emaciated, hideous, and loathsome.

Consider with what haste they will carry away this body, and hide it in the earth; which done, the world will think no more of you than you have thought of others; *God give him peace*, they will say, and that is all. O death, how forgetful art thou, and how pitiless!

Consider how the soul, on her departure from the body, takes her way to the right hand or to the left. Alas! whither will yours go? What way will it take? No other than that which it shall have begun here in this world.

Affections and Resolutions.

Pray to God, and cast yourself into His arms. Alas, O Lord, receive me into Thy protection at that dreadful day; make that hour happy and favourable to me, and rather let all the other days of my life be sad and sorrowful.

Despise the world. Since I know not the hour in which I must leave thee, O world, I will no more fix my love upon thee. O my dear friends and relations, pardon me if I love you no more, but with a holy friendship, which may last eternally; for why should I unite myself to you in such a way as to be forced to break and dissolve the tie.

I will prepare myself against that hour, and take all requisite care to make that journey happily: I will secure the state of my conscience to the utmost of my ability, and take immediate care to repair—such and such defects.

Conclusion.

Give thanks to God for these resolutions which He has given you.

Offer them to His Divine Majesty.

Be urgent with Him to give you a happy death, by the merits of that of His Son. Our Father.

Make a nosegay of myrrh.

Chapter XIV

SIXTH MEDITATION

On Judgment

Preparation.

PLACE yourself before God.

Beseech Him to inspire you.

Considerations.

At length, after the time which God has appointed for the duration of this world, and after many signs and horrible wonders, which will make men wither away for fear and dread, fire, coming like a deluge, shall burn and reduce to ashes the whole face of the earth, not sparing any one of the things which we see upon it.

After this deluge of flames and thunderings, all men shall rise from their graves (excepting those who are still on earth), and at the voice of the angel they shall be gathered together in the valley of Jehoshaphat, but alas! how different—some in glorious and resplendent bodies, some in bodies most frightful and horrible.

Consider the majesty with which the sovereign Judge will appear, surrounded by all the angels and saints; before Him His Cross, more brilliant than the sun, sign of mercy to the good, and of justice to the wicked.

This sovereign judge, by His dread command, which shall be instantly obeyed, will separate the good from the bad, placing the one on His right hand, and the other His left. O everlasting separation! after which never more shall these two companies meet again.

This separation being made, and the books of conscience opened, all men shall see clearly the malice of the wicked, and their contempt of God; and on the other hand, the penitence of the good, and the effects of God's grace which they have received; and nothing shall be hid. O God, what confusion for the one, and what consolation for the other.

Consider the last sentence of the wicked: *Depart, ye cursed into everlasting fire, prepared for the devil and his angels.* Weigh well these so weighty words. *Depart,* saith He; it is a word of perpetual rejection which God pronounces against those miserable ones, banishing them for ever from His family. He calls them *accursed.* O my soul, how dreadful a curse; a general curse, including all manner of woes; an irrevocable curse, comprehending all times, and eternity. He adds, *into everlasting fire.* Behold, O my heart, this vast eternity. O eternal eternity of pains, how dreadful art thou!

Consider the contrary sentence of the good. *Come,* saith the judge. O sweet word of salvation, by which God draws us to Himself, and receives us into the bosom of His goodness. *Ye blessed of my Father.* O dear blessing which comprehends all blessings! *Inherit the kingdom prepared for you from the foundation of the world.* O, good God, what mercy! for of this kingdom there shall be no end.

Affections and Resolutions.

Tremble, O my soul, at the remembrance of these things. O my God, who can assure me against that day, on which the pillars of heaven shall tremble for fear?

Detest your sins, which only can condemn you on that dreadful day.

Ah! I will judge myself now, that I may not be judged then. I will examine my conscience, and condemn myself. I will accuse and chastise myself, that the eternal Judge condemn me not on that dreadful day. I will therefore confess, and accept of all necessary counsel, etc.

Conclusion.

Thank God who has given you the means of assuring yourself against that day, and time to work out your repentance.

Offer Him your heart to perform it.

Pray Him to give you grace duly to accomplish it. Our Father.

Make your spiritual nosegay.

CHAPTER XV

SEVENTH MEDITATION

On Hell

Preparation.

PLACE yourself in the presence of God.

Humble yourself and implore His assistance.

Represent to yourself a dark city, all burning with brimstone and stinking pitch, and full of inhabitants who cannot make their escape.

Considerations.

The damned are in the infernal pit as in this woeful city, where they suffer unspeakable torments in all their senses and in all their members; because, as they have employed all their senses and all their members in sinning, so shall they suffer in all their members and in all their senses the pains due to sin. The eyes, for lascivious looks, shall endure the horrible sight of hell and devils. The ears, for having delighted in vicious discourses, shall hear nothing now but wailings, lamentations, and cries of despair. And so of the other senses.

Besides all these torments there is one still greater, which is the privation and loss of God's glory, from the sight of which they are excluded for ever. If Absalom found the privation of the sight of the face of his father David more grevious than his banishment, O God, what grief will it be to be for ever excluded from beholding Thy most sweet and gracious countenance?

Consider, above all, the eternity of these pains, which above all things makes hell intolerable. Alas! if a slight pain, or the heat of a little fever, makes one short night seem so long and tedious, how terrible will be the night of eternity with so many torments? From this eternity proceed eternal despair, blasphemy, and infinite rage.

Affections and Resolutions.

Terrify your soul with the words of holy Job.[1] O my soul, *who shall dwell with the devouring fire, who shall dwell with everlasting burnings?* wilt thou depart from thy God for ever?

Confess that you have deserved it, yea oftentimes. But henceforth I will choose the other way; for why should I descend into this bottomless pit?

I will therefore do—this and that, in order to avoid sin, which alone can bring me to this eternal death.

Give thanks; offer; pray. [As before.]

1 Should be Isaiah, viz., chapter xxxiii. 14.

CHAPTER XVI

EIGHTH MEDITATION

On Heaven

Preparation.

PLACE yourself in the presence of God.

Make the invocation.

Considerations.

Represent to yourself a beautiful and clear night, and think how delightful it is to behold the sky all spangled with that multitude and variety of stars; then add to this beauty that of a beautiful day, but so that the brightness of the sun may no way hinder the lustre of the stars and moon: and then you may say without hesitation, that all this put together is nothing compared with the glory of that great Paradise. O how that place is lovely and to be desired! O how glorious is that city!

Consider the glory, beauty, and multitude of the inhabitants of this happy country; those millions of millions of angels, cherubim, and seraphim; this company of apostles, prophets, martyrs, confessors, virgins, and holy matrons: their multitude is innumerable. O how blessed is this company! the meanest of them all is more beautiful to behold than all the world; what a sight then will it be see them all? But, O my God, how happy they are, they sing continually the sweet canticle of eternal love; they rejoice continually with an unchanging gladness; they impart to one another unspeakable contentments; and live in the consolation of a happy and indissoluble society.

Consider lastly how happy they are in the enjoyment of God, who delights them continually with his loving looks, and thereby opens in their hearts a fountain of delights. What happiness to be united everlastingly to their King? They are there like happy birds flying and singing perpetually in the atmosphere of divinity, which encompasses them on all sides with incredible pleasures. There each vies with other unweariedly in singing the Creator's praise:—Blessed be Thou for ever, O sweet and sovereign Creator and Redeemer, who art so bountiful to us, and dost communicate to us so liberally Thy glory. And in reply God blesses all His saints with a perpetual benediction:—Blessed be you for ever, says He, My beloved creatures, who have served Me, and shall praise Me everlastingly, with so great love and courage.

Affections and Resolutions.

Admire and praise this heavenly country. O how beautiful art thou, dear Jerusalem, and how happy are thy inhabitants!

Reproach your heart with the little courage it has had hitherto, in suffering itself to be turned so far out of the way to this glorious habitation. O why have I strayed so far from my sovereign good? Ah! wretch that I am, for these pleasures, so unpleasing and so vain, have I a thousand and a thousand times forsaken eternal and infinite delights! Was I mad to despise such precious blessings for desires so vain and contemptible.

Aspire, notwithstanding, with fervour to this delightful habitation. O my good and sovereign Lord, since it has pleased Thee at length to direct my steps into Thy right ways, never more will I turn back. Let us go, O my dear soul, let us go on to this eternal rest: let us journey towards this blessed land, which is promised us. What do we in this Egypt?

I will therefore disburden myself of all such things as may divert me from, or retard me in this journey.

I will do—such and such things which will lead me thither.

Give thanks: Offer: Pray.

CHAPTER XVII

NINTH MEDITATION

On the Election and Choice of Heaven

Preparation.

PLACE yourself in the presence of God.

Humble yourself before Him, and beseech Him to inspire you with His grace.

Considerations.

Imagine yourself to be in a level plain, alone with your good angel, as was young Tobias going to Rages; and that he shows you on high heaven opened, with all the pleasures represented in the meditation you have just made; that he then shows you beneath hell opened, with all the torments described in the meditation on hell. You being thus placed in imagination, and kneeling before your good angel:—

Consider that it is quite true that you are between heaven and hell; and that the one and the other is open to receive you, according to the choice which you shall make.

Consider that the choice which you make of one or the other in this world, will last for all eternity in the next.

And though both one and the other are open to receive you, according to your choice, yet God, who is ready to give you either the one by His justice, or the other by His mercy, desires, notwithstanding, with an incomparable desire, that you would make choice of heaven ; and your good angel also importunes you with all his power, offering you on God's behalf a thousand assistances, and a thousand graces to help you to gain heaven.

Consider, that Jesus Christ beholds you from heaven in His mercy, and graciously invites you, saying, Come, O dear soul, to everlasting rest, within the arms of My goodness ; I, who have prepared immortal delights for you in the abundance of my love. Behold likewise by faith the saints who exhort you, and millions of blessed souls who sweetly invite you, and wish nothing more than to see your heart united with theirs, to praise God for ever; assuring you that the way to heaven is not so hard as the world makes it. Courage, dear friend, say they, he who will diligently consider the way of devotion, by which we have ascended hither, shall see that we have come to these delights by pleasures incomparably more sweet than those of the world.

Election.

O hell, I detest thee now and for evermore ; I detest thy torments and pains ; I detest thy miserable and accursed eternity ; and above all, I detest those eternal blasphemies and maledictions which thou vomitest out eternally against my God. And turning my heart and soul to thee, O beautiful Paradise, everlasting glory, endless felicity, I choose irrevocably and for ever, to have my habitation and abode within Thy holy and most lovely tabernacles. I bless Thy mercy, O my God, and accept the offer which it pleaseth Thee to make me of it. O Jesus, my Saviour, I accept Thy everlasting love, and assent to the purchase which Thou hast made for me of a place in this blessed Jerusalem; not so much for any thing else as to love and bless thee for ever.

Promise that you will follow the saints in the way of holiness ; and give your hand to your good angel, that he may guide you thither.

Encourage your soul to make this choice.

Chapter XVIII

TENTH MEDITATION

By way of Election and choice which the Soul makes of a Devout Life

Preparation.

PLACE yourself in the presence of God. Humble yourself before Him, and implore His assistance.

Consideration.

Imagine yourself, again, to be in a level plain, all alone with your good angel; and that you see on the left hand the devil seated on a great high throne, attended by many infernal spirits, and surrounded with a great crowd of worldlings, who, bareheaded, acknowledge him for their lord, and do him homage, some by one sin and some by another. Observe the countenances of all the wretched courtiers of this abominable king: behold some of them transported with hatred, envy, and rage; others killing one another; others pale, thoughtful, and anxious, heaping up riches; others devoted to vanity, without any manner of pleasure but what is unprofitable and vain; others foul, abandoned, and corrupted in their brutish lusts. See how they are all without rest, order, and decency; see how they despise one another, and love but in pretence. See all this, and you will see the wretched kingdom of this world tyrannized over by this accursed king, so that it will move you to compassion.

On the other side, behold Jesus Christ crucified, who, with a cordial love, prays for these poor possessed ones that they may be freed from this tyranny, and calls them to Himself. Behold round about Him a great company of devout persons with their angels. Contemplate the beauty of this kingdom of devotion. O how beautiful it is to see this troop of virgins, men and women, whiter than the lily; that assembly of widows full of holy mortification and humility. See the ranks of many married people, who live so lovingly together with mutual respect, which cannot be without great charity. Consider how these devout souls join the exterior care of their households with the interior care of their souls, the love of the earthly with that of the celestial spouse. Look around on every side and you will see them all, with holy, sweet, and lovely mien, listening to our Lord, and desiring to have Him in the midst of their hearts. They are full of joy, but their joy is gracious, charitable, and well ordered; they love one another, but their love is most pure and holy, Such as suffer afflictions amongst this devout company do not vex themselves much, nor lose courage, for see how the eyes of the Saviour console them; and how they altogether aspire to Him.

You have already renounced Satan, with all his sad and wretched followers, by the good affections you have conceived; but you have not yet come to King Jesus yourself, nor united with His blessed and holy company of devout ones, but have hitherto halted between the one and the other.

A hundred thousand saints, who are of the company of those who attained to saintship though living in the world, invite and encourage you.

The crucified King calls you by name: *Come, My well beloved, come, that I may crown thee.*

Election.

O worldlings! O abominable company! no, never shall you see me under your banner. I have renounced for ever your follies and vanities. O king of pride, O king of misery, infernal spirit, I renounce thee with all thy vain pomps, I detest thee with all thy works.

And turning myself to thee, my dear Jesus, king of eternal happiness and glory, I embrace thee with all the powers of my soul, I adore thee with all my heart, I choose thee now and for ever for my king, I promise thee inviolable fidelity, I offer thee irrevocable homage, and submit myself to the obedience of thy holy laws and ordinances.

O my good angel, present me to this sacred assembly,

and forsake me not till I am associated with this blessed company, with whom I say, and will for ever say, in testimony of my choice, live Jesus, live Jesus.

CHAPTER XIX

How to make a General Confession

SUCH, then, my dear Philothea, are the meditations requisite for our purpose. When you have made them go on courageously in the spirit of humility to make your general confession. And pray suffer not yourself to be troubled with any kind of apprehension. The scorpion in its sting is venomous, but, being reduced into oil, it becomes a sovereign remedy against its own sting. So sin is shameful only in the committing; but being converted into confession and repentance, it becomes both honourable and wholesome. Contrition and confession are so beautiful and so fragrant that they efface the ugliness and disperse the ill savour of sin. Simon the leper said that the Magdalen was a sinner; but our Saviour said she was not so, and spoke of nothing but the ointment she poured out, and of the greatness of her love. If we are truly humble, O Philothea, our sins will infinitely displease us, because God is offended by them; but the confession of our sins will be sweet and pleasant to us, because God is honoured thereby. It is a kind of relief to acquaint the physician fully with the disease that torments us.

When you are before your spiritual father, imagine yourself on Mount Calvary, at the feet of Jesus Christ crucified, whose precious blood drops down from all His wounds to wash you from your iniquities. For though it be not the very blood of our Saviour, yet it is the merit of His blood shed for us, which is sprinkled abundantly on those who penitently confess their sins. Open then your heart freely, to cast out your sins by confession; for, in proportion as they are driven out of it, the precious merits of His divine passion will enter in, to replenish it with blessings.

But declare all, with simplicity and candour. Satisfy fully your conscience in this once for all; and having done so, then hearken to the counsels and injunctions of your ghostly Father, and say in your heart: *Speak, Lord, for thy servant heareth.*[1] Yes, Philothea, it is God whom you hear, since he has said to his ministers, *he that heareth you heareth me.*[2]

After that, take in hand the following protestation, which serves for a conclusion of all your contrition, and which you ought first to have meditated and considered. Read it attentively, and with the greatest compunction you possibly can.

Chapter XX

A formal Protestation for fixing in the Soul a firm Resolution to serve God

I THE undersigned, placed in the presence of the eternal God, and of the court of heaven, having considered the exceeding mercy of His divine goodness towards me, most unworthy and wretched creature; whom He has created out of nothing, preserved, sustained, and delivered from so many dangers, and loaded with so many benefits. But above all, having considered the incomprehensible gentleness and clemency with which this good God has so graciously spared me in my iniquities, so often and so lovingly inspired me, inviting me to amendment, and so patiently awaited my repentance and conversion until this —th year of my age, notwithstanding all my ingratitudes, disloyalties, and infidelities, whereby deferring my conversion, and despising His graces, I have so rashly offended Him: Having moreover considered, that on the

[1] 1 Kings iii. 9.

[2] Luke x. 16.

day of my holy baptism I was happily and holily vowed and dedicated to my God, to be his child, and that, contrary to the profession then made in my name, I have so greatly and so often, so execrably and detestably profaned and violated my understanding, applying and employing it against His divine Majesty: At length returning to myself, prostrate in heart and mind before the throne of the divine Justice, I acknowledge, confess, and avow myself lawfully attainted and convicted of high treason against His divine Majesty, and guilty of the death and passion of Jesus Christ, by reason of the sins I have committed, for which He died and suffered the torments of the Cross; so that consequently I deserve to be cast away, and damned for ever.

But turning myself toward the throne of the infinite mercy of the same eternal God, having detested with all my heart, and with all the powers of my soul, the transgressions of my past life, I most humbly beg and crave pardon, grace, and mercy, with entire absolution from my offences, by virtue of the death and passion of the same Saviour and Redeemer of my soul, resting on which, as the only foundation of my hope, I confirm again, and renew the sacred profession of allegiance made in my behalf to God at my baptism; renouncing the devil, the world, and the flesh, detesting their evil suggestions, vanities, and lusts, for all the time of this present life, and for all eternity. And turning myself to my most gracious and merciful God, I desire, determine, purpose, and resolve irrevocably to serve and love Him now and for ever; and to this end I give, dedicate, and consecrate to Him my spirit, with all its faculties, my soul, with all its powers, my heart, with all its affections, and my body, with all its senses; protesting that I will never more abuse any part of my being against His divine will and sovereign Majesty, to whom I offer up and sacrifice myself in spirit, to be for ever His loyal, obedient, and faithful creature, without ever unsaying, revoking, or repenting this resolution.

But if, alas! through the suggestion of my enemy, or through human frailty, it come to pass that I transgress in anything whatsoever this my vow and resolution, I protest and determine from this very hour, by the assistance of the Holy Ghost, to rise again as soon as I shall perceive my fall, and to return anew to the divine mercy, without any hesitation or delay whatsoever. This is my inviolable and irrevocable will, intention, and resolution, which I ratify and confirm, without reservation or exception, in the same sacred presence of my God, and in the sight of the Church Triumphant, and in the face of the Church Militant, my mother, who hears this my declaration in the person of him who, as her minister, hears me in this act.

May it please thee, O my eternal God, Almighty and all merciful, Father, Son, and Holy Ghost, to confirm me in this resolution, and to accept this my hearty and inward sacrifice in the odour of sweetness. And as it hath pleased Thee to give me the inspiration and will to do this, so grant me power and grace to perform it. O God, Thou art my God. God of my heart, God of my soul, and God of my spirit; so I acknowledge and adore Thee, now and evermore. Live, O Jesus.

Chapter XXI

Conclusion of this first Purgation

THIS protestation ended, be attentive, and open the ears of your heart to hear in spirit the sentence of your absolution, which the Saviour of your soul Himself, sitting on the throne of His mercy, will pronounce above in heaven before all the angels and saints, at the same time the priest in His Name absolves you here on earth. So that all the company of the blessed, rejoicing in your happiness, will sing a spiritual song with incomparable joy, and will all give the kiss of peace and fellowship to your heart, now re-established in grace and sanctified.

O Philothea, what a wonderful covenant is this, by which you make a happy treaty with the majesty of God; in giving yourself to Him you gain both Him and yourself for ever. Nothing now remains but to take pen in hand, and subscribe with a joyful heart the act of your protestation, and go to the altar, where God for His part will sign and seal your absolution and the promise He has made you of His heavenly kingdom, putting Himself, by His Holy Sacrament, as a sacred seal and signet upon your renewed heart.

Thus I hope, Philothea, your soul will be purged from sin, and all sinful affections. Yet because these affections do easily revive in the soul through our frailty and concupiscence, which may be mortified but can never be extinguished while we live here on earth, I will give you some counsels which, being well practised, will preserve you henceforth from mortal sin, and from all the affections thereto, so that it shall never again be able to take root in your heart. And because the same instructions serve also for a still more perfect purification, before I deliver them I will say somewhat of this more absolute purity to which I desire to conduct you.

Chapter XXII

That we must purify ourselves from the Affection to Venial Sins

As the dawn brightens, we see more clearly in the mirror the spots and soils on our face; so as the inward light of the Holy Ghost more and more illuminates our consciences, we see more plainly and distinctly the sins, the inclinations and imperfections, which hinder us from attaining to true devotion; and the selfsame light which makes us see those spots and blemishes, inflames us with a desire to cleanse and purify ourselves from them.

You will then discover, my dear Philothea, that besides mortal sins, and the affections to them (from which, by the foregoing exercises, you will have been purged), there remain yet in your soul many inclinations and affections to venial sins.

I do not say you will discover venial sins, but I say you will discover affections and inclinations to them. The two things are very different from one other: for we can never be free altogether from venial sins (at least we cannot continue in that purity for any long time), but we may well be free from all affection to venial sins; for it is one thing to say an untruth once or twice through thoughtlessness in matters of small importance, and another thing to take pleasure in lying and to be addicted to this sin.

I say then that it is necessary to purge the soul from all affections which she may have to venial sins; that is to say, we must not nourish voluntarily a will to continue and persevere in any kind of venial sin; for this would be a very great defect of will, knowingly to cherish in the heart a thing so displeasing to God as the will to displease Him. Venial sin, be it ever so little, displeases God, though not so highly that He will reject or damn us for it. If then, venial sin displeases Him, the will and affection to venial sin is no other than a resolution to be willing to displease His divine Majesty; and is it possible that a generous soul should not only displease her God, but also like to displease Him.

Such affections, my Philothea, are as directly contrary to devotion as affections to mortal sins are to charity; they enfeeble the powers of the spirit, hinder the course of divine consolations, open the door to temptations, and although they kill not the soul, yet they make it exceedingly sick. *Dead flies* (says the wise man) *cause the ointment of the apothecary to send forth a stinking savour;*[1] he means that flies, alighting for a moment upon the ointment, and tasting it in passing, spoil no more than they take, the rest remaining good; but when they die in the ointment, they make it loathsome and worthless. So,

1 Eccl. x. 1.

venial sins alighting upon a devout soul, and staying not long there, do not much harm; but if the same sins remain in the soul, because she has an affection to them, they make her without doubt lose the sweetness of the ointment —that is the holy devotion of the soul.

Spiders do not kill the bees, but they spoil and taint their honey, and if they remain in the hive they so entangle the comb with the webs they spin over it that the bees cannot go on with their work. So venial sin does not kill the soul, but when it takes up its abode in our soul through the affection we bear it, it spoils devotion, and entangles the powers of the soul with evil habits and inclinations, so that it can no longer exercise that prompitude of charity in which devotion consists.

It may not be of great consequence, Philothea, to tell some slight untruth; to exceed a little in words, in actions, in looks, in apparel, in mirth, in play, in dancing, provided that, as soon as the spiritual spiders are entered into our consciences, we chase and hunt them away, as the bees do the real spiders. But if we permit them to stay in our hearts, and not only so, but cherish them, so that they gain a hold and multiply there, we shall soon find our honey destroyed, and the hive of our conscience entangled and spoiled. But I say once again, what likelihood is there that a noble soul should take pleasure in displeasing God, and delight in becoming offensive to Him, or desire to do that which she knows to be disagreeable to Him?

CHAPTER XXIII

That we ought to purify ourselves from affections to things useless and dangerous

GAMES, balls, feasts, dress, shows, plays, are no evils in themselves, but indifferent, and may be used both well and ill; nevertheless, these things are always dangerous, and to entertain an affection to them is yet more dangerous. I say then, Philothea, that although it be lawful to play, to dance, to dress well, to be present at innocent comedies, to go into society; yet to be over fond of such things is contrary to devotion, and very injurious and dangerous. It is no sin to do such things, but it is a sin to set one's heart on them. It is a pity to sow in the garden of our hearts such vain and foolish affections, which take up the room of virtuous impressions, and hinder the sap of our souls from nourishing good inclinations.

The ancient Nazarites abstained not only from all that could inebriate, but also from grapes and from vinegar, not that grapes and vinegar intoxicate, but because that tasting the grape they would be tempted to drink wine. I do not say that we may never use these dangerous things; but I say that we can never set our affections on them without prejudice to devotion. The stags when they have become too gross and fat separate themselves from the herd and retire into the woods, knowing that being burthened with their own weight, they are not able to run if they should be hunted. The heart of man, overcharged with those superfluous, unprofitable, and dangerous affections, cannot run after God readily, swiftly, and lightly, which is the principal aim of devotion.

Little children delight to heat themselves in running after butterflies, and none think it ill in them, because they are little children; but is it not ridiculous, nay, rather lamentable, to see men in love with and eager after such unworthy trifles as those which I have named? which, besides their unprofitableness, put us in danger of committing disorders and extravagances in their pursuit. Wherefore, my dear Philothea, I say that we should purge ourselves from these affections; for though the acts are not always contrary to devotion, yet the affections for them are always prejudicial to it.

Chapter XXIV

That we must purge ourselves from Evil Inclinations

WE have, moreover, Philothea, certain natural inclinations, which, because they do not originate in our own sins, are not properly sins, either mortal or venial, but are called imperfections, and their acts are termed faults and omissions. For example, St. Paula, according to the account of St. Jerome, had a great tendency to grief and sadness, so that, at the death of her children and husband, she was in danger of dying of sorrow; this was an imperfection, but no sin, since it was against her desire and will.

Some are naturally cheerful, others morose; some hard to receive advice, others inclined to scorn; some prone to anger, others to love; and, in short, there are few persons in whom some such imperfections may not be observed. But although they are, as it were, common and natural to every one, yet, by care and the practice of the opposite virtues, we may correct and moderate them, and even free and purify our souls from them.

And I tell you, Philothea, we must do so. Men have found means to change the bitter almond trees into sweet, only by piercing them near the root, to let out their juice; and why may not we then let out perverse inclinations, and convert them into good ones? There is no nature however good which may not be corrupted by vicious customs; and there is no nature however perverse which may not, first by the grace of God, and next by industry and diligence, be subdued and overcome.

I will, therefore, now give you some counsels and propose some exercises, by means of which you may purge your soul from dangerous affections and natural imperfections and attachment to venial sins, and thus also secure your conscience more and more against all mortal sin. God give you grace to practise them well.

PART THE SECOND

CONTAINING INSTRUCTIONS FOR ELEVATING THE SOUL TO GOD BY PRAYER AND THE SACRAMENTS

CHAPTER I

Of the Necessity of Prayer

SINCE Prayer places our understanding in the divine brightness and light, and exposes our will to the warmth of heavenly love, there is nothing that so effectually purges our understanding from its ignorance, or our will from its depraved affections. It is the water of benediction, which, when sprinkled upon them, makes the plants of our good desires grow green and flourish, washes our souls from their imperfections, and quenches the thirst of passion in our hearts.

But, above all, I recommend to you mental prayer, and particularly that which has the life and passion of our Lord for its object. By making Him frequently the subject of meditation, your whole soul will be filled with Him; you will learn His ways, and frame all your actions on the model of His. He is the Light of the world, it is therefore in Him, by Him, and for Him, that we ought to be enlightened and illuminated. He is the Tree of desire, under whose shadow we ought to refresh ourselves. He is the living Well of Jacob, in which we may wash away all our stains. In fine, as little children by hearing their mothers talk, and by their childish prattle with them, learn at length to speak their language ; so we, by keeping close to our Saviour in meditation, and observing His words, actions, and affections, shall by means of His grace learn to speak, act, and will like Him. Here we must stay, Philothea, as we cannot come to God the Father but by this door; for as the looking-glass could never arrest our sight, if its back were not covered with tin or lead, so we could never in this world contemplate the divinity, had it not been united to the sacred humanity of our Saviour, whose life and death is the most fit, delightful, sweet and profitable object we can choose for our ordinary meditation. It is not without reason that our Saviour called Himself the Bread that came down from heaven; for as bread ought to be eaten with all sorts of meat, so our Saviour ought to be the subject of our meditation, consideration, and research, in all our prayers and actions. His life and death have been disposed and distributed into distinct points to assist meditation by several authors.

Employ in this spiritual exercise an hour every day before dinner, early in the morning if possible, because then your mind will be less distracted and more fresh after the repose of the night; but do not spend more than an hour in it, except by the express advice of your spiritual director.

If you can perform this exercise in church, and can find sufficient quiet there, it will be the most easy and fitting place, because neither father nor mother, wife nor husband, nor any other person whatsoever, can well hinder you from staying an hour in church ; whereas, at home, where you are not your own mistress, you could not be sure of so much leisure.

Begin all kinds of prayer, whether mental or vocal, by placing yourself in the presence of God. Observe this rule without exception, and you will soon find the great advantage of it.

If you will be advised by me, Philothea, say your *Pater* and *Credo* in Latin ; but at the same time learn perfectly to comprehend the meaning of the words in your own tongue, that, whilst you say them in the common language of the church, you may at the same time relish the admirable and delightful sense of those holy prayers. Say them, fixing your thoughts, and rousing your affections to their meaning, not saying many words, but studying to say what you do say from the heart; for a single *Our Father*, said with feeling and affection, is of more worth than ever so many run over in haste.

Such vocal prayers as may be found in approved Manuals and Hours may be profitably used, yet with this caution, that if you have the gift of mental prayer you always give it the chief place. So that if, after this, either through multiplicity of business, or some other cause, you cannot say your vocal prayers, you need not be troubled on that account, but rest contented with saying, either before or after your meditation, the Lord's Prayer and the Apostles' Creed.

If, whilst at vocal prayer, you feel your heart drawn and invited to interior or mental prayer, do not refuse the invitation, but quietly let your mind turn that way; do not be concerned at not finishing the vocal prayers you purposed to say: for the mental prayer which you have made is more pleasing to God, and more profitable to your soul; except however the office of the church, if you are bound to say that you must fulfil your obligation.

Should it happen, through a pressure of business, or some accidental cause, that all your morning should pass away without allowing you leisure for this holy exercise of mental prayer, which you must take care to avoid as much as may be, endeavour to repair this loss after dinner, and some time after, because by doing it before digestion is advanced, besides being heavy and drowsy, your health might be injured.

But if, in the whole course of the day, you can find no leisure for it, repair the loss by multiplying your ejaculatory prayers, and by reading some book of devotion; and make a firm resolution to resume the habit on the following day.

CHAPTER II

A short Method of Meditation. And first, of the Presence of God, the first point of the Preparation

BUT perhaps, Philothea, you know not how to make Mental Prayer, for it is a thing which, unhappily, few in our time do know; therefore I offer you a short and simple method for your use, until by the perusal of some of the good books which have been composed on this subject, and above all by practice, you may be more fully instructed.

I note down in the first place the preparation, which consists of two points the first is the putting one's-self in the presence of God, and the second is the invocation of His assistance. Now, for putting yourself in the presence of God, I shall set before you four principal means from which you may derive assistance at the outset.

The first consists in a lively and attentive apprehension of the Omnipresence of God, that is, that God is in all things and in every place, and that there is neither place nor thing in the world in which He is not by a most true presence; so that as the birds, wherever they fly, always meet with the air, so we, wherever we go, or wherever we are, find God present.

Every one knows this truth, but it is not every one who really grasps it. Blind men, though they see not their prince present among them, behave themselves nevertheless with respect when they are told of his presence; but the truth is that, because they see him not, they easily forget that he is present, and having forgot it, they still more easily lose their respectful and reverent behaviour. Alas! Philothea, we do not see God, who is present with us; and though faith assures us of His presence, yet not beholding Him with our eyes, we too often forget Him, and behave ourselves as though

He were far off from us; for although we know well that He is present in all things, yet not bearing it in mind, we act as if we did not know it. Therefore it is that before prayer it is always necessary to rouse our minds to attentive recollection and consideration of the presence of God. Thus David apprehended it when he exclaimed, *If I ascend up into heaven, thou art there: if I go down into hell, thou art there also.*[1] And thus we should use the words of Jacob, who, having seen the sacred ladder, said, *How dreadful is this place! Surely the Lord is in this place, and I knew it not.*[2] He means that he had not thought of it, for he could not be ignorant that God is in all things, and everywhere. When, therefore, you come to prayer, you must say with your whole heart unto your heart, O my heart, my heart! *Surely the Lord is in this place!*

The second means to place yourself in His sacred presence is, to reflect that God is not only in the place where you are, but that He is, after a most particular manner, in your heart, nay, in the very centre of your spirit, which He enlivens and animates by His divine presence, being there as the heart of your heart, and the spirit of your spirit: for as the soul, being diffused through the whole body, is present in every part thereof, and yet resides with a special residence in the heart, so likewise God being present to all things, yet resides in a more particular manner in our spirits; for which reason David says of Him, *God is the strength of my heart.*[3] And St. Paul says that it is in God *we live, and move, and have our being.*[4] By the consideration therefore of this truth you will excite in your heart a profound reverence towards God, who is there so intimately present.

The third means is, to consider our Saviour, who, in His humanity, looks down from heaven on all mankind, but especially on Christians, who are His children, and more particularly on such as are at prayer, whose actions and behaviour He minutely observes. This is by no means a mere imagination, but a most certain truth: for although we see Him not, yet

[1] Psa. cxxxix. [2] Gen. xxviii.

[3] Psa. lxxii. 26. [4] Acts xvii. 28.

He from on high beholds us. It was thus St. Stephen saw Him at the time of His martyrdom. So that we may truly say with the Spouse, *Behold he standeth behind our wall, he looketh forth at the windows, shewing himself through the lattice.*[5]

The fourth method consists, by an effort of the imagination, in representing to ourselves the Saviour in His sacred humanity, as if He were beside us, as we are accustomed to picture our friends, saying, I fancy to myself that I see him doing this or that, it seems as if I could see him, or some such speech. Use then one of these four means of placing your soul in the presence of God before prayer; do not use them all at once, but one at a time, and that briefly and simply.

[5] Cantic. ii. 9.

Chapter III

Of the Invocation, the second point of the Preparation

THE invocation is made in this manner: your soul, feeling itself in the presence of God, prostrates itself with the most profound reverence, acknowledging itself all-unworthy to appear before so sovereign a Majesty; yet, knowing His goodness wills it, humbly begs the grace to serve and worship Him in this meditation. To this end you may, if you please, use some short and impassioned words, like these of David: *Cast me not away from Thy presence: and take not Thy holy spirit from me. Make Thy face to shine upon Thy servant, and I will consider the wondrous things of Thy law. Give me understanding, and I will keep Thy law, yea I will keep it with my whole heart. I am Thy servant; give me understanding,*[1] or such like.

[1] Psa. cxix.

Chapter IV

Of the third point of Preparation, the Proposition of the Mystery.

AFTER these two general points of the preparation, there remains a third, not common to all kinds of meditations; it is that which some call the fabrication of the place, and others the interior lecture. This consists in representing to your imagination the subject of the mystery on which you desire to meditate, as if it really passed in your presence. For example, would you take for the subject of your meditation our Lord upon the cross, imagine yourself on Mount Calvary, and that you see and hear all that is done and said on the day of the Passion; or, which will be equally to the purpose, imagine our Lord's crucifixion, as the evangelists have described it, to take place in the very place where you are. Observe the same method as I have noted for this meditation when you meditate on death, or hell, or the like mysteries, which treat of visible and sensible objects; but as to other mysteries, such, for example, as the greatness of God, the excellence of virtue, the end for which we were created, which are invisible things, we must not attempt to make use of these kind of imaginations. We may, it is true, use some similitude or comparison to assist us in the consideration of them, but these are somewhat difficult to find, and I wish only to instruct you in so plain and easy a manner that your spirit may not be wearied in inventing comparisons. By means of this kind of imagination we confine our mind within the mystery we mean to meditate on, that it may not ramble to and fro; just as we shut up a bird in a cage, or rather as we tie a hawk by her jesses, that she may rest on the hand.

Yet some will say, "It is better to use the pure thought of faith, and a simple apprehension altogether mental and spiritual, in the representation of these mysteries, or else to imagine that the things are acted in your own spirit." But this manner is too subtle for beginners; therefore until such time as it shall please God to raise you higher, I advise you, Philothea, to remain in the lowly valley I have shown you.

Chapter V

Of the Considerations, which form the second part of the Meditation

AFTER the work of the imagination, follows the work of the understanding, which we call meditation; which consists in nothing else but in framing one or more considerations in order to stir up our affections to God and heavenly things. Hence meditation differs from study and other reflections and considerations, which are made not for the sake of acquiring virtue and the love of God, but for other ends and intentions, as to become learned, or to write or dispute upon them. Having then, as I have already said, confined your spirit within the bounds of the subject on which you desire to meditate; either by the imagination, if the matter be sensible, or by the simple proposition of it, if it be not an object of the senses; begin to form considerations on it; of which you will see examples ready made in the meditations which I have given you. But if your spirit find enough of relish, of light, and of fruit, in any one of them, stop there without going further; doing as the bees do, who never quit a flower so long as they can suck any honey from it; but if you do not find what you want in one consideration after you have turned it over and tried it a little, pass on to another; but go on quite calmly and simply with the work, without hurrying yourself.

Chapter VI

Of Affections and Resolutions; the third part of the Meditation

MEDITATION produces pious motions in the will, or affective part of our soul, such as the love of God and our neighbour; the desire of paradise and eternal glory; zeal for the salvation of souls; imitation of the life of our Lord; compassion, admiration, joy; fear of God's displeasure, of judgment, and of hell; hatred of sin; confidence in the goodness and mercy of God; confusion for the sins of our past life. In these affections our spirit should open itself out and expatiate to the utmost of its power.

You must not, however, Philothea, stop short at these general affections; you must reduce them to specific and particular resolutions for your own correction and amendment. For example; the first Word our Lord spoke on the Cross will doubtless excite in your soul a good affection to imitate it, namely, the desire to pardon your enemies and to love them; but I warn you that this will be to little purpose, if you do not add to it a particular resolution of this sort: Well, then, I will not hereafter be offended at annoying words which such a one—friend or neighbour, servant or ward—may say of me, nor resent this or that affront which such and such a one may put on me; on the contrary, I will say and do such and such a thing in order to win and soften him. And by this means, Philothea, you will correct your faults in a short time; whereas, by affections only, you will accomplish it but slowly, and with difficulty.

Chapter VII

Of the Conclusion, and Spiritual Nosegay

LASTLY, we must conclude our meditation by three acts, which must be done with the greatest humility we can: the first is an act of thanksgiving, giving thanks to God for the affections and resolutions which He has given us, and for His goodness and mercy, which we have found in the mystery of the meditation. The second is an act of oblation, by which we offer to God this His goodness and mercy, the death, the blood, and the virtues of His Son, and, together with them, our affections and resolutions. The third is one of supplication and petition, whereby we ask God and beseech Him to communicate to us the graces and virtues of His Son, and give His blessing upon our affections and resolutions, that we may be able faithfully to put them in execution. We then pray the same things for the church, our pastors, relations, friends, and others. And lastly, as I have already observed, we must conclude with the Lord's Prayer, which is the general and necessary prayer of all the faithful.

To all this I have added (p. 18) that you must gather a little nosegay of devotion; and this is what I mean. One who has been walking in a beautiful garden, does not willingly go away without gathering four or five flowers to keep and smell at the whole day after; so when our spirit has been expatiating in some mystery we ought to select one, or two or three points which we have found most pleasant, and which are most proper for our advancement, to think frequently on them, and to smell them, as it were, spiritually, for the rest of the day. This is to be done in the same place where we have been meditating, entertaining ourselves with it there, or whilst walking by ourselves for some time after.

Chapter VIII

Certain profitable counsels on the subject of Meditation

1. ABOVE all things, Philothea, when you go forth from your meditation, you must, as the occasion offers, remember the resolutions you have taken, in order carefully to reduce them to practice that very day. This is the great fruit of meditation, without which it is not only unprofitable, but frequently hurtful: because virtues meditated upon and not practised, often puff up the spirit and confidence, and make us imagine ourselves to be such as we have resolved and determined to be: which doubtless is true, when our resolutions are lively and solid; but how can they be really such, but rather vain and dangerous, if not reduced to practice? We must therefore, by all means endeavour to practise them, and seek for occasions, little or great, of putting them in execution. For example: if I have resolved by mildness to gain the goodwill of those who offend me, I will seek this very day an opportunity to meet them, and salute them kindly; or if I should not meet them, at least to speak well of them, and pray to God on their behalf.

2. As you go out from this heart-prayer you must take care not to give your heart a jolt, lest you spill the precious balm it has received by means of the prayer. I mean, that you must if possible keep silence a little, and gently remove your heart from prayer to your business, retaining, as long as you can, a feeling of the affections you have conceived. As a man who has received some precious liquor in a beautiful porcelain bowl, to carry home, walks gently, not looking aside, but sometimes he looks before him, for fear of stumbling against a stone, or making a false step, sometimes he looks at his bowl, for fear of not carrying

it level. So ought you to do when you go out from your meditation. Do not turn your attention at once to other things, but look simply before you. For instance, should you meet with any one with whom you are obliged to enter into conversation, it cannot be helped, you must accommodate yourself to it, but in such a way that you have an eye upon your heart, that as little as possible may be spilt of the liquor of holy prayer.

Nay, you must even accustom yourself to know how to pass from prayer to those occupations which your vocation and profession fairly and lawfully require, though they seem ever so distant from the affections you have received in prayer. For example, the lawyer ought to learn how to pass from prayer to pleading, the merchant to his traffic, and the married woman to her duty to her family, and the cares of her household, with so much gentleness and tranquillity that their spirits may not be disturbed : for, since both the one and the other are according to the will of God, we must learn to pass from the one to the other in the spirit of humility and devotion.

3. It may sometimes happen, that immediately after the preparation, your affection will feel itself aspiring up to God. In such a case, Philothea, you must let loose the reins without caring to follow the method which I have given; for although, generally speaking, the considerations ought to precede the affections and resolutions, yet if so be the Holy Ghost gives you the affections without the consideration, you ought not then to go back to seek the consideration, since its only use is to excite the affections. In a word, whenever affections present themselves, we must welcome them and make all give way to them, whether they come before or after all the considerations; and although I have placed affections after considerations, I have done so to distinguish more plainly the parts of prayer; for otherwise it is a general rule never to restrain the affections, but always to let them have their free course when they present themselves; and this I say, not only with regard to the other affections, but also with respect to the acts of thanksgiving, oblation, and petition which may likewise

be used in the midst of the considerations; for they must no more be restrained than the other affections; though afterwards, for the conclusion of the meditation, they must be repeated and taken up again. But as for resolutions, they are always to be made after the affections, and at the end of the meditation, before the conclusion; because as in these we have to represent to ourselves particular and familiar objects, they would put us in danger of distractions, should we mingle them with our affections.

Amidst our affections and resolutions, it is good to use colloquies, speaking sometimes to our Lord, sometimes to the angels, and the persons represented in the mysteries: to the saints, to ourselves, to our own hearts, to sinners, and even to insensible creatures, as one sees David did in his Psalms, and other saints in their meditations and prayers.

Chapter IX

Of the Dryness which is sometimes experienced in Meditation

SHOULD it happen, Philothea, that you feel no relish or comfort in meditation, I conjure you not to disturb yourself on that account, but sometimes open the door of your heart to vocal prayer, complain of yourself to our Lord, confess your unworthiness, beseech Him to assist you, kiss His picture if you have it at hand, say to Him those words of Jacob: *I will not let thee go except thou bless me;*[1] or those of the Canaanitish woman, *Lord, I am a dog; but the dogs eat of the crumbs which fall from their master's table.*[2]

At other times, take up some spiritual book, and read it with attention till your spirit be awakened, and return to you. Or sometimes stir up your heart by some attitude and gesture of

[1] Gen. xxxii. 26.
[2] Mat. xv. 27.

exterior devotion, such as prostrating yourself on the ground, crossing your hands upon your breast, or embracing a crucifix, provided you are alone, or in some private place. But if, after all, you receive no comfort, do not be troubled, however great the dryness, but continue to keep yourself in a devout posture before God. How many courtiers go a hundred times a-year into the prince's presence-chamber, without hopes of speaking to him, but only to be seen by him, and pay him their duty? So ought we, my dear Philothea, to come to holy prayer purely and simply to pay our duty, and testify our fidelity; should it please the divine Majesty to speak to us, and to converse with us by His holy aspirations and interior consolations, it would doubtless be to us a great honour and most delightful pleasure; but should it not please Him to do us this grace, but leave us without speaking to us, any more than if He did not see us, or we were not in His presence, we must not therefore depart, but, on the contrary, we must remain before His sovereign Goodness with a devout and quiet carriage. He will observe our diligence and perseverance, He will be pleased with our patience, and another time when we present ourselves before Him, He will show us grace and will converse with us, and make us experience the sweetness of holy prayer. Yet if He should not do so, let us rest content, Philothea, for it is too great an honour for us to be near Him and under His eye.

CHAPTER X

Morning Exercises

BESIDES this complete and formal mental prayer, and the other vocal prayers which you ought to say once every day, there are five other shorter kinds of prayers, which are, as it were, slips or suckers of the principal prayer; the first is that which is used in the morning as a general preparation for all the works of the day, which you may make in the following manner:

1. Adore God most profoundly, and return Him thanks for the grace He has done you in having preserved you during the past night; and if, during the course of it, you have committed any sin, crave His pardon.

2. Consider that the present day is given you, in order that in it you may gain the future day of eternity, make a firm purpose, therefore, to employ it well, with this intention.

3. Forecast what business, what conversation, what opportunities, you are likely to meet with to serve God; what temptations may befall you to offend Him, either by anger, by vanity, or any other irregularity; and prepare yourself with a firm resolution to make the best use of those means which may offer themselves to you to serve God and advance in devotion; as also on the other hand, dispose yourself carefully to avoid, resist, and overcome whatever may present itself that is prejudicial to your salvation, and the glory of God. And it is not enough to make this resolution; you must also prepare the means of putting it into execution. For example: if I foresee that I am to treat of any business with one that is passionate and easily angered, I will not only resolve to refrain from giving him any offence, but will also prepare words of meekness to prevent his anger, or use the assistance of some person who can keep him in temper. If I foresee that I shall have an opportunity to visit some sick person, I will arrange the time, and the comforts and assistances I may afford him: and so of the rest.

4. This done, humble yourself in the presence of God. Acknowledge that, of yourself, you can do nothing of what you have resolved upon, either as to avoiding evil or doing good; and, as if you held your heart in your hands, offer it, together with all your good designs, to the Divine Majesty, beseeching Him to take it under His protection, and to strengthen it, that it may proceed prosperously in His service, using these or the like words interiorly: "Behold, O Lord, this poor

miserable heart of mine, which, by Thy goodness, has conceived some good affections; but which, alas! is of itself too weak and wretched to execute the good which it desires, unless Thou impart to it Thy heavenly blessing, which for this end I humbly beg of Thee, O merciful Father, through the merits of the passion of thy Son, to whose honour I consecrate this day and all the remainder of my life."

But all these spiritual acts ought to be made briefly and fervently, and before you quit your chamber, if it be possible; that, by means of this exercise, all that you do throughout the whole day following may be watered with the blessing of God; and I beg of you, Philothea, never to fail herein.

Chapter XI

Of the Evening Exercise and Examination of Conscience

As before your corporal dinner you make a spiritual dinner, by means of meditation; so before supper, you must make a devout and spiritual supper or at least a collation. Make, then, some opportunity a little before supper, and then, prostrate before God, recollect your spirit in the presence of Jesus Christ crucified, whom you may represent to yourself by a single consideration and an interior glance of the eye; kindle again in your heart the fire of your morning meditation by a dozen of lively aspirations, humiliations, and loving ejaculations, which you shall make towards this Divine Saviour of your soul; or by repeating the points of your morning meditation which you relished most; or by stirring yourself up to devotion by some new spiritual subject, as you may like best.

As to the examination of conscience, which must be always made before bed-time, every one knows how to perform it. 1. We give thanks to God for having preserved us the day past. 2. We examine how we have behaved ourselves each hour of the day; and to do this more easily, we consider where we have been, with whom, and in what business we have been employed. 3. If we find that we have done any good, we make an act of thanksgiving to God for it; if, on the other hand, we have done any evil, in thought, in word, or in deed, we ask pardon for it of His Divine Majesty, firmly resolving to confess it the first opportunity and carefully to amend of it. 4. Afterwards we commend to the Divine Providence our soul, our body, the church, relations and friends; and 5. Finally, we ask God to watch over us and for us; and thus, with the blessing of God, we go to take the rest which His will has appointed for us.

This exercise, as well as that for the morning, must never be forgotten; since by that for the morning, you open the windows of your soul to the Sun of Righteousness; and by this for the evening, you close them against the darkness of hell.

Chapter XII

Of Spiritual Recollection

It is in this article, my dear Philothea, that I wish you with special affection to follow my counsel, for in it lies one of the most assured means of your spiritual advancement.

As often as you can in the course of the day recall your spirit into the presence of God, by one of the four ways I have marked out for you; observe what God is doing, and what you are doing: you will find his eyes turned towards you and perpetually fixed upon you by an incomparable love. Then say, O my God, why do I not turn my eyes always towards Thee, as Thou always lookest on me? Why dost Thou think incessantly of me, O my Lord, and why do I so seldom think of Thee? Where are we, O my soul? Our true place of rest is God, and where do we find ourselves?

As birds have nests on the trees to retire to when they need, and the deer thickets and coverts into which to retire and hide themselves and enjoy the cool shade in the heat of summer; even so our hearts, Philothea, ought to choose some place each day, either on Mount Calvary, or in the wounds of our Lord, or in some other place near him, to retreat to at every opportunity, there to refresh and recreate ourselves amidst our exterior business; and to take refuge there as in a covert, to seek safety from temptations. Blessed the soul that can say with truth to our Lord: *Thou art my house of defence and my castle, a refuge from the storm, a shadow from the heat.*[1]

Remember then, Philothea, to make occasional retreats into the solitude of your heart, whilst outwardly engaged in business or conversation. This mental solitude cannot be prevented by the multitude of those who are about you, for they are not about your heart but about your body: so your heart may remain alone, in the presence of God alone. This was the exercise of King David amidst his many occupations, as he testifies by a thousand passages in his Psalms, as when he says, *O Lord, as for me, I am always with Thee. I have set God always before me. Unto Thee lift I up mine eyes, O Thou that dwellest in the heavens. My eyes are ever looking unto the Lord.*[2] And indeed our occupations are not ordinarily so serious but that we may from time to time withdraw our heart from them, to replace it in this divine solitude.

When the father and mother of St. Catherine of Sienna had deprived her of every opportunity of place and leisure to pray and meditate, our Lord inspired her to make a little interior oratory within her soul, into which, retiring mentally, she might amidst her exterior affairs, have leisure in this holy solitude of the heart; and when ever the world afterwards assaulted her, she received no inconvenience from it, because, as she said, she shut herself up in her interior closet, where she comforted herself with her hea-

1 Psa. lxx. 3; Isaiah xxv. 4.

2 Psa. xvi. 9, cxxiii. 1, xxv. 14.

venly spouse. And so she afterwards counselled her spiritual children to make a chamber in their heart, and to dwell there.

Withdraw, then, your spirit from time to time into your heart, where, separated from all men, you may familiarly treat on the business of your soul with God. Say with David, *I am become like a pelican in the wilderness, like an owl that is in the desert. I have watched and am become as it were a sparrow that sitteth alone upon the house top.*[3] Which words, besides their literal meaning, which prove that this great king spent some solitary hours in the contemplation of spiritual things, do also point out in their mystical sense three excellent retreats, as it were three hermitages, wherein we may engage in solitude in imitation of our Saviour, who on Mount Calvary was like the *pelican* of the wilderness, which revives her dead young ones with her own blood ; in His *nativity*, in a desolate stable, He was like the *owl* in a ruinous building, mourning and weeping for our offences and sins ; and on the day of His *Ascension* He was like the *sparrow* withdrawing itself and flying up to heaven, which is, as it were, the house-top of the world. In these three solitudes we may make our spiritual retreats, even amidst the turmoil of our employments. The blessed Elzéar, Count of Arian in Provence, having been long absent from his devout and chaste Delphine, she sent an express to him to inform herself of his health, and he returned this answer: "I am very well, my dear wife, but if you desire to see me, seek me in the wound of the side of our sweet Saviour ; for it is there I dwell, and there you will find me ; elsewhere you will seek for me in vain." This was a Christian nobleman. indeed.

3 Psa. cii. 6, 7.

Chapter XIII

Of Aspirations, Ejaculatory Prayers, and Good Thoughts

We retire into God because we aspire to Him, and aspire to Him that we may retire into Him: so that the aspiring to God and the spiritual retiring into Him mutually support each other, and both proceed from and are born of good thoughts.

Aspire then frequently to God, Philothea, by short but ardent dartings of your heart; admire His beauty; invoke His aid; cast yourself in spirit at the foot of the cross; adore His Goodness; address Him frequently on your salvation; give your soul to Him a thousand times a day; fix your interior eye upon His sweetness; stretch out your hand as a little child to its father, that He may conduct you; place Him in your bosom like a delicious nosegay; plant Him in your soul like a standard; and make a thousand sorts of different motions of your heart, to enkindle the love of God and excite within yourself a passionate and tender affection for your divine Spouse. Thus one makes ejaculatory prayers, which the great St. Austin so strenuously recommended to the devout Lady Proba. Philothea, our spirit giving itself to habitual, confidential, and familiar intercourse with its God, will be altogether perfumed with His perfections. There is no difficulty in this exercise as it may be intermixed with our business and occupations without at all hindering them; the rather that whether in spiritual retreat or in interior ejaculations we only make little and short diversions, which nowise prevent but rather assist us in the pursuit of what we are about. The pilgrim who takes a little wine to cherish his heart and refresh his mouth, although he stops a moment for it does not interrupt his journey by so doing, but rather acquires strength to finish it with more ease and expedition, stopping only that he may go on the faster.

Many have collected together a store of vocal aspirations which no doubt are very useful, but if you follow my counsel you will not confine yourself to any set form of words, but pronounce, whether with your heart or mouth, such as love at the moment shall suggest to you; for it will furnish you with as many as you want. It is true, there are certain words which have a peculiar force to satisfy the heart in this respect. Such as the aspirations interspersed so copiously throughout the Psalms of David; the different invocations of the name of Jesus; the ejaculations of love expressed in the Song of Songs. Spiritual songs will also answer the same purpose when sung with attention.

In fine, as they that love with a human and natural affection have their thoughts always turned towards the object of their love, their heart full of affection for it, and their mouth filled with its praises; and when absent, they lose no opportunity to testify their affection by letters, and meet not a tree on whose bark they do not write the name of their beloved; even so, they who love God can never cease to think on Him, sigh for Him, aspire to Him, and speak to Him; and would if it were possible engrave the sacred name of Jesus on the breasts of all mankind.

To this all things invite them, as there is no creature that does not declare to them the praises of their beloved; and as St. Austin, after St. Anthony, says, everything in the world addresses them in a language very intelligible, though dumb, in favour of their love; all things excite them to good thoughts, which give birth to many flights and aspirations of the soul to God. Here are some examples:

St. Gregory, Bishop of Nazianzum, as he himself related to his people, walking on the sea shore, took notice how the waves, advancing upon the beach, left shells and little periwinkles, bunches of sea-weed, small oysters, and such like things, which the sea cast up, or so to say, spit out upon the shore, and then returning with other waves, took part of them back, and swallowed them up again, whilst the adjoining rocks continued firm and immoveable, though the billows beat against them with violence. Upon which he made this admirable reflection: that feeble souls, like shells and bits of weeds, suffer themselves to be borne away, sometimes by affliction and at other times by consolation, at the mercy of the inconstant billows of fortune, but that courageous souls continue firm and unmoved under all kinds of storms; and from this thought he proceeded to those aspirations of David: *Save me, O God, for the waters are come in, even unto my soul. O Lord, deliver me out of the deep waters; I am come into deep waters, so that the floods run over me;*[1] for at that time he was in affliction for the unhappy usurpation attempted by Maximus on his bishopric.

St. Fulgentius, bishop of Ruspa, being present at a general assembly of the Roman nobility, when Theodoric, king of the Goths, made an oration to them, and beholding the splendour of so many great lords, ranked each according to his quality, exclaimed, "O God, how glorious and beautiful must the heavenly Jerusalem be, since here below the earthly Rome appears in so much pomp! for, if in this world so much splendour is permitted to the lovers of vanity, what must that glory be which is reserved in the next world for those who shall behold the Truth!

St. Anselm, archbishop of Canterbury, by whose birth our mountains here were highly honoured,[2] is said to have been admirable in this application of good thoughts. A hare, pressed by hounds, as this holy prelate was proceeding on a journey, ran under his horse as to a place of refuge suggested by the imminent danger of death; and the hounds, barking around, did not attempt to violate the sanctuary to which their prey had had recourse. The sight was indeed extraordinary, and made the whole company laugh; whilst the saint, weeping and sighing, exclaimed: "Alas! you laugh, but the poor beast does not laugh; the enemies of the soul, after hunting and driving her by divers turnings and windings, through all sorts of sins, lie in wait for her at the narrow passage of death, to seize and devour her; and she, in terror, looks

1 Ps. lxix. 2, 15.

2 He was born at Aosta in Piedmont.

everywhere for succour and refuge, which if she find not, then her enemies mock and deride her. Which when the saint had said, he rode on sighing.

Constantine the Great wrote in terms of respect to St. Anthony, at which the religious about him being greatly astonished, "Why," said he, "do you wonder that a king should write to a man? Wonder rather that the eternal God has writ His law to mortal men, yea more, has spoken to them face to face in the person of His Son."

St. Francis, seeing a sheep alone amidst a flock of goats—"Observe," said he to his companion, "the poor little sheep, how mild it is amidst the goats; our blessed Lord was thus meek and humble among the Pharisees." At another time, seeing a little lamb devoured by a hog: "Ah! little lamb," said he, weeping, "how lively dost thou represent the death of my Saviour!"

That great personage of our own age, St. Francis Borgia, whilst yet duke of Gandia, going a hawking, made to himself a thousand devout conceptions. "I admired," he himself said afterwards, "how the falcons come to hand, suffer themselves to be hooded and to be tied to the perch; and that men are so untractable to the voice of God."

The great St. Basil said that the rose amid its thorns makes this remonstrance to men: "That which is most agreeable in this world, O ye mortals, is mingled with sorrow; nothing here is pure; regret is always attached to mirth; widowhood to marriage; care to fruitfulness; ignominy to glory; expense to honour; loathing to delight; and sickness to health. The rose is a fair flower," said this holy man, "yet it makes me very sorrowful, putting me in mind of my sin, for which the earth has been condemned to bring forth thorns."

A devout soul standing by a brook on a very clear night, and seeing the heaven reflected therein with all its stars, exclaimed: "O my God, these very stars I now behold, shall be one day beneath my feet, when thou shalt have lodged me in thy celestial tabernacles; and as the stars of heaven are here represented on the earth, even so are the men of this earth represented in the living fountain of divine charity."

Another, seeing a river flow swiftly by, cried out, "My soul will never be at rest till it be swallowed up in the sea of the Divinity which is its source." St. Frances contemplating a pleasant brook, upon the bank of which she was kneeling at her prayers, was rapt into an ecstasy, and softly repeated over and over again these words: "Thus the grace of my God flows gently and sweetly, like this little stream." Another, looking on the trees in bloom, sighed and said: "Ah! why am I alone without blossom in the garden of the Church?" Another, seeing little chickens gathered together under the hen, said: "Preserve us, O Lord, continually, under the shadow of thy wings." Another, seeing the sun-flower, "When (said he) shall the time come, O my God, that my soul shall thus follow the attractions of thy goodness!" And seeing some pansies, fair to the eye, but having no smell: "Ah," said he, "such are my thoughts, fine conceptions, fair to look upon, but useless and unproductive."

See, Philothea, how one may extract good thoughts and holy aspirations from everything that presents itself amidst the variety of this mortal life. Unhappy they who turn away the creatures from their Creator, to turn them into instruments of sin; and thrice happy they who turn the creatures to the glory of their Creator, and employ their emptiness to the honour of the truth. St. Gregory Nazianzen says: "I am wont to refer all things to my spiritual profit." Read the devout epitaph composed by St. Jerome for St. Paula; for it is charming to see how it is all over besprinkled with aspirations and holy thoughts which she used to draw from all sorts of occurrences.

Now, in these exercises of spiritual retreat and of ejaculatory prayers, the great work of devotion consists. They can supply the defect of all the other kinds of prayer; but failure in them can scarcely be repaired by any other means. Without them one hardly can lead the contemplative life, and can but badly lead the active life. Without them, repose is but idleness, and labour vexation. Therefore I conjure you to embrace them with all your heart, and never to abandon them.

CHAPTER XIV

Of the Holy Eucharist, and how we ought to take part in it

HITHERTO I have said nothing of the Sun of spiritual exercises, the most holy, sacred, and august sacrament and sacrifice of the Eucharist, the centre of the Christian religion, the heart of devotion, the soul of piety, the ineffable mystery which comprises within itself the abyss of divine love, by which God, applying Himself really to us, communicates abundantly His graces and favours.

2. Prayer, O Philothea, united with this divine sacrifice, has an unspeakable power, so that the soul hereby abounds in heavenly favours, as if stayed upon its Beloved, who so fills it with spiritual odours and delights, that it is *like a pillar of smoke perfumed with myrrh and frankincense, with all powders of the merchant*,[1] as it is said in the Song of Solomon.

3. Make every endeavour therefore to assist at the holy Eucharist every day, that you may offer with the priest the holy sacrifice for yourself and the whole church. St. John Chrysostom says the angels always attend in great numbers to honour this adorable mystery; and we, being there with them, and with the same intention, cannot but receive many favourable influences from such association. The choirs of the triumphant church, and those of the church militant unite themselves with our Lord in this divine act, that with Him, in Him, and through Him, they may ravish the heart of God the Father, and make His mercy all our own. What a happiness to a soul devoutly to contribute her affections for the obtaining so precious and desirable a treasure.

4. Should some cause make it impossible for you to assist in the celebration of this sovereign sacrifice by

[1] Song of Solomon, iii. 6.

your actual presence, you should at least send your heart thither; at the usual hour in the morning go to church in spirit if you cannot go otherwise; unite your intention with that of all the faithful; and make the same interior acts of devotion in your closet which you would make were you actually present at the service in some church, represented to your imagination.

5. Now, to assist at Holy Communion in a proper manner, either really or mentally, it is fitting[2]—1. From the beginning till the priest goes up to the altar, make with him your preparation, which consists in placing yourself in the presence of God, acknowledging your unworthiness, and begging pardon for your sins. 2. From the time he goes up to the altar, till the Gospel, consider the advent of our Lord and His life in this world, by a simple and general consideration. 3. From the Gospel till the end of the Creed, consider the preaching of our Saviour, and declare your desire to live and die in the faith and obedience of His holy word, and in the communion of the holy Catholic Church. 4. From the Creed to the Pater Noster, apply your heart to the mysteries of the death and passion of our Redeemer, actually and essentially represented in this holy sacrifice, and which, with the priest and the rest of the people, you must offer to God the Father for His honour and for your salvation. 5. From the Pater Noster to the Communion, strive to excite a thousand desires in your heart, wishing ardently to be for ever united to our Saviour by everlasting love. 6. From the Communion till the end, render thanks to His Divine Majesty for His incarnation, for His life, for His passion, for His death, and for the love He testifies in this holy sacrifice; conjuring Him by it to be for ever merciful to your relations, to your friends, and the whole Church. And finally, humbling yourself, with your whole heart, receive devoutly the benediction of God, which our Lord gives you by the ministry of His officer, the officiating priest.

But should you choose, during the Communion, to meditate upon a series of mysteries

2 It is thought right to retain this, though it does not apply to our Liturgy.

which you are taking in order from day to day, it is not required of you to turn aside to make all these particular acts; but it is enough that at the beginning you direct your attention to adore and offer up this holy sacrifice, by the exercise of your meditation and prayer, since in every meditation the aforesaid acts are contained throughout, either expressly, or tacitly and equivalently.

Chapter XV

Of other Public and Common Exercises

ON Sundays and holy days, besides going to Holy Communion, you ought also, Philothea, to be present at vespers, and other hours of the divine office, as far as your convenience will permit. For as these days are dedicated to God, we ought to perform more acts to His honour and glory on them than on other days. By this means you will feel a thousand sweetnesses of devotion, as St. Austin did, who testifies in his Confessions that hearing the divine offices in the beginning of his conversion, his heart melted into tenderness, and his eyes into tears of piety. And indeed, to say it once for all, there is always more benefit and comfort in the public offices of the Church than in private acts, God having so ordained, that community should be preferred before any kind of particularity.

Enter then willingly into the confraternities of the place wherein you reside, and especially those whose exercises are most productive of fruit and edification, as in so doing you practise a sort of obedience acceptable to God; for although these confraternities are not commanded, they are, nevertheless, recommended by the Church, which, to testify her approbation of them, grants certain privileges to such confraternities. Besides, it is always a charitable thing to concur with other people and to co-operate with others in their good designs; for although it may be that we should perform as good exercises by ourself as we can in the company of the confraternity, and perhaps take more pleasure in performing them in private, yet God is more glorified in our uniting and sharing our good deeds with our brethren and neighbours.

I say the same of all sorts of public prayers and devotions, in which as much as we can, we ought to contribute our good example for the edification of our neighbour, and our affections for the glory of God and the common intention.

CHAPTER XVI

How we ought to hear and read the Word of God

REVERENCE the Word of God, whether you hear it in familiar conversation with your spiritual friends, or whether you hear it at a sermon. Hear it always with attention and reverence. Make all the profit of it you possibly can, and suffer it not to fall to the ground, but receive it into your heart as a precious balm; imitating the Blessed Virgin, who kept and pondered in her heart all the things which were spoken in favour of her Son. Remember that our Lord gathers up the words we speak to Him in our prayers, in proportion as we gather up those He speaks to us by preaching.

Have always at hand some good book of devotion: such as the Spiritual Combat, the Confessions of St. Augustine, St. Jerome's Epistles, and the like, and read a little in them every day with great devotion, as if you were reading a letter which those saints had sent you from heaven to show you the way, and encourage you to come thither. Read also the histories and lives of the saints, in which, as in a looking-glass, you may see the image of the Christian life; and accommodate their actions to your own profit according to your state of life; for although many actions of the saints cannot absolutely be imitated by such as live in the midst of the world, yet they may all be followed at a greater or less distance. For example, the solitude of St. Paul, the first hermit, is imitated in your spiritual and real retreats, of which we have already spoken and shall hereafter speak; the extreme poverty of St. Francis, by the practices of poverty, of which we shall also speak; and so of the rest. It is true, there are some of their histories that give more light for the conduct of our lives than others, such as the life of the blessed mother Teresa, which is admirable in this respect, the lives of the first Jesuits, that of St. Charles Borromeo, archbishop of Milan, of St. Louis, of St. Bernard, the chronicles of St. Francis, and others. There are others, again, which contain more matter of admiration than imitation; as the life of St. Mary of Egypt, of St. Simeon Stylites, of the two Saints Catherine of Sienna and of Genoa, of St. Angela, and such like; which, nevertheless, fail not to give us a great relish in general for the love of God.

CHAPTER XVII

How we ought to receive Inspirations

BY inspirations are meant all those interior attractions, motions, reproaches, and remorses, illuminations and instructions, which God excites in us, preventing our heart with His blessings, through His fatherly care and love, in order to awaken, stimulate, urge, and attract us to the practice of holy virtues, to heavenly love, to good resolutions, and in a word, to everything that may help us on our way to eternal happiness. This is what the Spouse calls knocking at the door, and speaking to the heart of his Spouse, awaking her when she sleeps, calling after her when she is absent, inviting her to eat of his honey, gather apples and flowers in his garden, to sing, and cause her sweet voice to sound in his ears.

That you may the more perfectly comprehend me, I must use a comparison. To come to the full resolution of marriage, three circumstances must hold good together, with respect to the lady who is to be married: *first*, the person is proposed to her; *secondly*, she approves the proposition; *thirdly*, she gives her consent. In like manner, when God wills to do in us, by us, and with us, some act of great love, *first* He proposes it to us by inspiration: *secondly*, we are pleased with it; *thirdly*, we give our full consent to it. For, as there are three steps whereby we descend to the commission of sin—temptation, delectation, and consent—so there are also three steps whereby we ascend to the practice of virtue—inspiration, which is the opposite of temptation; the delectation conceived in the inspiration, which is the opposite of the delectation in the temptation; and the consent to the inspiration, which is the opposite of the consent to the temptation.

Now, though the inspiration should continue during our whole life, yet we should not render ourselves pleasing to God, if we took no pleasure in it; on the contrary, His Divine Majesty would be offended with us, as He was with the Israelites, with whom He was, as He says, forty years praying them to be converted, but they would not hear Him;[1] whereupon He swore in His wrath that they should not enter into His rest. In like manner, the gentleman that had for a long time addressed a lady would be very much disobliged if, after all, she would not hearken to the marriage he desired.

The pleasure we take in inspirations is a great step towards the glory of God; we thereby begin already to please His Divine Majesty; for although this delectation be not yet an entire consent, it is a certain disposition towards it; and if it be a good sign to take pleasure in hearing the Word of God, which is, as it were, an exterior inspiration, it must also be a good thing, and pleasing to

[1] Psa. xcv.

God, to take delight in His internal inspirations. It is this kind of pleasure of which the sacred Spouse speaks when she says, *My soul was melted when my beloved spake.*[2] So the gentleman is already well pleased with the lady whom he addresses, and esteems himself favoured, when he sees her take delight in his addresses.

But after all, it is the consent which perfects the virtuous act. For if, after receiving and taking pleasure in the inspiration, we nevertheless at last refuse our consent to God, we are extremely ungrateful, and highly offend His Divine Majesty, for we seem to despise His favours. Thus it happened to the Spouse; for though the sweet voice of her beloved had touched her heart with a holy pleasure, yet she would not open to him the door, but excused herself with a frivolous excuse; with which her Spouse being justly displeased, went his way, and left her.[3] So the gentleman, who has for a long time sought a lady, and made his addresses agreeable, should he at last be shaken off and despised, would have much more occasion of discontent than if his suit had never been permitted and encouraged.

Resolve, then, Philothea, to accept heartily all the inspirations it shall please God to send you; and when they arrive receive them as the ambassadors of the King of Heaven, who desires to enter into a contract of marriage with you. Attend calmly to their propositions; consider the love with which you are inspired, and cherish the holy inspirations; consent, but with an entire, loving, and steadfast consent; for by this means God, whom you cannot oblige, will hold Himself greatly obliged to your good will. But before you consent to inspirations in things that are of great importance, or that are out of the ordinary way, always consult your spiritual guide, that he may determine whether it is a true or false inspiration; because the enemy, seeing a soul ready to consent to inspirations, often proposes false ones to deceive her, which he can never do so long as she with humility obeys her guide.

The consent being given, you must be diligent to obtain the results and hasten the

2 Song of Sol. v. 6.
3 Song of Sol. v. 2-7.

execution of the inspiration, which is the height of true virtue; for to have the consent in the heart, without proceeding to the result, would be like planting a vine, and not intending that it should bring forth fruit.

Now what contributes wonderfully to all this, is the due practice of the morning exercise and the spiritual retreats above recommended, as by these means we prepare ourselves to do what is good, not only by a general, but also by a particular preparation.

Chapter XVIII

Of Holy Confession

OUR Saviour has left the use of confession to His church, that in it we might cleanse ourselves from all our iniquities, as often as we should be defiled by them. Never suffer your heart, then, Philothea, to remain long infected with sin, since you have a remedy so easy and accessible. As the lioness, having been with the leopard, runs in haste to wash herself, and get rid of the foulness which that contact has left, lest the lion coming should be offended and provoked thereby; so the soul which has consented to sin, ought to conceive a horror of herself, and cleanse herself as quickly as possible, out of the respect she ought to bear to the Divine Majesty, who incessantly beholds her. Ah! why should we die a spiritual death, since we have so sovereign a remedy herein.

Have always a sincere sorrow for the sins you confess, be they ever so small, with a firm resolution to correct yourself of them in future. Many who confess their venial sins merely out of custom, and for the sake of order, without any thought of amendment, continue their whole lifetime under the guilt of them, and by this means lose many spiritual benefits and advantages. If then you confess that you have spoken some untruth, though without malice, or have said some improper word, or have played excessively, repent, and be firmly resolved to amend; for it is an abuse to confess any kind of sin, whether mortal or venial, without the desire to be delivered from it, since confession was instituted for no other end.

Do not make only those superfluous accusations, which some make as a matter of course:—I have not loved God so much as I ought; I have not prayed with so much devotion as I ought; I have not loved my neighbour as I ought; I have not received the sacraments with so great reverence as I ought, and such like; for in saying this you will say nothing definite which can make your confessor understand the state of your conscience; since every saint in heaven, and every man on earth might say the same things if they were to come to confession. Examine, then, what particular cause you may have to make these accusations; and when you have discovered it, accuse yourself of the fault which you have done simply and ingenuously. For example: you accuse yourself of not having loved your neighbour so much as you ought; perhaps, because having seen some poor person in distress, whom you might easily have helped and comforted, you took no notice of him; well, then, accuse yourself of this definite thing, and say, "Having seen a poor man in necessity, I did not assist him as I might have done, through negligence, or through hard-heartedness, or through contempt, acccording to what you know to have been the cause of this fault. In like manner, do not accuse yourself of not having prayed to God with as much devotion as you ought; but if you have admitted any voluntary distractions, or neglected to take the place, or the time, or the posture requisite for insuring attention in prayer, accuse yourself simply of the fault whatever you find it to have been, without those general allegations which are neither one thing nor another in confession.

Do not content yourself with confessing your venial sins, merely as to the fact; but assure yourself also of the motive which induced you to commit them. For example: do not content yourself with saying you have told an untruth without injury to any person; but also declare whether it was out of vain-glory, to praise or excuse yourself; or in jest, or through obstinacy. If you have sinned in play, express whether it was for the desire of gain, or for the pleasure of conversation: and so of the rest. Tell also how long a time you continued in your sin; for the length of time is ordinarily a great aggravation of the sin, there being a great difference betwixt a vain thought which has passed through the soul in a quarter of an hour, and one which she has indulged for one or two or three days. We must then tell the fact, the motive, and continuance of our sins. For though commonly we are not bound to be so punctilious in declaring venial sins, and indeed are not absolutely obliged to confess them at all, yet such as desire to cleanse their souls perfectly, the better to attain to holy devotion, should be careful to make their spiritual physician acquainted with the evil, be it ever so small, of which they desire to be cured.

Fail not then to tell what is requisite that he may perfectly understand the nature of your offence. For example: a man whom I dislike says some light word in jest, and I take it in bad part, and I put myself in a passion; whereas, if another whom I liked had said something more harsh, I should have taken it in good part; in such case I should not fail to say, I have spoken angry words against a certain person, having taken in bad part some things he said to me, not so much on account of the nature of the words, as because I dislike the person. Moreover, if, to make the matter more clear, it be necessary to state what the words were, I think it would be right to declare them, as by accusing yourself thus ingenuously you not only discover your sin, but also your evil inclinations, customs, habits, and other roots of the sin; by means of which your spiritual father acquires a more perfect knowledge of the heart he deals with, and of the remedies most proper to be applied. But you must always conceal the third person who has had any part in your sin, as much as lies in your power.

Beware of a number of sins that often live and reign insensibly in the soul, in order that you may confess them, and be able to purge yourself of them. To this end, read attentively the 6th, 27th, 28th, 29th, 35th, and 36th chapters of the Third Part, and the 7th chapter of the Fourth Part.

Do not lightly change your confessor; but having made choice of one, continue on the appointed days to give him an account of the state of your conscience, telling him ingenuously and frankly the sins you have committed, and from time to time, once every month or two months, let him also know the state of your inclinations, though you may not have sinned by them: for instance, if you have been tormented with sadness or with melancholy, or if you have been inclined to pleasure, or to the desire of acquiring worldly goods; and such like inclinations.

Chapter XIX

Of Frequent Communion

It is said that Mithridates, king of Pontus, having invented the mithridate, so strengthened his body thereby, that afterwards when he endeavoured to poison himself, to avoid falling into the hands of the Romans, he could not. Our Saviour has instituted the most venerable sacrament of the Eucharist, which contains really His flesh and His blood, that whosoever eateth may live for ever. Whosoever, therefore, frequently eateth thereof, with devotion, so confirms the health and life of his soul, that it is almost impossible he should be poisoned by any kind of evil affection: for we cannot be nourished with this flesh of life, and at the same time live with the affections of death. Thus as men, dwelling in the terrestrial paradise, might have avoided corporal death, by the power of the fruit of the tree of life which God hath planted therein, so they may also avoid spiritual death, by the virtue of this sacrament of life. If the most tender fruits, and such as are most subject to corruption, as cherries, strawberries, and apricots, can be easily kept the whole year, when preserved with sugar or honey, no wonder that our hearts, although frail and weak, are preserved from the corruption of sin, when sugared and honied with the incorruptible flesh and blood of the Son of God? O Philothea, Christians who shall be condemned will be speechless when the just Judge shall upbraid them with their folly in having involved themselves in eternal death, since it was so easy to have maintained themselves in spiritual life and health by feeding on his body, which he left them for this end—Miserable wretches! will he say, why did you die, having the fruit and the food of life at your command.

"The practice of receiving the holy communion every day I neither praise nor blame; but to communicate every Sunday, I persuade and exhort every one, provided his soul be without any affection to sin." These are the very words of St. Augustine, with whom I neither absolutely blame nor approve of the practice of communicating daily, but leave it to the discretion of the ghostly father of him that would be resolved on this point; for as extraordinary dispositions are required for daily communion, it is not prudent to recommend it generally; and since these dispositions, although extraordinary, are found in many pious souls, it is not advisable to dissuade generally from it; but it must be regulated by the consideration of the inward state of each individual. It would be imprudent to advise every one without distinction to so frequent communion, but it would also be imprudent also to blame any one for it, especially if he is following the advice of a prudent director. The reply of St. Catherine of Sienna was happy, when it was objected to her frequent communion that St. Augustine neither praised nor blamed daily communion—"Well, then," said she, "since St. Austin blamed it not, I pray do not you blame it any more than he, and I shall be content."

But, Philothea, you see that St. Augustine strongly advises and exhorts us to communicate every Sunday; comply with his advice as far as you may be able; for since, I assume, you have no affection to either mortal or venial sin, you are in that disposition which St. Augustine requires, yea, and in a more excellent degree, since you not only have no desire to commit sin, but retain in you not even an affection to sin; so that, should your ghostly father think it proper, you may profitably communicate still more frequently than every Sunday.

However, many lawful impediments may occur, not, perhaps, on your own part, but on the part of those with whom you live, which may occasion a discreet guide to advise you not to communicate so often. For example: if you live in a state of subjection, and they to whom you owe obedience or reverence are so ill instructed, or so capricious, as to be troubled or disquieted to see you communicate so frequently; in such a case it would, all things considered, be advisable to condescend to their infirmity, and communicate but once a fortnight; but this is to be understood when you can by no means remove the difficulty. It is not possible to lay down any general rule in this case; we must, therefore, act according to the advice of our spiritual director; though I may say assuredly, that the distance between the times of communicating, for such as desire to serve God devoutly, should not exceed a month.

If you act with proper prudence, neither father, mother, husband, nor wife, will prevent you from communicating often; for if, on the day of your communion, you are not less diligent in the duties of your calling, if you are more gentle and kind towards others, and if you do not refuse any sort of duties which you owe them, there can be no likelihood that they should seek to prevent you from an exercise which brings them no kind of inconvenience, except they should be of a spirit extremely froward and unreasonable; and in that case, as I have said already, your director will advise you to use some condescension.

The primitive Christians communicated every day, although married, and blessed with children; from whence I infer, that frequent communion is by no means inconsistent with the state of a parent, husband, or wife, provided the party that communicates be prudent and discreet. As for bodily diseases, there are none which can be a lawful impediment to this holy devotion, excepting that which provokes to frequent vomiting.

To communicate every week, it is requisite that one should be free from mortal sin, and without any affection to venial sin, and have, moreover, a great desire to communicate; but to communicate every day, it is necessary that we should have overcome the greatest part of our evil inclinations, and that it should be by the advice of our spiritual director.

Chapter XX

How we ought to Communicate

BEGIN to prepare yourself for the holy communion the evening before, by many aspirations and ejaculations of love, retiring earlier, that you may rise sooner in the morning. Should you awake in the night, fill your heart and mouth immediately with some odorous words, in order that your soul may be perfumed for the reception of her spouse, who, waking while you are sleeping, is preparing a thousand graces and favours for you, if on your part your are disposed to receive them. In the morning, rise with great joy on account of the happiness you hope for; and, having confessed, go with great confidence, but also with great humility, to receive this heavenly meat, which nourishes your soul to immortality; and when the time comes, after repeating, *Lord, I am not worthy that Thou shouldest come under my roof*, full of faith, hope, and charity, receive Him, in whom, by whom, and for whom you believe, hope, and love. O

Philothea, represent to yourself, that as the bee, after gathering from the flowers the dew of heaven, and the choicest juice of the earth, and reducing them into honey, carries them into her hive, so the priest, having taken from the altar the body and blood of the Saviour of the world, the true Son of God, who, like the dew, is descended from heaven, and the true Son of the Virgin, who like a flower, is sprung from the earth of our humanity, puts them as delicious food into your mouth and body.

Having received Him, rouse up your heart to do homage to the King of your salvation, treat with Him concerning your spiritual affairs; consider that He is within you, where He has taken up His abode for your happiness; make Him all the welcome you possibly can; and conduct yourself in such a manner that it may appear in all your actions that God is with you.

But when you cannot have the advantage of communicating really at the holy Eucharist, communicate at least spiritually, uniting yourself by an ardent desire to this life-giving flesh of our Saviour.

Your principal intention in communicating should be to advance, strengthen and comfort yourself in the love of God; for you must receive through love that which love alone caused to be given to you. You cannot consider our Saviour in an action either more full of love, or more tender than this in which He annihilates Himself, as it were, and changes Himself into meat, that so He may penetrate our souls, and unite Himself intimately to the hearts and to the bodies of His faithful ones.

If worldings ask you why you communicate so often, tell them it is to learn to love God, to purify yourself from your imperfections, to be delivered from your miseries, to be comforted in your afflictions and supported in your weaknesses. Tell them that two sorts of persons ought to communicate frequently, the perfect, because being well disposed, they would be greatly to blame not to approach to the source and fountain of perfection; and the imperfect, to the end they may be able to aspire to perfection; the strong, lest they should become weak; and the weak, that they may become strong; the sick, that they may be healed; and the healthy, lest they fall into sickness; that for your part being imperfect, weak, and sick, you have need of frequent communion with Him who is your perfection, your strength and your medicine. Tell them, that such as have not many worldly affairs to look after ought to communicate often, because they have leisure for it; that such as have much business on their hands should also communicate often, because they have need of it; that he who labours much, and is loaded with cares, ought to eat solid meats, and that frequently. Tell them that you receive the holy sacrament frequently, to learn to receive it well; because one hardly performs an action well, which he does not often practise.

Communicate frequently, then, Philothea, and as often as you can, with the advice of your spiritual Father; and believe me, as hares in our mountains become white in winter, because they neither see nor eat anything but snow; so, by approaching to, and eating beauty, purity, and goodness itself in this divine sacrament, you will become fair and pure and good.

PART THE THIRD

CONTAINING CERTAIN COUNSELS CONCERNING THE PRACTICE OF THE VIRTUES

CHAPTER I

Of the Choice we ought to make as to the exercise of the Virtues

AS the queen of the bees never goes abroad without being surrounded by all her little subjects, so charity never enters the heart without bringing all the other virtues in her train, arraying and manœuvring them, as a captain does his soldiers. But she does not employ them all at once, nor all alike, nor at all times, nor in every place. The righteous man *is like a tree planted by the water side, which brings forth his fruit in due season,*[1] because charity, watering the soul, produces in it good works, each in its season. *A tale out of season is as music in mourning,*[2] says the proverb. It is a great fault in many, who undertaking the practice of some particular virtue, are determined to exercise it on all occasions. Like the ancient philosophers, they are always weeping or laughing; nay they are worse than they, for they blame and reprove all who do not always exercise the same virtues as themselves; whereas we should *rejoice with them that do rejoice, and weep with them that weep,*[3] says the apostle, for *charity*, says he, *suffereth long and is kind, envieth not,*

1 Psa. i. 3.

2 Ecclus. xxii. 6.

3 Rom. xii. 15.

vaunteth not itself, is not puffed up.[4]

There are, however, some virtues of general utility, which ought not only to be exercised by themselves, but ought also to communicate their qualities to the practice of all other virtues. Occasions are seldom presented for the exercise of fortitude, magnanimity, and munificence; but meekness, temperance, modesty and humility are virtues wherewith all the actions of our life ought to be tinged. There are virtues more excellent than these, but the use of these is more necessary. Sugar is more excellent than salt, but the use of salt is more frequent and general. We must always therefore have a good store of these general virtues in readiness, since we have occasion to use them almost continually.

In the exercise of the virtues, we should always prefer that which is most conformable to our duty, not that which is most agreeable to our inclination. St. Paula's inclination was to use rigour in corporal mortifications, that she might more easily enjoy spiritual sweetnesses, but she was under a greater obligation to obey her superiors; and therefore St. Jerome blamed her for using immoderate abstinences against her bishop's advice. The apostles, on the other hand, being commissioned to preach the gospel and distribute the bread of heaven to the souls of men, judged that they should be wrong to interrupt these holy exercises for the love of the poor, though that is an excellent virtue. Every condition of life has its own peculiar virtue. A prelate has his peculiar virtues, a prince his, and a soldier his, a married woman has hers, a widow hers. Though all ought to possess all the virtues, yet all are not bound to exercise them equally, but each ought to practise, in a more particular maner, those virtues which are most requisite for the state of life to which he is called.

Among the virtues, unconnected with our particular duty, we ought to prefer the most excellent, not the most showy. Comets usually appear greater than stars, and occupy a greater space in our eyes, whereas in reality, they cannot, either in magnitude or quality, be compared with

[4] 1 Cor. xiii. 4.

the stars; and only seem greater because they are nearer, and of a grosser nature than the stars; so there are certain virtues which because they are near, and easily seen, and so to say material, are highly esteemed, and always preferred by the vulgar. Thus they commonly prefer corporal alms-giving before spiritual; the hair shirt, fasting, going barefoot, using the discipline, and other such corporal mortifications, before meekness, gentleness, modesty, and other mortifications of the heart, which are nevertheless much more excellent. Choose then, Philothea, the best virtues, not the most highly thought of; the mostexcellent, not the most apparent; those which are really the best, not those which are the most showy.

It is profitable for every one to select some particular virtue for special cultivation, yet not so as to abandon the rest, but to keep his spirit more justly ordered and occupied. A beautiful virgin, in royal attire and ornaments brighter than the sun, crowned with a crown of olives, appeared to St. John, bishop of Alexandria, and said to him: *I am the eldest daughter of the king; if thou canst have me for thy friend I shall conduct thee to his presence.* He understood that she was mercy towards the poor, which God recommended to him; and, therefore, ever after he give himself up so absolutely to the practice of this virtue, as on that account to be everywhere called St. John the Almoner. Eulogius the Alexandrian, desiring to do some particular service to God, and not having strength enough to embrace a solitary life, nor to subject himself to the obedience of another, took into his house a poor wretch all diseased and disfigured with leprosy, that he might exercise on him the virtues of charity and mortification; and that he might perform them the more worthily, he made a vow to honour him as a servant does his master, and so to treat and wait upon him; and when a temptation happened as well to the leper as to Eulogius, to depart the one from the other, they addressed themselves to the great St. Anthony, who said: "Take care, my children, not to depart from one another, for you are both near your end, and if the angel do not find you together, you run a great risk of losing your crowns."

The king St. Louis visited hospitals, and served the sick with his own hands as diligently as if he had served for wages. St. Francis loved poverty above all virtues, and called her his Lady. St. Dominick loved preaching, from which his order has taken its name. St. Gregory the Great, following the example of the great Abraham, took pleasure in entertaining pilgrims, and, like him, received the King of Glory in the form of a pilgrim. Tobias practised the charity of burying the dead. St. Elizabeth, though a great princess, loved above all to humble herself. St. Catherine of Genoa, in her widowhood, dedicated herself to serve an hospital. Cassian relates, that a devout lady desirous to be exercised in the virtue of patience, had recourse to St. Athanasius, who, at her request placed her with a poor widow, exceedingly peevish, choleric, passionate, disagreeable, and unbearable, who continually scolding this devout lady, gave her ample occasion to exercise the virtues of meekness and endurance.

Thus, among the servants of God, some apply themselves to serve the sick; others to relieve the poor; others to advance the knowledge of Christian truth amongst children; others to reclaim lost and wandering souls; others to adorn churches and deck altars; others to restoring peace and concord among such as have been at variance. In this they are like embroiderers who upon different grounds lay in beautiful variety silks and gold and silver to resemble all kinds of flowers; for thus these pious souls who make choice of some particular exercise of devotion make it the ground for the spiritual embroidery, upon which they practise the variety of all other virtues; holding by this means all their actions and affections better united and ordered, by referring them to their principal exercise; and thus they show forth their spirit *in a vesture of gold wrought about with divers colours.*[5]

When assaulted by any vice, we must as earnestly as we can embrace the practice of the contrary virtue, and refer all others to it; by which means we shall over-

[5] Ps. xlv. 9.

come our enemy, and at the same time advance in all the virtues. Thus, if assaulted by pride or anger, I must in all my actions turn and bend to the side of humility and meekness, and make all my other exercises of prayer and sacraments, of prudence, constancy, and sobriety subservient to this end. For as the wild boar, to sharpen his tusks, whets and polishes them with his other teeth, which are themselves also pointed and sharpened thereby; so a virtuous man, having undertaken to perfect himself in that virtue of which he stands in most need for his defence, files and polishes it by the exercise of the other virtues, which, whilst they help to refine that one, become all of them more excellent, and better polished. Thus it happened to Job, who exercising himself particularly in patience, against the many temptations whereby he was assaulted, became perfectly established and confirmed in all kinds of virtues. Thus, says St. Gregory Nazianzen, it has happened that by a simple act of some virtue perfectly practised, a person has attained to the height of all virtue; alleging the example of Rahab, who having perfectly practised the virtue of hospitality, arrived at a great degree of glory. But this is to be understood when such a virtue is practised with great fervour and charity.

Chapter II

A continuation of the same Discourse about the Choice of Virtues

St. Augustine well says, that young beginners in devotion commit certain faults, which according to the rigour of the laws of perfection are blameable, and yet commendable on account of the presage they give of future excellence in piety, to which they serve as a disposition. That low and servile fear which begets excessive scruples in the souls of new converts from a course of sin, is commendable in beginners, and a certain presage of a future purity of conscience; but the same fear would be blameable in those who are far advanced, in whose heart love ought to reign, which, little by little, drives away this kind of servile fear.

St. Bernard, when he began was full of rigour and harshness towards those who put themselves under his direction; he told them to begin with that they must leave the body behind, and come to him only with the spirit. When he heard their confessions, he treated with extraordinary severity all sorts of faults, however small; and so vehemently urged these poor novices on to perfection, that instead of helping them forward, he drove them back; for they lost heart and breath to see themselves so earnestly pressed up so steep and high an ascent. Observe, Philothea, it was an ardent zeal for perfect purity that induced this great saint to adopt this manner of proceeding, and this zeal was a great virtue which did not fall short, nevertheless, of being reprehensible; so that God Himself corrected him for it in a holy vision, pouring at the same time into his soul a meek, gentle, amiable, and tender spirit, so that, being totally changed, he repented of his former rigour and severity, and became so gracious and condescending to every one, as to make himself all to all, that he might gain all. St. Jerome having related how his dear daughter St. Paula, was not only excessive, but obstinate, in the exercise of bodily mortification, to such a degree that she would not yield to the contrary advice which St. Epiphanius, her bishop, had given her on this subject; and moreover, that she suffered herself to be carried away with such excessive grief for the death of her friends as to be herself frequently in danger of death; concludes at length with these words: "Some will say, that instead of writing the praises of this holy woman, I write dispraises and censures of her; but I call Jesus to witness, whom she served, and whom I desire to serve, that I lie not either on one side or on the other, but set down sincerely what relates to her, as one Christian of another; that is to say, I write her history, not her panegyric; and her vices are the virtues of others." He meaning that the failings and defects of St. Paula would have been virtues in a soul less perfect; and that there are actions esteemed imperfections in the perfect which would be held great perfections in those who are imperfect.

It is a good sign when, at the end of sickness, the legs of the sick person swell, for it shows that nature, now acquiring strength, casts out the superfluous humours; but this would be a bad symptom in one that was not sick, as it would show that nature had not sufficient strength to resolve and dissipate the humours. We must, my Philothea, have a good opinion of those who practise virtues, though with imperfections, since we see the saints themselves have often practised them in this manner. But as to ourselves, we must be careful to exercise them, not only faithfully, but discreetly; and to this end we must strictly observe the advice of the wise man, *not to lean on our own understanding*,[1] but on the judgment of those whom God has given us for conductors.

There are certain things which many esteem as virtues, which in reality are not virtues at all, concerning which I must say a word to you; I mean ecstacies or raptures, insensibilities, impassibilities, deifical unions, elevations, transformations, and such like perfections, treated of in certain books, which promise to elevate the soul to a contemplation purely intellectual, to an essential application of the spirit, and a supernatural life. But observe well, Philothea, these perfections are not virtues, but rather the recompences which God gives for virtues, or still rather they are specimens of the happinesses of the life to come, which God sometimes presents to men, to make them desire the entireties which are above in heaven.

But, for all that, we must not aspire to such favours, since they are by no means necessary to the serving and loving of God well, which ought to be our only pretension; neither are they such as can be obtained by labour and industry, since they are

[1] Prov. iii. 5.

rather passions than actions; which we may indeed receive, but cannot produce in ourselves. I add, that we have only undertaken to make ourselves good, devout, and pious men and women, and it is necessary to occupy ourselves diligently in this; but if it should please God to elevate us to these angelic perfections, we shall then be also good angels; but in the meantime, let us endeavour simply, humbly, and devoutly to acquire those simple virtues, those self-conquests, which our Saviour has put within the reach of our care and labour; such as patience, meekness, mortification of the heart, humility, obedience, poverty, chastity, tenderness toward our neighbours, bearing with their imperfections, diligence, and holy fervour. Let us willingly leave those supereminent favours to elevated souls; we merit not so high a rank in the service of God; too happy shall we be to serve Him in His kitchen or pantry, to be His porters or His pages. It is for Him hereafter, if he should think proper, to admit us into His cabinet or privy council. Yea, Philothea, this King of glory does not recompense His servants according to the dignity of the offices they hold, but according to the love and humility with which they exercise them. Saul, seeking his father's asses, found the kingdom of Israel. Rebecca, watering the camels of Abraham, became the spouse of his son. Ruth gleaning after the reapers of Boaz, and lying down at his feet, was advanced to his side and made his wife. High and elevated pretensions to extraordinary favours are very much subject to illusions, deceits, and falsities; and it sometimes happens that those who think themselves angels, are not so much as good men, and that in truth there is more sublimity in their words and expressions, than in their manner of thinking and acting. We must, however, neither despise nor censure anything rashly; but blessing God for the supereminence of others, keep ourselves in our lower but safer way, less eminent, and better suited to our insufficiency and littleness; in which if we conduct ourselves with humility and fidelity, God will infallibly elevate us to greatness that will be great indeed.

CHAPTER III

Of Patience

YE *have need of patience, that after ye have done the will of God, ye might receive the promise,*[1] says the Apostle. Yea, our Saviour Himself has said, *In your patience possess ye your souls.*[2] It is a man's great happiness, Philothea, to possess his soul; and the more perfect our patience, the more perfectly do we possess them. Let us frequently call to mind that as our Lord has saved us by patient suffering, we also must work out our salvation by sufferings and afflictions; enduring injuries, and contradictions, and afflictions with all possible meekness.

Do not limit your patience to such or such kind of injuries and afflictions, but extend it to all such as it shall please God to send, or permit to befall you. Some are unwilling to suffer any other tribulations but such as are honourable; as, for example, to be wounded in battle, to be prisoners of war, to be persecuted for religion, or to be impoverished by some lawsuit determined in their favour. These people do not love the tribulation, but the honour wherewith it is accompanied; whereas he that is truly patient, and the servant of God, suffers indifferently tribulations accompanied by ignominy or by honour. To be despised, reprehended, or accursed by wicked men, is only pleasant to a man of good heart; but to be blamed, accursed, and ill-treated by the good or by our friends and relatives, herein true patience may be shown. I estimate the meekness with which the great St. Charles Borromeo suffered a long time the public reprehensions that a great preacher, of a strictly reformed order, uttered against him in the pulpit, more highly than that with which he bore all the assaults he received from others; for just as the stinging of bees is far more pain-

[1] Heb. x. 36. [2] Luke xxi. 19.

ful than that of flies, so the evils we suffer from good men and their contradictions are much more insupportable than what we suffer from others; and yet it often happens that two good men, having each of them the best intentions, through a diversity of opinion, foment great persecutions and contradictions against each other.

Be patient, not only with respect to the afflictions which may befall you, but also with respect to their accessories or accidental circumstances. Many could be content to encounter evils, provided they might not be incommoded by them. I should not be vexed, says one, at being poor, were it not that it disables me from serving my friends, from giving my children a proper education, and from living as respectably as I could wish. It would give me no concern, says another, were it not that the world will think it happened through my own fault. Another would be content to be slandered, and would bear it quite patiently, provided no one would believe the detractor. Others are willing to suffer some part of the inconvenience of evil, but not the whole; they do not fret on account of their sickness, but for the want of money to get themselves cured, or because they are so troublesome to those about them. Now I say, Philothea, we must not only have patience to be sick, but also be content to be sick of whatever disorder God pleases, in whatever place, amongst such persons as He pleases, and with such inconveniences as He pleases; and so of other tribulations. When any evil befals you, apply such remedies as may be in your power, and agreeable to the will of God; for to act otherwise would be to tempt His Divine Majesty; but having done this, wait with entire resignation for the success it may please God to send; and if it please Him that the remedies overcome the evil, return Him thanks with humility; but if it please Him that the evil should overcome the remedies, bless Him with patience.

I agree with the counsel of St. Gregory: Whenever you are justly accused of a fault, humble yourself very heartily, and candidly confess that you deserve the accusation that is brought against you: but if the charge be false, excuse yourself meekly, denying your guilt; for you owe this respect to the truth, and to the edification of your neighbour. But if, after your true and lawful excuse, they continue to accuse you, do not at all trouble yourself, and do not strive to get your excuse admitted; for having discharged your duty to truth, you must also do the same to humility; by which means you neither offend against the care you ought to have of your reputation, nor the love you owe to peace, meekness of heart, and humility.

Complain as little as possible of the wrongs done you; for, commonly speaking, he who complains sins, because self-love always makes us believe the injuries done to us greater than they really are. But above all, do not make complaints to persons who are easily angered or apt to think evil; but if complaints be necessary, either to remedy the offence, or to restore quiet to your mind, let them be made to the meek and such as truly love God; otherwise, instead of easing your heart, they will provoke it to greater pain; for instead of pulling out the thorn which pricks you, they will thrust it further into your foot.

Many, when sick, afflicted, or injured by others, refrain from complaining, or showing a sensibility of that they suffer, because that, as they think—and they are right in thinking so — would show plainly a want of fortitude and nobleness; but they greatly desire, and try to bring it about by various artifices, that every one should complain for them, and have great commiseration for them, and admire their patience and fortitude. Now this is a patience, but not true patience, rather it is a refined ambition and subtle vanity. *They have whereof to glory*, says the apostle, *but not before God.*[3] The truly patient man neither complains himself, nor desires to be pitied by others; he speaks of his sufferings with truth and sincerity, without murmuring, complaining, or aggravating the matter; he patiently permits himself to be condoled by others, unless they pity him for an evil which he has not; for then he will modestly declare that he suffers not that evil; and thus he continues peaceable

[3] Rom. iii. 2.

between truth and patience, keeping his trouble to himself, and not complaining of it.

Amidst the contradictions which will befal you in the exercise of devotion, for this will not fail to be the case, remember the words of our Lord, *A woman when she is in travail hath sorrow, because her hour is come; but when she hath brought forth her child, she remembereth no more the anguish, for joy that a man is born into the world.*[4] For you have conceived in your soul the noblest child in the world, which is Jesus Christ, and until He be quite brought forth, you cannot but suffer in labour; but be of good courage, these sorrows once past, everlasting joy will remain to you for having born such a man into the world. Now, you will have wholly brought Him forth when you have entirely formed Him in your heart, and in your works, by the imitation of His life.

In sickness offer up all your griefs, and pains, and languors as a sacrifice to our Lord, and beseech him to unite them with the torments He suffered for you. Obey your physician; take your medicines, food, and other remedies, for the love of God; remembering the gall He took for the love of you; desire to be cured that you may serve Him, but refuse not to continue sick that you may obey Him; and dispose yourself to die, if it be His pleasure, that you may praise and enjoy Him for ever.

Remember that as bees whilst making their honey, live upon bitter food, so we can never perform acts of greater sweetness, nor better compose the honey of excellent virtues, than whilst we eat the bread of bitterness, and live in the midst of afflictions. And as the honey that is gathered from the flowers of thyme, a small bitter herb, is the best of all honeys, so the virtue which is exercised in the bitterness of the meanest and most abject tribulations is the most excellent of all virtues.

Look frequently with the spiritual eye on Christ Jesus crucified, naked, blasphemed, slandered, forsaken, and overwhelmed with all sorts of troubles, sorrows, and labours; and consider that all your sufferings, neither in quality nor quantity, are to

[4] John xvi. 21.

be compared with His, and that you can never suffer anything for Him equal to what He has endured for you.

Consider the torments which the martyrs of old have suffered, and those which so many persons now endure, more grievous beyond comparison than yours, and then say: Alas! are not my sufferings consolations, and my pains pleasures, in comparison of those who, without any relief, assistance, or mitigation, live in a continual death, overwhelmed with afflictions infinitely greater than mine.

CHAPTER IV

Of Exterior Humility

BORROW *empty vessels not a few*, said Elisha, *and pour oil into them.*[1] To receive the grace of God into our hearts, they must be emptied of vainglory. The kestrel, by crying and looking on the birds of prey, affrights them by a secret property peculiar to herself, which makes the doves love it above all other birds, and live in security near it; so humility repels Satan, and preserves the graces and gifts of the Holy Ghost within us; and therefore all the saints, but particularly the King of Saints and His Mother, have always honoured and loved this blessed virtue more than any other amongst the moral virtues. We call that glory *vain* which we assume to ourselves, either for what is not in us, or for what is in us, but does not deserve that we should glory in it. The nobility of our ancestors, the favour of great men, popular honour, these are things not in us, but either in our progenitors, or in the esteem of other men. There are people who are made proud and insolent by riding a good horse, wearing a feather in their hat, or being dressed in a fine suit of clothes: but who sees not the folly of this?

[1] 2 Kings iv. 3.

for if there be any glory in such things, the glory belongs to the horse, the bird, and the tailor; and what a meanness of spirit must it be to take one's value from a horse, a feather, or the fashion of one's coat? Others value and admire themselves for a turned-up moustache, for a well-trimmed beard, for curled locks, or soft hands; or because they can dance, sing, or play; but are not these poor-spirited men, who seek to increase their value and raise their reputation by such frivolous and foolish things? Others for a little learning would be honoured and respected by the whole world, as if every one ought to go to school to them and take them for their masters; and therefore we call them pedants. Others strut like peacocks in the consciousness of their beauty, and think that all the world is in love with them. All this is extremely vain, foolish, and impertinent; and the glory which they derive from such poor causes is justly esteemed vain, foolish, and frivolous.

True goodness is proved like true balm: we try balm by distilling it in water; if it sinks and rests at the bottom, it is accounted to be of the most excellent and precious kind; so, would you know whether a man is truly wise, learned, generous, or noble, observe whether his good qualities tend to humility, modesty, and submission, for then they are good indeed; but if they swim on the surface, and strive to appear above water, their real value is less in the proportion in which they are more displayed. Pearls that are conceived and nourished by the wind, or by the noise of thunder, have nothing of the substance, but only the outside appearance of pearl, so the virtues and good qualities of men that are bred and nourished by pride, ostentation, and vanity, have nothing but the appearance of good, without juice, marrow, or substance.

Honours, rank, and dignities are like saffron, which thrives best and grows more plentifully for being trodden under foot. It is no longer honour to be handsome when a man prizes himself for it; beauty, to have a good grace, should be disregarded; and learning is a disgrace to us, when it puffs us up and degenerates into pedantry.

If we are punctilious for rank, precedence, and titles, besides exposing our qualities to be examined, scrutinized, and contradicted, we render them vile and contemptible; for as honour is beautiful when freely given, so it becomes base when exacted or sought after and demanded. When the peacock spreads his tail to admire himself, in raising up his beautiful feathers, he ruffles all the rest, and discovers his deformities. Flowers that are beautiful whilst they grow in the earth, wither when handled; and as they who smell the mandrake at a distance, in passing by, perceive a most agreeable odour, whilst they who smell it near, and for a long time, become stupified and sick; so honours give a pleasant gratification to those who smell them slightly and afar off, without stopping to amuse themselves with them, or taking trouble about them; but they who affect them and feed on them, are exceedingly blameable and worthy of reprehension.

The pursuit and love of virtue tends to make us virtuous; but the pursuit and love of honours tends to make us contemptible and worthy of blame. Generous minds dc not amuse themselves about the petty toys of rank, and honours, and salutations; they have other things to do; that is the mark of degenerate spirits.

He that can have pearls does not load himself with shells; and they who aspire to virtue do not trouble themselves about honours. Every one, indeed, may take and keep his own place, without prejudice to humility, so that it be done without care and without contention. For as they who come from Peru, besides gold and silver which they bring back from thence, bring also apes and parrots, because they neither cost much, nor add much to the ship's lading; so they who aspire to virtue, refuse not the rank and honours due to them, provided always that they do not cost them too much care and attention, nor involve them in trouble, anxiety, disputes, or contentions. Nevertheless, I do not here allude to those whose dignity concerns the public, nor to certain particular occasions which involve important consequences; for in these every one ought to maintain what belongs to him with prudence and discretion, accompanied by charity and courtesy.

Chapter V

Of Interior Humility

BUT you desire, Philothea, that I should lead you still deeper into humility; for what I have hitherto said rather belongs to wisdom than humility. Now then I will pass on further. Many will not and dare not consider the particular favours God has done them, lest it should excite vainglory and self-complacency; but in so doing they deceive themselves: for since the best means to attain to the love of God (says the great angelical doctor) is the consideration of His benefits, the more we know them, the more we shall love Him; and as particular benefits more powerfully move us than those that are common to others, so ought they to be more attentively considered. Certainly, nothing can so effectually humble us before the mercy of God, as the multitude of His benefits; nor anything so much humble us before His justice, as the multitude of our misdeeds. Let us then consider what He has done for us, and what we have done against Him; and as we reflect on our sins one by one, so let us consider one by one His favours. We need not fear that the knowledge of His gifts will puff us up, so long as we are attentive to this truth, that whatever is good in us is not ours. Alas! do mules cease to be stupid and stinking beasts, for being laden with the precious furniture and perfumes of the prince? *What hast thou that thou didst not receive? And if thou didst receive it, why dost thou glory?*[1] Nay, on the contrary, the lively consideration of favours received, makes us humble, because a knowledge of them begets acknowledgment. But if, in considering the favours that God has conferred on us, any thoughts of vanity

[1] 1 Cor. iv. 7.

should begin to arise in us, it will be an infallible remedy to recur to the consideration of our ingratitudes, our imperfections, and our miseries. If we consider what we have done when God was not with us, we shall see very well that what we do while He is with us, is not of our making nor of our growth; we shall, indeed, enjoy it and rejoice in it, because we have it, but we shall glorify God alone for it, because He alone is the author of it. Thus the Blessed Virgin confesses that God had done great things for her, but it is only to take occasion to humble herself and to glorify God. *My soul*, says she, *doth magnify the Lord, because He has done to me great things.*[2]

We very often say that we are nothing, that we are misery itself, and the refuse of the world; but would be very sorry that any one should take us at our word, or tell others that we are such as we say we are. On the contrary, we pretend to run away and hide ourselves, to the end that the world should run after us and seek us out. We make-believe to be last, and sit down in the lowest place, but it is in order that we may be desired to go up higher. True humility never makes a show of being humble, nor uses many humble words; for she not only desires to conceal all other virtues, but still more and above all she wishes to conceal herself; and were it lawful to feign or to scandalize her neighbour, she would perform actions of arrogancy and haughtiness, that she might conceal herself beneath them, and remain altogether unknown and concealed.

My advice, therefore, Philothea, is that we should either not use words of humility, or else use them with a sincere interior sentiment conformable to what we pronounce outwardly. Let us never cast down our eyes but when we humble our hearts; never seem to desire to be the lowest, unless we really desire it. Now I think this rule so general as to admit of no exception. I only add, that civility requires we should sometimes offer precedence to those who will doubtless refuse it; and yet this is neither double-dealing nor false humility; for in this case the mere offer of pre-

2 Luke i. 46, 49.

cedence is the beginning of honour, and since we cannot give it them entirely, we do well to give them the beginning of it. I say the same of some words of honour or respect which in strictness do not seem conformable to the truth, yet they are sufficiently so, provided the heart of him that pronounces them has a sincere intention to honour and respect him to whom they are addressed; for although the words signify with some excess that which we would say, yet we do not ill to make use of them, when common custom requires it. I would, indeed, that our words were always as near as possible suited to our affections, that so we might follow in all things and everywhere a cordial sincerity and candour. A man that is truly humble would rather another should say of him that he is miserable, that he is nothing, and that he is good for nothing, than say it himself; at least, if he knows that any man says so, he does not contradict it, but heartily agrees to it: for believing it himself firmly, he is glad to have others of the same opinion.

Many say that they leave mental prayer to those who are perfect; that as for them they are unworthy to use it. Others protest they dare not communicate often, because they do not think themselves sufficiently pure. Others fear they should bring disgrace upon devotion if they meddled with it, by reason of their great misery and frailty. Others refuse to employ their talents in the service of God and their neighbour, because, say they, they know their own weakness, and fear they should become proud if they proved instruments of any good; and that, in giving light to others, they should consume themselves in the flames of vanity. All this is nothing but artifice, and a sort of humility not only false but malicious, whereby they tacitly and subtlely seek to find fault with the things of God; or at the best, to cover, under the pretext of humility, the love of their own opinion, of their own humour, and of sloth. *Ask thee a sign of the Lord thy God, ask it either in the depth or in the height above,* said the prophet to unhappy Ahaz; and he answered, *I will not ask, neither will I tempt the Lord.*[3] O the

[3] Isa. vii. 11.

wicked man! He pretends to have an extreme reverence for God, and excuses himself, under colour of humility, from aspiring to that grace which divine goodness offers him: but does he not see, that when God desires to give us His graces, it is pride to refuse them? that the gifts of God oblige us to receive them? and that it is humility to obey and to comply as nearly as we can with His desires? Now, the desire of God is that we should be perfect, uniting ourselves to Him, and imitating Him as nearly as we possibly can. The proud man, who trusts in himself, has just reason not to attempt anything; but the humble is so much the more courageous by how much the more he recognises his own inability; and the more wretched he esteems himself the more confident he becomes; because he places all his trust in God, who delights to display His omnipotence in our weakness, and to elevate His mercy upon our misery. We may, then, humbly and devoutly, presume to undertake all that is judged proper for our advancement by those who conduct our souls.

To imagine we know what we know not, is positive folly: to desire to pass for knowing that of which we are ignorant, is an intolerable vanity. For my part, I would not make a parade even of the knowledge which I have, neither, on the other hand, would I pretend to be ignorant thereof. When charity requires it, we must plainly and mildly communicate to our neighbour, not only what is necessary for his instruction, but also what is necessary for his consolation; for humility, which conceals virtues in order to preserve them, discovers them, nevertheless, when charity requires it, in order that we may enlarge, increase, and perfect them; in which she imitates that tree in the isles of Tylos, which at night closes her beautiful carnation flowers, and only opens them to the rising sun, so that the inhabitants of the country say that these flowers sleep by night; for thus humility covers and conceals all our virtues and human perfections, and never lets them appear but for the sake of charity, which being not a human and moral, but a divine and heavenly virtue, is the true sun of all other virtues, over which she ought always to have dominion. So that those humilities which are prejudicial to charity are assuredly false.

I would neither pretend to be a fool nor a wise man; for if humility forbids me to play the sage, candour and sincerity also forbid me to counterfeit the fool; and if vanity is opposite to humility, so artifice, affectation, and dissimulation are contrary to plain-dealing and sincerity. But if some great servants of God have pretended to be fools, to render themselves more abject in the eyes of the world, we must admire, but not imitate them; for they had such peculiar and extraordinary motives for going to this excess, that no one ought from thence to draw any conclusions for himself. David, when he danced and leaped before the ark of the covenant somewhat more than ordinary decorum required, had no design to make the world believe he was a fool, but with all simplicity, and devoid of artifice, he made use of these exterior motions in conformity with the extraordinary and excessive joy he felt in his heart. It is true that when Michal, his wife, reproached him for it, as an act of folly, he did not regret to hear himself vilified, but, continuing in a true and sincere representation of his joy, he testified that he was glad to receive some reproach for his God. Wherefore I tell you, that if for acts of a true and sincere devotion the world shall esteem you mean, abject, or foolish, humility will make you rejoice at this happy reproach, the cause of which is not in you but in those that reproach you.

CHAPTER VI

That Humility makes us love our own Abjection

I PASS on still further, and tell you, Philothea, that in all, and through all, you should love your own abjection. But you will ask me, what is it to love your own abjection? In Latin *abjection* signifies *humility*, and *humility* signifies *abjection*, so that when the Blessed Virgin, in her sacred canticle, says that *all generations shall call her blessed*, because our Lord had regarded the *humility of His handmaiden*, her meaning is, that our Lord had graciously looked down on her abjection, her meanness, and lowliness, to heap His graces and favours upon her. Nevertheless, there is a difference between the virtue of *humility* and *abjection* for *abjection* is the littleness, baseness and vileness, which are in us without our being aware of it; whereas the virtue of *humility* is a true knowledge, and a voluntary acknowledgment of our abjection. Now the height of this humility consists in not only being willing to acknowledge our abjection, but in loving and delighting in it; and this, not through want of spirit and nobleness, but for the sake of the greater exaltation of the Divine Majesty, and holding our neighbour in greater estimation than ourselves. To this I exhort you; and that you may comprehend me the better, I tell you that among the evils which we suffer, some are abject, and others honourable; many accommodate themselves to such as are honourable, but scarce any one is willing to accommodate himself to such as are abject. You see a devout old hermit all ragged and exposed to the cold; every one honours his tattered habit and compassionates his endurance: but if a poor tradesman, a poor gentleman, or a poor lady be in the like case, the world despises and scoffs at them for it; and thus you see how their poverty is abject. A religious receives a sharp reproof from his superior, or a child from his father with meekness, and every one calls this mortification, obedience, and wisdom; should a gentlemen or lady receive a like rebuke from some one in the same spirit, then, although it be for the love of God, it is called cowardice and want of spirit. Here then is another evil that is abject. One has a cancer in his arm, and another in his face; the first has only the disease, but the other, together with the disease, has contempt, disdain, and abjection. I say, then, that we must not only love the evil, which is done by the virtue of patience, but also embrace the abjection, which is done by the virtue of humility. There are, moreover, virtues which are abject, and virtues which are honourable. Patience, meekness, simplicity, and even humility itself, are virtues which worldly people consider mean and abject; while on the contrary, they hold prudence, fortitude, and liberality in great esteem. There are also actions of one and the same virtue some of which are despised, and others are honoured: to give alms and forgive injuries, are both of them acts of charity; yet the first is honoured by every one, whilst the latter is despised in the eyes of the world. A young lady or gentleman who refuses to join in the disorders of a dissolute company, or to talk, play, dance, drink, or dress as the rest do, will be taunted and blamed by the others, and their modesty will be termed bigotry and affectation; to love this is to love our abjection.

Here is an abjection of another kind. We go to visit the sick; if I am sent to the most miserable, it will be to me an abjection according to the world, for which reason I will love it. If I am sent to people of quality, it is an abjection according to the spirit, for there is not so much virtue nor merit in it, and therefore I will love this abjection also. If one falls in the midst of the street, besides the fall one has the shame also, we must love this abjection. There are even faults which have no other ill in them but only the abjection; and humility does not require that we should deliberately commit them, but it does require that we should not vex ourselves when we have committed them. Such are certain follies, incivilities, and inadvertencies, which we ought to avoid, before they are committed, for the sake of civility and discretion; but when they are committed, we ought to put up with the abjection they bring us, and accept it willingly, for the sake of practising holy humility.

I say yet more: if I have been disordered by anger or lewdness, or passion, have spoken any unbecoming words, whereby God and my neighbour have been offended, I will earnestly repent, and be very sorry for the offence, and endeavour to make the best reparation I can; but I will not fail to accept the abjection and the contempt which it has brought upon me; and could the one be separated from the other, I would heartily cast away the sin, and humbly retain the abjection.

But though we love the abjection that follows the evil, yet we must not neglect, by fit and lawful means, to redress the evil that caused it, especially when the evil is of consequence; as for example, should I have some disagreeable disorder in my face, I will endeavour to have it cured, but not with an intent to get rid of the abjection I receive by it. If I have been guilty of some fault which has given no one offence, I will make no apology for it; because, although a fault, it is not one which affects others, I could therefore only make excuses in order to get rid of the abjection, which would be contrary to humility. But, if, through inadvertence, or through folly, I should have offended or scandalized any one I will repair the offence by some true excuse; because the fault affects others, and charity obliges me to remove it. Besides, it happens sometimes that charity requires we should remove the abjection for the good of our neighbour, to whom our reputation is necessary; but in such a case, though we remove the abjection from before our neighbours' eyes, to prevent scandal, yet we must carefully shut it up in our own heart for its edification.

But would you know, Philothea, which are the best abjections, I tell you plainly, that those are the most profitable to our souls, and most acceptable to God, which befall us by accident, or by our condition of life; because we have not chosen them ourselves, but have received such as God has sent us, whose choice is always better than our own. But were we to choose any, the greatest are the best; and those are esteemed the greatest that are most contrary to our inclinations, provided they are comformable to our vocation: for—to say it once for all—our own choice and election spoil or lessen almost all our virtues. Oh!

who will give us grace to be able with the great King to say: *I had rather be a door-keeper in the house of my God, than to dwell in the tents of wickedness.*[1] No one can do it, dear Philothea, but He who, to exalt us, lived and died in such manner as to be the reproach of men, and the outcast of the people. I have said many things to you, which may seem hard to you in theory, but believe me, they will be sweeter than sugar or honey when you put them in practice.

[1] Ps. lxxxi. 11.

CHAPTER VII

That we must preserve our Good Name while practising Humility

PRAISE, honour, and glory are not given to men for simple virtue, but for excellence in virtue, for by praise we endeavour to persuade others to esteem the excellence of those whom we praise; by honour we testify that we ourselves esteem them; and glory, in my opinion, is nothing else but a certain lustre of reputation, which arises from the concurrence of many praises and honours; so that honours and praises are like precious stones, of which a number set together form the jewel glory. Now, humility, not enduring that we should have any opinion of our own excellence, or think ourselves worthy to be preferred before others, consequently cannot permit that we should hunt after praise, honour, or glory, which are only due to excellence; yet, she consents to the counsel of the wise man, who admonishes us to be careful of our good name;[1] because a good name is the repute not of excellence, but only of an ordinary honesty and integrity of life, which humility does not hinder us from acknowledging in ourselves, nor consequently from desiring the reputation of it. It is true, humility would despise a good name, if charity stood not in need of

[1] Eccles. xii. 15.

it; but because it is one of the foundations of human society, and without it we should not only not be profitable but prejudicial to the public, by reason of the scandal it would receive thereby, charity requires, and humility consents, that we should desire it, and carefully preserve it. Moreover, as the leaves of trees, which in themselves are of little value, are nevertheless very useful, not only to beautify the tree, but also to preserve its fruits while they are still tender; so a good reputation, which of itself is not a thing much to be desired, is notwithstanding very useful, not only for the ornament of life, but also for the preservation of our special virtues, especially of such virtues as are as yet but weak and tender.

The obligation of preserving our reputation, and of being actually such as we are thought to be, presses a generous spirit forward with a strong and gentle violence. Let us preserve our virtues, dear Philothea, because they are acceptable to God, the supreme object of all our actions. But as they who desire to preserve fruits are not content to candy them with sugar, but also put them into vessels which are proper to keep them; so, although the love of God be the principal preserver of our virtue, yet we may further employ our good name as very convenient and profitable for that purpose.

Yet we must not be over eager, exact and punctilious with respect to the preservation of our good name; for such as are over tender and sensible in this point, are like those who for every slight indisposition take physic, for they, thinking to preserve their health, destroy it altogether; and those others, by endeavouring so delicately to maintain their reputation, entirely lose it; for by this tenderness they become whimsical, quarrelsome, insupportable, and provoke the malice of detractors.

To overlook and despise attack and calumny is generally speaking a far more effectual remedy than resentment, contention, and revenge; contempt causes them to vanish; whereas, if we are angry at them, we seem to own them. Crocodiles hurt none, but those who fear them, nor does detraction hurt any but those who trouble themselves about it. An excessive fear of losing our good name, betrays a great distrust of its foundation, which is the truth of a good life. Towns which have wooden bridges over great rivers, fear their being carried away by every flood, but they which have bridges of stone apprehend only extraordinary inundations: so they who have a soul solidly grounded in Christian virtue, despise the overflowing of injurious tongues, but they who feel themselves weak, are disturbed by every idle story. In a word, Philothea, he who is over anxious to be in repute with everybody loses it with everybody; and he deserves to lose honour, who seeks to receive it from those whose vices rendered themselves truly infamous and dishonourable.

Reputation is but a sign to point out where virtue resides: it is virtue, then, that must be preferred in all, and through all. Wherefore should any one call you a hypocrite because you addict yourself to devotion, or a coward because you have pardoned an injury, laugh at all that; for, besides that such judgments are passed on us by the weak and foolish, we must not forsake or turn aside out of the way of virtue, although we were to lose our reputation, because we must prefer the fruit before the leaves, viz., interior and spiritual graces before all exterior advantages. It is lawful to be careful of our reputation, but not to idolize it; and as we should not offend the eyes of the good, so it is not necessary that we should care to satisfy those of the wicked. The beard is an ornament to the face of man, and the hair to that of a woman: if one pluck up by the roots the beard from the chin, or the hair from the head, it will hardly grow again; but if it be only cut, nay, though it be close shaved, it will soon shoot forth again, and grow stronger and thicker than ever; so, although our reputation be cut, or even shaved close, by the tongue of detractors, which says David *is like a sharp razor*, we must not make ourselves uneasy, for it will soon shoot forth again, not only as fair as before, but much more firm and durable. But if our vices, our neglects, and evil life take away our reputation, it will hardly ever return, because it is pulled up by the root; for the root of a good name is virtue and probity, which as long as they remain in us, may always recover the honour due to them.

We must give up any conversation, any idle habit, any foolish affection or any improper company, which injure our reputation, for our good name is of more value than all such idle gratifications. But if for the exercise of piety, for advancement in devotion, for making our way towards our eternal welfare, men grumble, murmur, and speak evil of us, let us leave them to bark like dogs against the moon; for should they be able to cast an aspersion on our good name, and by that means cut and shave the hair and beard of our reputation, it will quickly spring up again, and the razor of detraction will be as advantageous to our honour, as the pruning knife is to the vine, which makes it abound and multiply in fruit.

Fixing our eyes constantly on Jesus Christ crucified, let us march on in His service with confidence and simplicity, yet with wisdom and discretion; He will be the protector of our reputation; and should He suffer it to be taken from us, it will be either to restore it with advantage, or to make us profit in holy humility, one ounce of which is preferable to ten thousand pounds of honours. Are we blamed unjustly? let us peaceably oppose truth against calumny; does the calumny continue? let us also continue to humble ourselves, thus resigning our reputation, together with our soul into the hands of God; we cannot secure it better. Let us serve God *in evil report and good report*,[2] according to the example of St. Paul, that we may be able to say with David, *For thy sake, O Lord, I have suffered reproach, shame hath covered my face.*[3] I except, nevertheless, certain crimes, so horrid and infamous, that no man ought to suffer the false imputation of them, if he can justly acquit himself; and also certain persons, on whose reputation depends the edification of many; for in these cases, according to the opinion of divines, we must quietly seek a reparation of the wrong received.

[2] 2 Cor. vi. [3] Ps. xviii.

Chapter VIII

Of Meekness towards our Neighbour and Remedies against Anger

THE holy chrism, which by ancient tradition, we use in the Church of God for confirmations and consecrations, is composed of oil of olives mingled with balm, which represent, among other things, the two favourite and well-beloved virtues which shone forth in the sacred person of our Lord, and which He has especially recommended to us; as if by them our heart ought to be in a particular manner consecrated to His service, and dedicated to His imitation: *Learn of Me*, said He, *for I am meek and humble of heart.*[1] *Humility* perfects us towards God, and *meekness* towards our neighbour. The balm, which, as I have before observed, always takes the lowest place when poured into other liquors, represents humility: and the oil of olives, which always swims uppermost, represents meekness and kindness, which surmounts all things, and excels amongst virtues, as being the flower of charity, which according to St. Bernard, is then in its perfection, when it is not only patient, but when over and above that it is also meek and kind. But take care, Philothea, that this mystical chrism, compounded of meekness and humility, be within your heart: for it is one of the great artifices of the enemy, to make many deceive themselves with the expressions and exterior appearance of these two virtues, who not examining thoroughly their interior affections, think themselves to be humble and meek, whereas in truth they are nothing of the kind; and this may be easily discovered, for notwithstanding all their ceremonious mildness and humility, at the least cross word which any one says to them, or the smallest injury they receive, they puff themselves up with an unparalleled

[1] Matt. xii. 29.

arrogance. It is said, that those who have taken the preservative, which is commonly called the *Fat of St. Paul*, do not swell when bit and stung by a viper, provided the preservative be of the best sort: in like manner, when humility and meekness are good and true, they preserve us from the swelling and burning heat which injuries are wont to raise in our hearts. But if, being stung and bit by detractors and enemies, we fly out, swell, and are enraged, it is a certain sign that neither our humility nor meekness are true and sincere, but only apparent and artificial.

The holy and illustrious patriarch Joseph, sending back his brethren from Egypt to his father's house, gave them this one counsel only: *See that ye fall not out by the way.*[2] I say the same to you, Philothea; this, wretched life is but a journey to the happy life to come; let us not then fall out with each other by the way, but rather march on with the troop of our brethren and companions, meekly, peaceably, and lovingly; nay, I say to you, absolutely and without exception, be not angry at all if it be possible, and admit no pretext whatever for opening the gate of your heart to anger; for St. James tells us positively, and without reservation: *The wrath of man worketh not the righteousness of God.*[3] We must, indeed, resist evil, and restrain the vices of those under our charge constantly and courageously, but yet with meekness and quietness. Nothing so soon appeases the enraged elephant as the sight of a little lamb, and nothing so easily breaks the force of cannon-shot as wool. We do not take the correction which proceeds from passion, though it be accompanied with reason, so readily as that which proceeds from reason alone; for the reasonable soul, being naturally subject to reason, never subjects itself to passion, but through tyranny; and consequently when reason is accompanied by passion she makes herself odious, her just government being debased by the fellowship of tyranny. Princes do honour to their people, and make them rejoice exceedingly, when they visit them with a peaceful train; but when

[2] Gen. xlv. 29.

[3] St. James ii. 20.

they come at the head of armies, though it be for the common good, their visits are always disagreeable and oppressive; for although they cause military discipline to be rigorously observed among their soldiers, yet they can never do it so effectually but that some disorders will happen, by which the countryman is oppressed. In like manner, as long as reason rules, and peaceably deals out chastisements, corrections, and reprehensions, although severely and exactly, every one loves and approves it; but when she brings anger, passion, and rage, which St. Augustin calls her soldiers, along with her, she makes herself more feared than loved, and even her own disordered heart is oppressed and maltreated. It is better, says the same St. Augustin, writing to Profuturus, to deny entrance to just and reasonable anger than to admit it, be it ever so little; because being once admitted, it is with difficulty driven out again; for it enters as a little twig, and in no time it grows and becomes a beam. So if anger can but once gain the night of us, and *the sun go down upon our wrath*, which the apostle forbids, it turns into hatred, from which we have scarcely any means of ridding ourselves; for it nourishes itself under a thousand false pretexts, since no angry man ever thought his anger unjust.

It is better then to endeavour to live without anger, than to resolve to make a moderate and discreet use of it; and when, through imperfection and frailty, we find ourselves surprised by it, it is better to drive it away at once than to enter into a parley with it; for, if we give it ever so little leisure, it will become mistress of the place, like the serpent which easily draws in its whole body where it can get in its head.

But how shall I drive it away? you will say. You must, my dear Philothea, at the first sensation of it which you perceive, muster your forces, not hastily and impetuously, but mildly, and yet seriously; for as we see in public halls and courts of justice the ushers crying "Silence!" make more noise than those whom they wish to silence, so it frequently happens, that by endeavouring with violence to restrain our anger, we stir up more disturbance in our heart than the anger had excited before, and the heart thus agitated is no longer master of itself. After this meek effort, practise the advice which St. Augustin, being then old, gave to the young bishop Auxilius: Do, says he, that which a man should do; if that befal you which the man of God speaks of in the Psalms: *My eye is consumed with wrath*,[1] have recourse to God, crying out: *Have mercy upon me, O Lord*, that he may stretch forth his right hand to repress your anger. I mean we must invoke the assistance of God when we find ourselves excited to wrath, in imitation of the apostles, when they were tossed by the wind and the storm upon the waters; for he will command our passions to cease, and there will be a great calm. But I warn you that the prayer which is made against present and pressing danger, must always be performed calmly and quietly, and not violently, and this must be observed in all the remedies against this evil. Moreover, as soon as ever you perceive that you have been guilty of an act of anger, repair the fault immediately, by an act of meekness towards the same person against whom you were angry. For as it is a sovereign remedy against a lie, to contradict it upon the spot as soon as we perceive we have told it; so it is an excellent remedy against anger to repair it instantly by a contrary act of meekness; for green wounds, they say, are most easily cured.

Again, when your mind is in a state of tranquillity, and without any cause for anger, lay in a plentiful store of meekness and good nature, speaking all your words and doing all your actions, little and great, in the mildest manner possible; calling to mind that the spouse in the Canticles[2] has not only honey on her lips, and on her tongue, but also under her tongue, that is, in her breast; and she has not only honey but milk also; so we must not only have our words sweet towards our neighbour, but also our whole breast, that is to say, the whole interior of our soul; neither must we have the sweetness of honey only, which is aromatic and

1 Ps. xxx.

2 Song of Sol. iv. 11.

fragrant, that is to say, the sweetness of civil conversation with strangers, but also the sweetness of milk amongst our family and neighbours; in which they fail greatly, who abroad are like angels, and like devils at home.

CHAPTER IX

Of Meekness towards Ourselves

ONE of the best exercises of meekness we can perform, is that whose subject is ourselves, in never fretting against ourselves and our imperfections. For though reason requires that we should be displeased and sorry for it when we commit any fault, yet we must refrain from a bitter, gloomy, spiteful, and passionate displeasure. For many make a great mistake in this respect, who, being overcome by anger, are angry for having been angry, and vexed at having given way to vexation, and fretful for having been fretful. For by this means they keep their heart perpetually laid and steeped in anger; and though it seems as if the second anger destroyed the first, it serves nevertheless to open a passage for fresh anger on the first occasion that shall present itself. Besides these, angers, spites, and vexations against ourselves tend to pride, and flow from no other source than self-love, which is troubled and disquieted to see ourselves imperfect. We must then be displeased at our faults, in a peaceable, calm, and steadfast manner; for, as a judge punishes malefactors much better when he is guided in his sentences by reason, and proceeds in a spirit of tranquillity, than when he acts with violence and passion, because judging in passion, he punishes the faults not according as they are, but according as he is himself, so we correct ourselves much better by calm and steady repentances than by those which are harsh, eager, and passionate; for repentances made with violence proceed not according to the quality of our faults, but according to our inclinations. For example, he who affects chastity will vex himself with disproportioned bitterness at the least fault he commits against that virtue, and will but laugh at a gross detraction he has been guilty of; on the other hand, he who hates detraction, torments himself about a little grumbling, and makes no account of a gross fault committed against chastity; and so of others. Now all this springs from no other cause than this, that, in judging their consciences, these men are not guided by reason, but by passion.

Believe me, Philothea, as the reproofs of a father made in a mild and affectionate manner have far greater power over a child for his correction than rage and passion, so when our heart has committed any fault, if we reprehend it with mild and calm remonstrances, having more compassion for it than passion against it, encouraging it to amendment, the repentance it will thereby conceive will go much further, and sink deeper than a fretful, scolding, and stormy repentance.

If I myself, for example, had formed a strong resolution not to yield to the sin of vanity, and yet had fallen into some great instance of it, I would not reprove my heart after this manner: "Art thou not wretched and abominable, that after so many resolutions, thou hast suffered thyself to be thus carried away by vanity? Die with shame, lift up no more thy eyes to heaven, blind, impudent traitor that thou art, and rebel to thy God;" and such like things. But I would correct it thus, rationally and compassionately, saying: "Alas, my poor heart, behold we have fallen into the fault we had so firmly resolved to avoid. Oh! let us rouse ourselves and quit it for ever; let us call again upon the mercy of God, and hope that it will assist us to be more constant for the time to come; and let us put ourselves again into the way of humility. Courage! Let us from this day forward be more upon our guard; God will help us, we shall do better;" and on this reprehension I would build a firm and constant resolution never more to relapse into that fault, using the proper means to avoid it, and seeking the advice of my director.

However, if any one should find his heart not sufficiently moved with this mild correction, he may use reproaches and correction more sharp and severe, to excite it to deeper confusion, provided that after he has roundly blamed and chided his heart, he finish with some encouragement, ending all his grief and anger with a sweet and consoling confidence in God, in imitation of that illustrious penitent, who, seeing his soul afflicted, encouraged it in this manner, *Why art thou cast down, O my soul, and why art thou so disquieted within me? Hope in God, for I shall yet praise him, who is the help of my countenance, and my God.*[1]

When then your heart falls, raise it up gently; humbling yourself greatly before God, and acknowledging your misery, but without being surprised at your fall; for it is no wonder that infirmity should be infirm, or weakness weak, or misery wretched. Detest, nevertheless, with all your power the offence God has received from you, and return to the way of virtue which you had forsaken with great courage and confidence in his mercy.

[1] Ps. xlii. 5.

Chapter X

That we must do our business with Diligence, but without Eagerness or Anxiety

THE pains and diligence with which we ought to attend to our concerns are very different things from care, anxiety, and eagerness. The angels take pains about our salvation, and pursue it with diligence, yet they are never agitated by care, anxiety, or eagerness; for painstaking and diligence naturally result from their charity, whereas anxiety, eagerness, and care are utterly incompatible with their felicity; because painstaking and diligence may be accompanied by a calm and tranquil state of mind, whereas anxiety and care, and still less eagerness, never can be.

Be painstaking and diligent then, O Philothea, in all those affairs which are under your care; for God having entrusted them to you, wills that you should take great pains about them; but if possible do not be anxious and careful about them; that is to say, do not set about them with disquiet, anxiety, and haste; do not be eager about your work, for all eagerness disturbs the reason and judgment, and prevents us from doing that properly about which we are so eager.

When our Lord reprehended Martha, he said—*Martha, Martha, thou art careful and troubled about many things.* Observe that, had she been simply painstaking, she would not have been troubled; but being careful and disquieted, she was eager and troubled, and it was for this that our Lord blamed her.

Rivers that flow gently through the plains bear large vessels and rich merchandize; and rain, which falls gently on the fields, makes them fruitful in grass and corn; but torrents and rivers which run rapidly, inundate the country, overflow the neighbourhood, and are useless for traffic; and vehement and tempestuous rains ruin both corn-field and meadow. Work done with too much eagerness and hurry is never well done. We must hasten leisurely, says the old proverb: *He that is in haste*, says Solomon, *is in danger of stumbling.*[1] We always do our business soon enough when we do it well. Drones make more noise and fuss than bees, but they make only wax, and no honey; so they who hurry themselves with an eager care and noisy anxiety always do little and do it ill.

Flies trouble us not by their strength but by their multitude, so affairs of importance do not give us so much trouble as trifling ones when they are many in number. Take your affairs in hand quietly, and try to do them in order, one after another; for if you want to do them all at once, or in disorder, you will make efforts which will so overcharge and depress your spirit, that it will probably lie down under

1 Prov. xix. 2.

the burden without effecting anything.

In all your affairs rely wholly on the providence of God, through which alone any of your undertakings can succeed; labour, nevertheless, quietly on your part to co-operate with it, and then you may be assured, if you trust as you ought in God, the event which will come to you will be always that which is the most profitable for you, whether it appear good or bad according to your own judgment. Do as the little children do; little children who, with one hand hold fast by their father, and with the other gather strawberries or blackberries along the hedges; do you, while gathering and managing the goods of this world with one hand, with the other always hold fast the hand of your heavenly Father, turning to Him from time to time to see if your actions or occupations are pleasing to Him; but take heed, above all things, that you never let go His hand, thinking to gather more; for should He let you go, you will not be able to take another step without falling. My meaning is, Philothea, that amidst those ordinary affairs and occupations which do not require very earnest attention, you should look more to God than to your affairs; and when they are of such importance as to require your whole attention to do them properly, you should look to God from time to time, like mariners, who, to arrive at the port to which they are bound, look more up towards heaven than down on the sea on which they sail; thus will God work with you, in you, and for you, and your labour shall be followed by consolation.

Chapter XI

Of Obedience

CHARITY alone can place us in a state of perfection, but obedience, chastity, and poverty, are the three principal means to acquire it. Obedience consecrates our will, chastity our body, and poverty our means to the love and service of God. These are the three branches of the spiritual cross, all three being based upon the fourth, which is humility. I shall say nothing of these three virtues as they are solemnly vowed, because that concerns professed Religious only; nor even as they are simply vowed, for though a vow adds many graces and merits to virtues, yet, to make us perfect, it is not necessary they should be vowed, provided they be observed. For though being vowed, and especially solemnly, they place a man in the state of perfection; yet to place him in perfection itself, it suffices that they be observed, there being a material difference between the state of perfection and perfection itself, for all bishops and religious are in the state of perfection, but all are not arrived at perfection itself, as is only too plainly to be seen. Let us endeavour then, Philothea, to practise these virtues well, each according to his vocation; for though they do not place us in the state of perfection, yet they will nevertheless make us perfect; and, indeed, we are all obliged to practise these three virtues, though not all in the same way.

There are two sorts of obedience; the one necessary, the other voluntary. By that which is necessary you are bound to obey your ecclesiastical superiors, as the Bishop, the parish Priest, and such as are commissioned by them; you must also obey your civil superiors, such as your Sovereign, and the magistrates who are put in authority under him; lastly, you must obey your domestic superiors, viz. your father and mother, master and mistress. This obedience is called necessary, because no man can exempt himself from the duty of obeying these superiors, God having placed them in authority to command and govern us, each in the department which is assigned to him. Obey their commands for this is of necessity; but to be perfect, follow their counsels also; and even their desires and inclinations, so far as charity and discretion will permit. Obey them when they order that which is agreeable, as to eat or to take recreation; for though it seems no great virtue to obey on such occasions, it would be a great vice to disobey. Obey them in things indifferent, as to wear this or that dress; to go one way or another; to sing or be silent; and this will be a very commendable obedience. Obey them in things hard, troublesome, and disagreeable, and this will be a perfect obedience. Lastly, obey meekly without reply, readily without delay, cheerfully without repining; and above all obey lovingly, for the love of Him, who for love of us, made Himself obedient unto death, even the death of the cross, and who, as St. Bernard says, rather chose to part with His life than His obedience.

That you may learn effectually to obey your superiors, comply readily with the will of your equals, yielding to their opinions in what is not wrong, without being contentious or obstinate. Accommodate yourself cheerfully to the desires of your inferiors, as far as it is reasonable to do so, never exercising an imperious authority over them so long as they are good. It is an illusion to believe that we should obey with ease, i we were Religious, if we find ourselves backward and stubborn in obedience to those whom God has placed over us.

Voluntary obedience is that to which we oblige ourselves by our own choice, and which is not imposed upon us by another. We do not commonly choose our prince, our bishop, our father or mother, nor even do wives generally choose their husbands, but we choose our confessor and our director; and if in choosing we make a vow to obey, as it is said the holy mother Teresa did, who, besides the obedience solemnly vowed to the superior of her order, bound herself by a simple vow to obey Father Gratian, or if, without a vow, we dedicate ourselves to the obedience of any one, this obedience is called voluntary, on account of its being grounded on our own free will and choice.

We must obey all our superiors, each according to the kind of authority which is given him over us. In political matters we must obey our prince; in ecclesiastical, our prelates; in domestic, our father, master, or husband; and, in what regards the private conduct of the soul, our ghostly father or director.

Request your spiritual father to order you all the actions of piety you are to perform, because they will be better and have double grace and goodness, the one of themselves, because they are works of piety, the other of obedience, which requires them, and in virtue of which they are performed. Blessed are the obedient, for God will never suffer them to go astray.

Chapter XII

Of the Necessity of Chastity

CHASTITY is the lily of virtues; it makes men almost equal to angels. Nothing is beautiful but by its purity, and the purity of men is chastity. Chastity is called *honesty*, and the possession of it *honour;* it is also called *integrity*, and its contrary *corruption*. In short, it has this peculiar glory, to be the fair and unspotted virtue of both soul and body.

The chaste heart is like the mother pearl, that can receive no drop of water but such as comes from heaven; for it can accept of no pleasure but that of marriage, which is ordained from heaven; out of which it is not allowed so much as to think of it, so as to take a voluntary and deliberate delight in the thought.

For the *first degree* of this

virtue, Philothea, beware of admitting any kind of forbidden pleasure, as all those are which are taken out of marriage, or even in marriage, when they are taken contrary to the rule of marriage. For the *second*, refrain as much as possible from all unprofitable and superfluous pleasures, although lawful and permitted. For the *third*, set not your affection on pleasures and delights which are ordained and commanded; for, although we must take those delectations that are necessary, I mean those which concern the end and institution of holy matrimony, yet we must never set our heart and mind upon them.

As to the rest, every one stands in great need of this virtue. They who are in a state of widowhood ought to have a courageous chastity, to despise not only present or future objects, but to resist also the imaginations which former pleasures may produce in their minds. For this cause St. Augustin admires the purity of his friend Alipius, who had wholly forgotten and despised the pleasures of the flesh, of which nevertheless he had some experience in his youth.

In effect, as while fruits are entire and sound, they may be preserved, some in straw, some in sand, and some in their own leaves, but being once cut or bruised, it is almost impossible to preserve them, but by honey and sugar, in the way of sweetmeats; so untainted chastity may many ways be kept, but after it has once been violated nothing can preserve it but an extraordinary devotion, which, as I have often repeated, is the true honey and sugar of the spirit.

Virgins have need of a chastity extremely innocent and delicate, to banish from their hearts all sorts of curious thoughts, and to despise, with an absolute contempt, all sorts of unclean pleasures; which, in truth, deserve not to be desired by men, since they are better enjoyed by asses and swine. Let then these pure souls take heed never to make the least doubt but that chastity is incomparably better than all that which is incompatible with it.

For, as the little butterfly, seeing the flame, hovers with curiosity about it, to try whether it be as sweet as it is fair, and being borne away with this fancy, ceases not until it is destroyed at the very first trial; so young people suffer themselves frequently to be so possessed with the false and foolish opinion they have of the pleasure of voluptuous desires, that after many curious thoughts, they at length ruin themselves, and perish in the flames; more foolish in this than the butterflies, for these have some cause to imagine that the fire is sweet, because it is so beautiful; but those, knowing that which they seek to be extremely dishonourable, cease not, nevertheless, to set a value on that brutish pleasure.

As for those who are married, it is most true, though the vulgar cannot conceive it, that chastity is very necessary also for them; because, in respect of them, it consists not in abstaining absolutely from carnal pleasures, but in containing themselves in the midst of pleasures. Now, as this commandment, *be angry and sin not*, is, in my opinion, harder than this, *be not angry;* and as one may easier keep from anger than regulate it, so it is easier to keep ourselves altogether from carnal pleasures than to preserve a moderation in them. It is true that the holy liberty of marriage has a peculiar force to extinguish the fire of concupiscence; but the frailty of those who enjoy this liberty passes easily from permission to usurpation, and from use to abuse; and as we see many rich men steal, not through want, but avarice, so also we may observe many married people exceed by mere intemperance and incontinency, notwithstanding the lawful object to which they ought and might confine themselves; their concupiscence being like wild fire, which runs burning here and there, without resting in any one place. It is always dangerous to take violent medicines; for if we take more than we should, or if they be not well prepared, they may be attended by fatal consequences. Marriage was blessed and ordained in part as a remedy for concupiscence, and doubtless it is a very good remedy, but yet violent, and consequently very dangerous, if it be not used with discretion.

I add, that the variety of

human affairs, besides long diseases, oftentimes separate husbands from their wives; and therefore married people have need of two kinds of chastity: the one for absolute abstinence, when they are separated upon the occasions of which I have been speaking; the other for moderation, when they are together in the ordinary course. St. Catherine of Sienna, saw amongst the damned many souls grievously tormented for having violated the sanctity of marriage, which happened, said she, not for the enormity of the sin, for murders and blasphemies are more enormous; but because they who commit it make no conscience of it, and therefore continue long in it.

You see, then, that chastity is necessary for all sorts of people; *Follow peace with all men*, says the apostle, *and holiness, without which no man shall see God;* by holiness is here understood *chastity*, as St. Jerome and St. Chrysostom observe. No; Philothea, no one shall see God without chastity; no one shall dwell in His holy tabernacle who is not clean of heart: and as our Saviour himself says, *Dogs, and the unchaste shall be banished thence:*[1] and, *Blessed are the pure in heart, for they shall see God.*[2]

1 Rev. xxii. 15.
2 Matt. v. 8.

CHAPTER XIII

Advices how to preserve Chastity

BE exceedingly diligent in turning yourself aside from all the approaches and allurements of incontinency; for this evil works insensibly, and, from small beginnings, advances to great results, which are always more easily avoided than cured.

Human bodies are like glasses, which cannot be carried together, touching one another, without running the risk of being broken, or like fruits, which, though ever so sound and seasonable, yet by touching one another are impaired. Water itself, in a vessel, be it ever so fresh, being once touched by any beast of the earth, cannot long retain its freshness. Never suffer any one, Philothea, to touch you familiarly, either in the way of sport, or in the way of love; for though perhaps chastity may be preserved in those actions rather light than lewd, yet the freshness and flower of chastity always receives some detriment and loss; but to suffer yourself to be touched immodestly is the utter ruin of chastity.

The source of chastity is the heart, and the body is its subject; and therefore it may be lost either by the exterior senses of the body, or the interior thoughts and desires of the heart. It is impurity to behold, to hear, to speak, to smell, or touch any thing immodest, the heart entertaining itself, and taking pleasure in it. St. Paul says positively, *let not fornication be so much as once named amongst you.*

The bees not only have an aversion to carrion, but avoid and hate extremely all sorts of stench which proceed from it. The sacred spouse in the Canticles[1] has her hands distilling myrrh, which is the antidote against corruption; her lips are bound with a scarlet ribbon, the mark of her modesty in her words; she has the eyes of a dove, to signify their cleanliness; her ears have gold ear-rings in token of their purity; her nose is amongst the cedars of Lebanon, which are incorruptible wood. Such ought to be the devout soul; chaste, clean, and pure in hands, lips, ears, eyes, and in all her body.

Chastity may be lost as many ways as there are kinds of immodesty and wantonness; so that, according as they are great or little, some weaken it, others wound it, and others kill it outright. There are certain indiscreet and sensual familiarities and passions which, to speak properly, do not destroy chastity, and yet they weaken it, leave it languishing, and stain its beautiful whiteness. There are other familiarities and passions not only indiscreet, but vicious; not only fond, but dishonest; not only sensual, but carnal; and by these chastity is, at least, grievously wounded. I say, *at least;* because it dies by them, and perishes altogether, when these fooleries and wan-

[1] Cant. v. 5, iv. 3, iv. 1, i. 10, vii. 4.

ton dalliances are carried to extremity.

Frequent not the company of immodest persons, especially if they be also imprudent, as they generally are; for as the he-goats, touching the sweet almond trees with their tongues, make them become bitter, so these corrupted souls and infected hearts scarcely speak to any, either of the same or a different sex, but they cause them to fall in some degree from purity: they have poison in their eyes and in their breath, like basilisks. On the contrary, keep company with the chaste and virtuous; often meditate upon and read holy things; for the word of God is chaste, and makes those also chaste who delight in it; which made David compare it to the topaz, a precious stone which has the property of assuaging the heat of concupiscence.

Keep yourself always near to Jesus Christ crucified, both spiritually by meditation and really by the holy communion. For as they who lie on the herb called *agnus castus*, become chaste and modest, so you, laying down your heart to rest upon our Lord, who is the true, chaste, and immaculate Lamb, will see that your soul and your heart will soon be cleansed from all the defilements of impurity.

CHAPTER XIV

Of Poverty of Spirit to be observed in the midst of Riches

BLESSED *are the poor in spirit, for theirs is the kingdom of heaven.*[1] Cursed then are the rich in spirit, for the misery of hell is their portion. He is rich in spirit, who has riches in his spirit, or his spirit in riches; he is poor in spirit who has no riches in his spirit, nor his spirit in riches. The halcyons form their nests like an apple, and leave only a

[1] Matt. v. 3.

little opening at the top; they build them on the sea-shore, but make them so firm and impenetrable, that, when the waves surprise them, the water can never get into them, but keeping always afloat, they remain in the midst of the sea, upon the sea, and masters of the sea. Your heart, dear Philothea, ought to be like this nest, open only to heaven, and impenetrable to riches and all transitory things. If you have them, keep your heart free from the least affection towards them; keep it always floating above them, so that amidst riches it is empty of riches, and the master of riches. Ah! no; do not put this heavenly spirit into earthly goods; let it be always superior to them, above them, not in them.

There is a difference between having poison, and being poisoned; apothecaries have almost all kinds of poison for use on different occasions, but they are not poisoned, because they have not the poison in their bodies, but in their shops; so you may possess riches without being poisoned by them, if you have them in your house or in your purse, and not in your heart. To be rich in fact, and poor in spirit, is the great happiness of a Christian; for by this means he has the conveniency of riches for this world, and the merit of poverty for the world to come.

Alas! Philothea, no one ever acknowledges himself to be covetous; every one disavows this baseness and meanness of heart; they excuse themselves on account of the expense of children which weighs upon them; on account of the prudence which requires that they should lay by some capital; they never have too much, they always find some reason or other for having a little more; even the most covetous not only do not confess that they are so, but think in their conscience they are not so. No; for covetousness is a malignant fever, which becomes the more insensible, the more violent and ardent it is. Moses saw the sacred fire which burned the bush, and yet consumed it not; but this profane fire of avarice, on the contrary, consumes and devours the covetous person, and yet burns him not; at least in the midst of the most excessive heats of his avarice, he boasts of the most agreeable coolness in the world ; and esteems his insatiable drought to be a natural and pleasing thirst.

If you have a continual, ardent, and restless desire to possess the goods which you have not, it is in vain for you to say that you do not wish to obtain them improperly, you do not, for all that, fall short of being truly covetous. If a man has a constant, ardent, and restless desire to drink, although he wants to drink nothing but water, yet it is a sign that he has fever.

O Philothea, I know not whether it is a justifiable desire to desire to have that justly which another justly possesses : for it seems by this desire, we wish to convenience ourselves by the inconvenience of another. If a man possesses anything justly, has he not more right to keep it justly than we have to desire it justly? Why then do we extend our desires to his possessions, to deprive him of them? At the best, if this desire be just, yet certainly it is not charitable, for we would not in any case, that another man should desire, although justly, that which we have a desire to keep justly. This was the sin of Ahab, who desired to have Naboth's vineyard justly, which Naboth much more justly desired to keep; Ahab had an ardent, constant, and restless desire for it, and thereby he offended God.

It is time enough, dear Philothea, to desire your neighbour's goods, when he is desirous to part with them : for then his desire will make yours not only just, but charitable also; yes, for I am willing you should take care to increase your substance, provided it may be done, not only justly, but with meekness and charity.

If you have a strong attachment to the goods you possess, if you are very solicitous about them, setting your heart on them, giving your thoughts to them, having a lively and anxious fear of losing them, believe me you have some sort of fever ; for they who have a fever, drink the water that is given them with a certain eagerness and earnestness and satisfaction, which the healthy are not accustomed to have. It is impossible to take much pleasure in anything without having a good deal of affection for it.

If any loss of goods befall you, and you find your heart very grieved and disconsolate, believe me, Philothea, you have too great an affection for them; for nothing can be a stronger proof of affection for anything than grief for the loss of it.

Desire, not then, with a full and express desire, the wealth which you have not, nor fix your heart much on what you have; grieve not for the losses which may befall you; and then you will have some reason to believe, that though rich in fact, you are not so in desire, but that you are poor in spirit, and consequently blessed, for the kingdom of heaven is yours.

Chapter XV

How to practise true Poverty, being, notwithstanding, really rich

THE painter, Parrhasius, painted the Athenian people, by a an ingenious contrivance representing them as diverse and variable in character, choleric, unjust, inconstant, courteous, gentle, merciful, haughty, proud, humble, resolute, and timorous, and all this together; and I, dear Philothea, would put together into your heart riches and poverty, a great care and a great contempt of worldly things.

Be much more careful to make your goods profitable and fruitful than worldly men are. Tell me, are not the gardeners of great princes more curious and diligent in cultivating and embellishing the gardens committed to their charge than if they were their own. And why is this? No doubt it is because they consider them as the gardens of kings and princes, to whom they desire to make themselves acceptable by these services. Philothea, our possessions are not our own; God has given us them to cultivate, and wishes that we should render them fruitful and profitable, and therefore we do Him acceptable service in being careful of them.

But then it must be a greater and more solid care than that which worldly people have of their goods; for they labour only for love of themselves, but we must labour for the love of God. Now as self-love is violent, and turbulent and impetuous, so the care which proceeds therefrom is full of trouble, uneasiness, and disquiet; and as the love of God is sweet, peaceable, and calm, so the care which proceeds from it, although it be for worldly goods, is yet amiable, sweet and gracious. Let us then exercise this gracious care to preserve, nay even to increase our temporal goods, whenever proper occasions present themselves, and as far as our condition requires, for God wishes us to do so for the love of Him.

But beware lest self-love deceive you; for sometimes it counterfeits the love of God so well that one would declare it is the love of God. To prevent it from deceiving you, and the care of your temporal goods from degenerating into covetousness, besides what I said in the former chapter, we must very often practise real and effective poverty in the midst of all the means and riches that God has given us.

Give up, then, always some part of your means, by bestowing it on the poor with a willing heart; for to give away what we have, is to impoverish ourselves by so much as we give; and the more we give, the poorer we make ourselves. It is true, God will repay it you again, not only in the next world, but even in this; for nothing so much makes us prosper in this world as alms; but, till such time as God shall restore it you will be always so much the poorer by what you have given. O how holy and rich is that poverty which is occasioned by giving alms!

Love the poor and poverty, for by this love you will become truly poor, since, as the Scripture says, *we are made like things which we love.* Love makes the lovers equals; *Who is weak*, saith St. Paul, *and I am not weak?* He might have likewise said, who is poor, and I am not poor? For love made him resemble those whom he loved. If then you love the poor, you will be truly a partaker of their poverty, and poor like them.

Now if you love the poor, be often in their company, be glad to see them in your house, and to visit them in theirs; converse willingly with them; be pleased to have them near you in the church, in the streets, and elsewhere. Be poor in tongue with them, speaking to them as one of them; but be rich in hand, by imparting your goods to them, as having more abundance.

Do you wish to go still further, Philothea? Then do not content yourself with being as the poor, but be poorer than the poor. And how can that be? The servant is less than his master; make yourself then a servant of the poor; go and serve them in their beds when they are sick; serve them, I say, with your own hands; be their cook yourself, and at your own expense; be their sempstress and laundress. O my Philothea, this service is more glorious than a kingdom.

I cannot sufficiently admire the ardour with which this counsel was put in practice by St. Louis, one of the greatest kings the sun ever saw. I say, a great king in every kind of greatness. He very often served at table the poor whom he maintained, and caused three poor men almost every day to dine with him, and many times eat the remainder of their pottage with an incomparable love. When he visited the hospitals, which he frequently did, he commonly set himself to serve those who had the most loathsome diseases, such as the leprous, and ulcerous, and served them kneeling on the ground with naked knee, respecting in their persons the Saviour of the world, and cherishing them as tenderly as any fond mother could cherish her own child.

St. Elizabeth, daughter of the king of Hungary, was in the habit of associating with the poor, and for her recreation, sometimes clothed herself like a poor woman among her ladies, saying to them: "If I were a poor woman, I would dress in this manner." Ah! Philothea, how poor were this prince and princess in the midst of their riches, and how rich in their poverty. Blessed are they who are poor in this manner, for to them belongs the kingdom of heaven. *I was hungry, and ye gave Me meat; I was naked, and ye clothed Me; inherit the kingdom prepared for you from the foundation of the world,*[1] will the King of the Poor and of Kings say in His great judgment.

There is no one but upon some occasion or other has some failure or want of some conveniency. Sometimes we receive a visit from a guest, whom we wish and ought to entertain well, but at the time have not the means; at other times, our best clothes are in one place, whilst we want them in another place where it is necessary to go into company. It happens that all the wines in our cellar ferment and turn, so that there remain only such as are bad or green. We find ourselves in the country at some poor village where all things are wanting, where we have neither bed, chamber, table, nor attendance. In short, it is very often easy to suffer for the want of something, however rich we may be. Now this is to be poor in effect, with regard to the things we want. Philothea, be glad of these occasions, acccept them heartily, and endure them cheerfully.

But should you meet with losses which impoverish you more or less, as tempests, fires, innundations, dearths, robberies, or lawsuits; O then is the proper season to practise poverty, receiving those losses with meekness, and accommodating yourself with patience and constancy to your impoverishments. Esau presented himself to his father with his hands covered with hair, and Jacob did the same; but since the hair on Jacob's hands did not stick to his skin, but to his gloves, one might take away the hair without flaying or hurting him; on the contrary, because the hair on the hands of Esau stuck to his skin, which was hairy by nature, he who should have attempted to pluck off his hair would have put him to pain; he would have cried aloud, and been very warm in his own defence. Thus, when our worldly goods cleave to our heart, if tempest, a thief, or a cheat, should pluck any part of them from us, what complaints, trouble, and impatience do we not fall into? But when our goods are only held by the care God would

1 Matt. xxv. 34, 35.

have us take of them, and not by our hearts, should they be taken from us, we lose neither our senses nor our peace. It is the difference between beasts and men, as to their clothing; for the clothing of the former sticks to their flesh, and that of men is only put on, so that it can be put off at pleasure.

CHAPTER XVI

How to practise Richness of Spirit in real Poverty

BUT if you are really poor, dear Philothea, be likewise poor in spirit; make a virtue of necessity, and use this precious jewel of poverty according to its worth; its lustre is not recognised in this world, yet, nevertheless, it is exceedingly rich and beautiful.

Be patient, you are in good company; our Lord Himself, His blessed mother, the apostles, and innumerable saints both men and women, have been poor; and even when they might have been rich, have not cared to be so. How many great personages have there been, who, in spite of opposition, have with care gone to seek after holy poverty in cloisters and hospitals, and have taken indefatigable pains to find her! Witness St. Alexius, St. Paula, St. Paulinus, St. Angela, and so many others, and see, Philothea, how, more gracious towards you, she has come to offer herself to you; you have found her without being at the trouble of seeking after her; embrace her then as the dear friend of Jesus Christ, who was born, lived, and died with poverty, who was His nurse during the whole course of His life.

Your poverty, Philothea, has two great advantages, by means of which you may greatly profit. The first is, that it did not come to you by your own choice, but by the will of God alone, who has made you poor without any concurrence of your own will. Now that which we receive purely from the will of God is always very agreeable to Him, provided that we receive it with all our heart, and for the love of His holy will; where there is least of our own, there is most of God's; the simple and pure acceptance of God's will makes any suffering extremely pure.

The second advantage of this kind of poverty is, that it is a poverty really poor. Poverty which is praised, caressed, esteemed, succoured and assisted, is near akin to riches, at least, it is not altogether poverty; but the poverty which is despised, rejected, reproached, and abandoned, is really poor. Now such is ordinarily the poverty of secular persons; for since they are not poor by their own choice, but from necessity, their poverty is not much esteemed, and just because it is not esteemed their poverty is poorer than that of the religious; although otherwise the poverty of the religious has a very great excellency, and is much more commendable, by reason of the vow, and of the intention for which it is chosen.

Do not complain then, my dear Philothea, of your poverty; for we never complain but of that which displeases us, and if poverty displeases you, you are no longer poor in spirit, but rich in desire.

Be not disconsolate because you are not so well assisted as might appear necessary, for in this consists the excellence of poverty. To wish to be poor and not to feel the hardships of poverty, is a too great ambition, for it is to wish for the honour of poverty with the convenience ot riches.

Be not ashamed to be poor, nor to ask alms in charity. Receive with humility what shall be given you, and bear denial with meekness. Remember frequently the journey the Blessed Virgin took into Egypt to carry her dear Child there, and how much contempt, poverty, and misery she was obliged to suffer. If you live thus, you will be very rich in your poverty.

Chapter XVII

Of Friendship: and, first, of that which is evil and frivolous

LOVE holds the first rank among the passions of the soul; it is the king of all the motions of the heart; assimilates all the rest to itself, and makes us like that which it loves. Be careful then, Philothea, to entertain no evil love, for if you do, you will presently become evil. Now friendship is the most dangerous love of all; because other loves may be without communication, but friendship, being wholly grounded upon it, we can hardly be on terms of friendship with any person without partaking of his qualities.

All love is not friendship; for one may love without being beloved again, then there is love but not friendship; because friendship is a mutual love, if it is not mutual, it is not friendship. Nor is it enough that it be mutual, but the persons who love each other must know their reciprocal affection; for if they know it not, they have love but not friendship. There must be also some kind of communication between them, which may be the ground of friendship. Now according to the diversity of the communications, the friendship also differs, and the communications are different according to the difference of the good offices they communicate to each other. If they be false and vain, the friendship is also false and vain; if they be true, the friendship is likewise true; and the more excellent the offices, the more excellent also is the friendship. For as that honey is best, which is gathered from the bosom of the most exquisite flowers, so that love which is founded upon the most exquisite communication is the most excellent. And as there is honey in Heraclea of Pontus, which is poisonous, and makes those mad who eat it, because it is gathered from the aconite, which abounds in that country; so the friendship founded upon the communication of false and vicious offices, is altogether false and vicious.

The communication of carnal pleasures is a mutual inclination and brutish allurement, which can no more bear the name of friendship among men, than the similar inclinations of asses and horses; and if there were no other communication in marriage, there would be no friendship at all in it; but because, besides that, there is a communication in marriage, of life, of industry, of goods, of affections, and of an indissoluble fidelity, therefore the friendship of marriage is a true and holy friendship.

A friendship that is grounded on the communication of sensual pleasure is utterly gross, and unworthy of the name of friendship; and so is that which is founded on perfections which are frivolous and vain; because these perfections also depend on the senses. I call those pleasures sensual which are immediately and principally annexed to the exterior senses; such as the pleasure to behold a beautiful person, to hear a sweet voice, and the like. I call frivolous perfections certain vain endowments and qualities, which weak minds call virtues and perfections. Listen how the greater part of silly girls, women, and young people talk: they do not at all hesitate to say: Such a gentleman has many virtues and perfections, for he dances gracefully, he plays well at all sorts of games, he dresses fashionably, he sings delightfully, speaks eloquently, and is good looking; thus mountebanks esteem those the most perfect among themselves who are the greatest buffoons.

But as all these things regard the senses, so the friendships which proceed from them are termed sensual, vain, and frivolous, and deserve rather the name of foolish fondness than of friendship; such are the ordinary friendships of young people, which are grounded on moustaches, locks, and glances, on clothes, affectation and chatter; friendships suited to the age of those lovers whose virtues are yet only tendrils, and their judgment only in the bud; such friendships are only temporary, and melt away like snow in the sun.

CHAPTER XVIII

Of Fond Love

WHEN these foolish friendships are carried on between persons of different sexes, without any view of marriage, they are called flirtations: for being but embryos, or rather phantoms of friendship, they cannot be called either friendship or love, because of their excessive vanity and imperfection. Now, by means of these fondnesses, the hearts of men and of women are caught, involved, and entangled with each other in vain and foolish affections, founded upon these frivolous communications, and wretched complacencies, of which I have just been speaking.

And although these silly loves, commonly speaking, terminate at last in sensualities and shameful lasciviousness, yet that is not the first design or intention of the persons between whom they are carried on; otherwise they would not be merely flirtations, but downright indecencies. Sometimes even many years pass before anything directly contrary to the chastity of the body shall happen between those who are engaged in this folly, they stop short at distempering their hearts with wishes, sighs, amorous entertainments, and such like fooleries and vanities; and this upon different pretensions.

Some have no other design than to satisfy their hearts with loving and being loved, following in this their amorous inclination; and these regard nothing in the choice of their loves but their own taste and instinct: so that on meeting with an agreeable object, without examining the character or conduct of the person, they will begin this commerce of flirtation, and entangle themselves in these wretched nets, out of which afterwards they find it difficult to disengage themselves. Others suffer themselves to be carried into this folly by vanity, esteeming it no small glory to catch and blind hearts by love. And these, aiming at their own glory in the choice they make, set their nets and lay their snares, in conspicuous, high, rare and illustrious places. Others are led away both by their amorous inclination and by vanity; for though their hearts are inclined to love, yet they will not engage themselves in it without some advantage of glory. These friendships are all evil, foolish, and vain: because they ever at length tend and terminate in the sin of the flesh; and because they rob God, the wife, and the husband, of that love, and consequently of that heart, which belonged to them; foolish because they have neither foundation nor reason; vain because they yield neither profit, honour, nor content; on the contrary, they waste time, entangle honour, and bring no other pleasure than that of an eagerness in pursuit and without knowing what they pursue, or what they would have. For these wretched and weak minds still imagine, they have I know not what to hope for, from the testimonies which are given them of reciprocal love; but yet they cannot tell what this is; the desire of which can never end, but goes on continually, oppressing their hearts with perpetual distrusts, jealousies, and disquietudes.

St. Gregory Nazianzen, writing against vain women, said wonders on this subject. Here is a sentence, which he addressed indeed to women, but which is also applicable to men. "Thy natural beauty is sufficient for thy husband: but if it be for many men, like a net spread out for a flock of birds, what will be the consequences? He will be pleasing to thee who shall please himself with thy beauty; thou wilt return him glance for glance, look for look; presently will follow sighs and little amorous words; dropped by stealth at the beginning, but soon after they will become more familiar, and pass to an open courtship. Take heed, O my talking tongue, of telling what will follow: yet, will I say this one truth; nothing of all those things which young men and women say or do together in these foolish complacencies is exempted from grievous stings. All the links of wanton loves hold one by another, and follow one another, as one piece of iron, touched by the loadstone, draws divers others after it."

O how wisely has this great bishop spoken? What is it you think to do? To give love? No; for no one gives love voluntarily, without of necessity receiving it also. He that catches in this game is caught. The herb *aproxis* receives and conceives fire as soon as it sees it; our hearts are like it; as soon as they see a soul inflamed with love for them, they are at once set on fire with love for it. But some one will say, I am willing to entertain some of this love, but not too much. Alas! you deceive yourself, this fire of love is more active and penetrating than you imagine; you think to receive but a spark, and will be astonished to see how in a moment it will take possession of your whole heart, reduce all your resolution to ashes, and your reputation to smoke. *Who will pity a charmer that is bitten with a serpent?*[1] And I also, after the wise man, cry out, O foolish and senseless people, think you to charm love so as to be able to manage it at pleasure? You would play with it, but it will sting and torment you cruelly; and do you not know what every one will say about it? Every one will laugh at and deride you for having thought you could charm love; and for having in this false security put into your bosom a dangerous serpent, which has ruined and destroyed both your soul and honour.

O God! what blindness is this, to play away thus at hazard against such frivolous stakes the principal power of our soul? Yes, Philothea, for God regards not man, but for his soul; nor his soul, but for his will; nor his will, but for his love. Alas! we have not nearly so much love as we need; I mean to say, that we fall infinitely short of having enough to love God with; and yet, wretches that we are, we lavish it away and pour it forth on foolish, vain, and frivolous things, as if we had enough and to spare. Ah!

[1] Ecclus. xii. 13.

this great God, who hath reserved to himself the whole love of our souls in acknowledgment of our creation, preservation, and redemption, will exact a most strict account of all these foolish deductions we make from it; for, if he will make so rigorous an examination into our idle words, how strictly will he not examine into our idle, improper, foolish, and pernicious friendships.

The walnut tree is very prejudicial to the vines and fields wherein it is planted; because, being so large, it attracts all the moisture of the surrounding earth, and renders it incapable of nourishing the other plants; its foliage is also so thick that it makes a large and close shade; and lastly it attracts the passers by, who, to beat down the fruit, spoil and trample upon all about it. These fond loves do the same injury to the soul, for they so take possession of it, and so strongly draw its motions to themselves, that it has no strength left to produce any good work; the leaves, viz., the idle conversations, amusements, and dalliance, are so frequent, that all leisure time is taken up in them; and finally, they beget so many temptations, distractions, suspicions, and other evil consequences, that the whole heart is trampled down and ruined by them. In a word, these fond loves banish not only heavenly love, but also the fear of God from the soul; enervate the spirit, and undermine the reputation; they are the sport of courts, but the plague of hearts.

CHAPTER XIX

Of True Friendship

LOVE every one, Philothea, with a great love of charity, but have no friendships but with those who can communicate with you in virtues; and the more exquisite the virtues are which shall be the matter of your communications, the more perfect shall your friendship also be. If this communication be in the sciences, the friendship is certainly very commendable ; but still more so, if it be in the virtues, in prudence, discretion, fortitude, and justice ; but should your reciprocal communications relate to charity, devotion, and Christian perfection, how precious will your friendship be ! It will be excellent, because it comes from God ; excellent, because it tends to God ; excellent, because its bond is God ; excellent, because it shall last eternally in God. O how good it is to love on earth as they love in heaven ; to learn to cherish each other in this world as we shall do eternally in the next.

I speak not here of the simple love of charity, for that we ought to have for all men ; but I speak of that spiritual friendship by which two or three or more souls communicate one to another their devotion and spiritual affections, and make themselves but one spirit. How good a right have such happy souls to sing : *Behold how good and pleasant it is for brethren to dwell together in unity.*[1] Yes, for the delicious balm of devotion distils out of one heart into another, by a participation so continual, that it may be said that God has poured out upon this friendship *His blessing and life for evermore.* I consider all other friendships but shadows beside this, and their bonds but chains of glass or of jet, in comparison of this great bond of holy devotion, which is all of gold.

Make no other kind of friendship than this. I speak of such friendships as you choose yourself ; for you must not forsake or neglect the friendships which nature or former duties oblige you to cultivate, with relations, kindred, benefactors, neighbours, and others.

Some perhaps will tell you : "You should have no kind of particular affection and friendship, because it occupies the heart, distracts the mind, and begets envy ;" but they are mistaken in their counsels ; because they have seen, in the writings of some devout authors, that particular friendships and extraordinary affections are of infinite prejudice to Religious,

1 Ps. cxxxiii 1. 2 Ibid. 3.

they therefore imagine that it is the same with other people. But there is a material difference; for as in a well-ordered monastery the common design of all tends to true devotion, it is not needful then to make these particular communications, lest, seeking among individuals for that which is common to the whole, they should fall from particularities to partialities. But for such as dwell among worldly people, and desire true virtue, it is necessary for them to unite themselves together by a holy and sacred friendship, since by this means they encourage, assist, and support each other in good: for as they who walk on plain ground need not to lend each other a hand, whilst they who are in rugged and slippery roads hold one by the other to walk more securely; so they who are in a religious community stand in no want of particular friendships, but they who are in the world have need of them to secure and assist each other amidst the many dangerous places through which they are to pass. In the world all are not aiming at the same end, all are not actuated by the same spirit; we must therefore separate ourselves, and contract friendships, according to our several aims. This particularity begets, indeed, a partiality; but it is a holy partiality, which creates no division, except that between good and evil, sheep and goats, bees and hornets, a very necessary division.

No one surely can deny that our Lord loved St. John, Lazarus, Martha, and Magdalen, with a more tender and special friendship, for the Scripture testifies it. We know that St. Peter tenderly cherished St. Mark and St. Petronilla, as St. Paul did Timothy and St. Thecla. St. Gregory Nazianzen boasts a hundred times of the incomparable friendship he had with the great St. Basil, and describes it in this manner: "It seemed that in both of us there was but one soul dwelling in two bodies. And if they are not to be believed, who say that all things are in all things, yet of us two you may believe that we were both in each of us, and one in the other: we had each of us only one aim, to cultivate virtue, and to accommodate all the designs of our life to future hopes; going in this manner out of this mortal earth before death." St. Augustin testifies that St. Ambrose loved St. Monica entirely for the rare virtues he saw in her, and that she reciprocally loved him as an angel of God. But I am to blame to detain you so long in a matter so clear. St. Jerome, St. Augustin, St. Gregory, St. Bernard, and all the greatest servants of God have had very particular friendships, without prejudice to their perfection. St. Paul, reproaching the disorders of the Gentiles, accuses them of being people without natural affection, that is to say that they had no true friendship. And St. Thomas, with all true philosophers, acknowledges that friendship is a virtue; and he speaks of particular friendship, since, as he says, perfect friendship cannot be extended to a great many persons. Perfection therefore consists, not in having no friendships, but in having none but such as are good, holy, and sacred.

CHAPTER XX

Of the difference between true and vain Friendships

OBSERVE, Philothea, this important admonition. The poisonous honey of Heraclea looks like the other that is wholesome; there is great danger in mistaking the one for the other, or in taking them mixed together, for the goodness of the one cannot counteract the poison of the other. So we must be upon our guard, not to be deceived in our friendships, particularly when they are contracted between persons of different sexes, under what pretext soever. For the devil often imposes upon those who love. They begin with virtuous love; but unless they are very discreet, fond love will begin to intermingle, then sensual love, and afterwards carnal love. Yea, there is even danger in spiritual love, if we are not extremely upon our guard: though in this it is more difficult to be imposed upon, because its purity and whiteness make more apparent the stains which Satan seeks to mingle with it; and therefore when he takes this in hand he does it more subtlely, and endeavours to slip in impurities by almost insensible degrees.

You may distinguish worldly friendship from that which is holy and virtuous, as the poisonous honey of Heraclea is known from the other. The honey of Heraclea is sweeter to the tongue than the ordinary honey, because of the juice of the aconite, which gives it an additional sweetness; so worldly friendship ordinarily produces a great profusion of sweet words, a caressing of impassioned expressions, praises of beauty, grace, and other sensuous qualities; whereas holy friendship speaks a plain and sincere language, and commends nothing but virtue and the grace of God, the only foundation on which it subsists. The honey of Heraclea, when swallowed, occasions a giddiness in the head, so false friendship breeds a vertigo in the mind, which makes its subjects stagger in chastity and devotion, hurrying them on to affected, wanton, and unregulated looks, sensual caresses, inordinate sighs, and complaints of not being beloved, a studied and enticing carriage, gallantries, interchanging of kisses, with other familiarities and improper favours, the certain and unquestionable presages of the approaching ruin of chastity. But holy friendship has no looks but what are simple and modest, no caresses but pure and sincere, no sighs but for heaven, no familiarities but spiritual, no complaints but when God is not loved, infallible marks of chastity. The honey of Heraclea troubles the sight, so this worldly friendship dazzles the judgment to such a degree, that they who are affected by it think they do well when they do ill, and believe their excuses and pretexts and assertions are true reasons. They fear the light and love darkness. But holy friendship is clear-sighted, and never hides herself, but appears willingly before those who are good. In fine, the honey of Heraclea leaves a great bitterness in the mouth; so false friendships change, and end with lewd and foul words and demands; or, in case of refusal, with injuries, slanders, deceits, sadness, confusions, and jealousies, which often terminate in violence and madness. But chaste friendship is always equally honourable, modest, and amiable, and never changes, but into a more perfect and pure union of spirits; a lively image of the blessed friendship exercised in heaven.

St. Gregory Nazianzen says that the cry of the peacock, when he struts and spreads his tail, excites the peahen to lust; so, when we see a man, dressed in his best feathers and strutting like a peacock, approach to flatter, and wheedle and whisper in the ears of women, or of maidens, without aiming at lawful marriage, without doubt, it is but to incite her to some immodesty; and every virtuous woman will stop her ears against the cry of this peacock, the voice of this enchanter, who seeks thus subtlely to charm her; but should she hearken to him, alas! what an evil presage of the future loss of her heart!

Young people, who use gestures, glances, and caresses, or speak words, in which they would not willingly be surprised by their fathers, mothers, husbands, wives or confessors, testify hereby that they are treating of something contrary to honour and conscience. The Blessed Virgin was troubled when she saw an angel in the shape of a man, because she was alone, and he gave her extraordinary, though heavenly praises. O Saviour of the world! purity itself was afraid of an angel in the shape of a man, should not impurity then fear a man though he come in the shape of an angel, when he praises her with sensual and earthly praises.

Chapter XXI

Counsels and Remedies against Evil Friendships

But what remedies are there against this brood and spawn of fond loves, follies, and impurities? As soon as you feel the first symptoms of them, turn completely away, with an absolute detestation of this vanity; run to the cross of your Saviour, and take His crown of thorns, and put it about your heart, so that these little foxes may not come near it. Take good heed of coming to any kind of compromise with this enemy; do not say, I will listen to him, but will do nothing he shall say to me; I will lend him my ears, but will refuse him my heart: O Philothea, for God's sake, be resolute on these occasions; the heart and ears correspond with each other, and as it is impossible to stop a torrent that has taken its leap from the mountain's brow, so it is hard to prevent the love which has entered in at the ear from falling headlong down into the heart.

According to Alcmæon goats breathe by the ears, and not by the nostrils. Aristotle indeed denies it; and I know not how it is: but this I know well, that our heart breathes by the ear; and as it expires and sends forth its own thoughts by the tongue, so it inspires and draws in the thoughts of others by the ear. Let us then guard carefully our ears from the breath of foolish words, for otherwise our hearts will on a sudden be infected. Hearken to no kind of terms, under any pretext whatever: in this case alone there is no danger of being rude and uncivil.

Remember that you have dedicated your heart to God, and that your love having been sacrificed to Him, it would be a sacrilege to deprive Him of the least particle. Rather sacrifice it to Him anew, by a thousand resolutions and protestations; and keeping yourself close within them, as a deer within its covert, call upon God, and he will help you, and his love will take yours under its protection, that it may live for Him alone.

But if you are already caught in the nets of such foolish loves, ah! how difficult will it be to extricate yourself from them! Place yourself before His Divine Majesty, acknowledge in His presence the excess of your misery, frailty, and vanity. Then, with the greatest effort of which your heart is capable, detest this love which you have begun; abjure the vain declaration of it which you have made; renounce the promises you have received; and with the greatest and most absolute resolution, arrest in your heart, and determine never again to admit, the attempts and pleadings of this love.

If you could withdraw yourself to a distance from the object, I should very strongly recommend it; for as they who have been bitten by a serpent cannot easily be cured in the presence of those who have been wounded by the same reptile; so the person stung with love will hardly be cured of this passion as long as he is near the other who has been wounded with the same sting. Change of place contributes very much to allay the heat and pains either of grief or of love. The youth of whom St. Ambrose speaks in his second book of Penance, having made a long journey, returned home altogether, freed from those fond loves he had formerly entertained, and so much changed that his foolish mistress meeting him, and saying: Dost thou not know me? I am really myself. Yes, answered he, but I am not myself. Absence had wrought in him this happy change. And St. Austin witnesses, that to mitigate the grief he suffered for the death of his friend, he withdrew himself from Tagasta, the place where his friend died, and went to Carthage.

But what must he do who cannot withdraw himself? He must absolutely abstain from all secret interviews, all private conversation, all amorous looks, all sighs, and in general all sorts of communications and allurements which may nourish this stinking and smoky fire; or, at least, if he is compelled to speak to the other party, let it be only to declare with a bold, short, and serious protestation, the eternal divorce which he has sworn. I cry aloud to every one who has fallen into these wretched snares: Cut them, break them, tear them; you must not wait to unravel these criminal friendships, you must rend them asunder; you must not untie the knots, but break them or cut them, so that the cords and strings may be worth nothing; we must not deal gently with a love which is so contrary to the love of God.

But after I have thus

broken the chains of this infamous bondage, there will still remain some traces; the marks and scars of the iron will still be impressed upon my feet, that is to say, upon my affections. No, Philothea, they will not, if you have conceived as great a detestation of the evil as it deserves; for in that case you will now be excited by no other emotion but that of an extreme horror of this infamous love, and of all that relates thereto; and will remain free from all other affection towards the forsaken object, but that of a most pure charity for God's sake. But if, through the imperfection of your repentance, there should yet remain in you any evil inclination, procure a mental solitude for your soul, according to what I have taught you before, and withdraw yourself into it as often as you can, and by a thousand reiterated ejaculations of the spirit renounce all your criminal inclinations; reject them with your whole force; read pious books more than usual; go to confession, and communicate more frequently than is your custom; confer humbly and sincerely concerning all the suggestions and temptations of this kind which may befall you, with your director if possible, or some prudent, faithful soul; and doubt not that God will deliver you from all evil passions, provided you continue faithfully in these good exercises.

Alas! you will say, but will it not be ingratitude to break off a friendship so unmercifully? O how blessed is that ingratitude which makes us pleasing to God! But no, Philothea, I tell you in the name of God, this will be no ingratitude, but a great benefit which you will do to your lover; for in breaking your own bonds asunder, you will also break his, since it was the same bonds which bound you both; and though for the present he may not be sensible of his happiness, yet he will acknowledge it soon, and join with you in singing, as an act of thanksgiving: *O Lord, thou hast broken my bonds in sunder; I will offer to thee the sacrifice of thanksgiving, and will call upon the name of the Lord.*[1]

[1] Ps. cxvi. 14, 15.

Chapter XXII

Further Counsels on the subject of Friendship

FRIENDSHIP requires much intercourse between the friends, otherwise it can neither be born nor subsist. Wherefore it often happens that with this communication of friendship many other communications pass insensibly and glide from heart to heart, by a mutual infusion and reciprocal intercourse of affections, inclinations, and impressions. But this happens especially when we have a high esteem for him whom we love; for then we open our heart in such manner to his friendship, that with it his inclinations and impressions enter easily in all their entirety, be they good or bad. Certainly the bees which gather the honey of Heraclea seek nothing but honey; but with the honey they insensibly suck the poisonous qualities of the aconite from which they gather it. We must then, Philothea, in these things carefully practise the counsel which, as the ancients have told us, the Saviour of our souls was accustomed to give: Be ye good changers of money, that is to say, receive not bad money with good, nor base gold with the fine; separate that which is precious from that which is vile; for there is scarcely any person who has not some imperfection. For why should we receive promiscuously the faults and imperfections of a friend, together with his friendship? We must love him indeed, notwithstanding his imperfections, but we must neither love nor receive his imperfections; for friendship requires a communication of good, not of evil. Wherefore as they who draw gravel out of the Tagus, separate the gold which they find and carry it away, and leave the sand on the banks; so they who have the communication of some good friendship, ought to separate from it the sand of imperfections, and not suffer it to enter into their souls. St. Gregory Nazianzen testifies that many, loving and admiring St. Basil, allowed themselves to be led to imitate him, even in his outward imperfections, as in speaking slowly and with an abstracted and pensive spirit, in the fashion of his beard, and in his gait. And we often see husbands, wives, children, and friends, who, having a great esteem of their friends, parents, husbands, and wives, get a thousand little imperfections, either through complaisance or by imitation, in the intercourse of friendship, which they have with one another. Now this they ought by no means to do, for every one has evil inclinations enough of his own, without loading himself besides with those of others; and friendship is so far from requiring it, that on the contrary it obliges us to aid one another, in order to our being mutually freed from all kind of imperfections. We must indeed meekly bear with our friend in his imperfections, but we must not lead him into them, much less transplant them into ourselves. But I speak only of imperfections; for as to sins we must neither occasion them, nor tolerate them in our friends. It is either a weak or a wicked friendship to behold our friend perish, and not to help him; to see him die of an imposthume, and not to dare to open it with the lancet of correction, to save his life. True and living friendship cannot subsist in the midst of sins. They say that the salamander extinguishes the fire in which it lies, so sin destroys the friendship in which it lodges. If it be but a transient sin, friendship will presently put it to flight by correction; but if it remain, and take up its abode, friendship immediately perishes; for it cannot subsist but upon true virtue. How much less, then, ought we to commit sin for friendship's sake. Our friend becomes our enemy, when he would lead us to sin; and deserves to lose his friendship when he would ruin and destroy his friend. So it is one of the most infallible marks of false friendship to see it exercised towards a sinful person, of whatever kind his sins; for if he whom we love is vicious, without doubt our friendship is vicious also; for since it cannot be based on true virtue, it must needs be grounded on some frivolous perfection, or some sensual quality. Society formed for temporal profit among merchants is but a shadow of true friendship, since it is not made for the love of persons, but for the love of gain.

Finally, these two divine sentences are the two main pillars to secure the Christian life; the one is that of the wise man: *Whoso feareth the Lord shall direct his friendship aright:*[1] the other is that of the apostle, St. James: *The friendship of the world is enmity with God.*[2]

[1] Ecclus. vi. 17. [2] Jas. iv. 4.

Chapter XXIII

Of the exercises of Exterior Mortification

THEY who treat of husbandry and rural affairs, assure us, that if one writes any word upon a very sound almond, and encloses it again in the shell, folding and closing it properly, and then plants it, all the fruit of the tree which grows from it will have the same word engraven upon it. For my part, Philothea, I have never been able to approve of the method of those, who, to reform a man, begin with his exterior, such as his gestures, his dress, or his hair. I think we ought, on the contrary, to begin with his interior, *Turn ye to Me,* (said God,)[1] *with all your heart. My son, give Me thine heart.*[2] For the heart being the source of our actions, they will be such as it is. The divine Spouse inviting the soul,[3] says, *Set me as a seal upon thine heart, as a seal upon thine arm.* Yes, verily; for whosoever has Jesus Christ in his heart, will soon have Him in all his exterior actions. It is therefore, dear Philothea, I have desired above all things to engrave upon your heart this holy and sacred motto, *Live Jesus;* assured that your life, which proceeds from the heart as an almond tree from its kernel, will bring forth all its actions, which are its fruits, written and graven with the same words of salvation;

[1] Joel ii.

[2] Prov. xxiii. [3] Cant. viii. 6.

and that, as this sweet Jesus lives within your heart, so will He also live in all your actions, in your eyes, in your mouth, in your hands, and even in the hair of your head: so that you will be able to say with St. Paul, *I live, yet not I, but Christ liveth in me.* In a word, he who has gained the heart of a man, has gained the whole man. But the heart itself, by which we are to begin, requires to be instructed how it ought to frame its outward behaviour, so that men may not only behold holy devotion therein, but also great wisdom and discretion. For this end I am about briefly to give you some counsels.

If you are able to endure fasting, you would do well to fast some days besides those which are commanded by the Church; for besides the usual effects of fasting, viz., to elevate the spirit, to keep the flesh in subjection, and to facilitate the exercise of virtue, it is a great means to restrain gluttony, and keep the sensual appetite and the body subject to the law of the spirit: and even though we do not fast much, yet the enemy fears us, when he knows we know how to fast. Wednesdays, Fridays, and Saturdays are the days on which the ancient Christians exercised themselves most in abstinence; choose then some one of these fast days to fast on, as far as your devotion and the discretion of your director shall advise you.

I would willingly say to you as St. Jerome said to the good Lady Læta: *Long and immoderate fastings displease me much, especially in those that are yet of tender age.* I have learned by experience, that the young ass when wearied in a journey, seeks to go out of the way; that is to say, that young people, being brought into infirmities through excess of fasting easily turn themselves to delicacies. The deer cannot run well in the two seasons of the year, when they are too fat and when they are too lean. We are greatly exposed to temptations, both when our body is too much pampered, and when it is too much weakened; for the one makes it insolent with ease, and the other desperate with affliction; and as we cannot bear it when it is too fat, so it cannot bear us when it is too lean. The want of this moderation in the use of fasting, discipline, hair shirts, and other austerities, has rendered the best years of many unprofitable in the service of charity; as it did in St. Bernard, who repented that he had used overmuch austerity; and the more they ill treated their bodies in the beginning, the more they were constrained to indulge them in the end. Would they not have done better to have mortified their bodies moderately, and in proportion to the offices and labours to which their condition obliged them?

Labour, as well as fasting, serves to mortify and subdue the flesh. If the labour you undertake is necessary to you or useful for the glory of God, I had rather you would suffer the pain of labour than of fasting. This is the sense of the Church, since, on account of such labours as contribute to the service of God and our neighbour, she discharges those who do them even from the fasts commanded. One has the pain to fast; another to serve the sick, or visit prisoners; to hear confessions, to preach, pray and perform such like exercises; these latter kind of pains are of more value than the former; for, besides that they subdue the body equally well, they produce fruits much more desirable. Therefore, generally speaking, it is better to preserve our bodily strength more than may be necessary, than to weaken it too much; for we may always abate it when we will, but we cannot always repair it when we would.

It seems to me that we should hold in great reverence the word which our Saviour and Redeemer Jesus Christ said to His disciples,[1] *Eat such things as are set before you.* It is, in my opinion, a greater virtue to eat, without choice, that which is laid before you, and in the same order as it is presented, whether it be agreeable to your taste or not, than always to choose the worst; for although this latter way of living seems more austere, yet the former has, notwithstanding, more resignation, since by it we renounce not only our own taste, but even our own choice; and it is no small mortification to accomodate one's taste to every kind of meat, and keep it in

1 Luke x. 8.

subjection to all occurrences. Besides this kind of mortification passes unobserved, gives no trouble to any one, and is especially adapted to ordinary life. To set one kind of meat aside, and take another, to pick and taste off every dish, to think nothing properly cooked or sufficiently plain, to make a mystery about every morsel, bespeaks a heart over nice, and caring too much about dishes and platters. I think more highly of St. Bernard's having once unconsciously drunk oil by mistake for water or wine, than if he had drunk wormwood water on purpose, for it was a plain sign that he thought not of what he drank; and in this indifference respecting what we eat and what we drink, consists the perfection of the practice of the sacred rule, *Eat such things as are set before you.* I except, however, such meats as may prejudice the health, or even incommode the spirit, such as hot, high-seasoned, and flatulent meats; as also certain occasions in which nature requires recreation and assistance, in order to be able to support some labour for the glory of God. A continual and moderate sobriety is preferable to violent abstinences practised by fits, and alternated with great relaxations.

We must take from the night for sleep, every one according to his constitution, as much time as is requisite to enable him to spend the day profitably. And because the Holy Scripture in a hundred places, the examples of the saints, and natural reasons, strenuously recommend the morning hours as the best and most fruitful part of our days, and our Lord Himself is named the Orient, or rising sun, I think it a point of virtue to take care to go to rest early in the evening, that we may be enabled to awake and rise early in the morning. Certainly, that time is the most favourable, the most agreeable, and the least subject to disturbance. The very birds invite us to awake and praise God; so that early rising is equally serviceable to health and holiness.

Balaam, mounted on his ass, was going to king Balak, but because he had not a right intention, the angel waited for him in the way, with a sword in his hand to kill him. The ass, seeing the angel, stood still three several times as if restive; Balaam, therefore, beat her cruelly with his staff, to make her go, until, at the third time, the beast falling quite down under Balaam, by an extraordinary miracle, spoke to him,[1] *What have I done to thee? wherefore hast thou smitten me, lo, these three times?* And immediately Balaam's eyes were opened, and he saw the angel, who said to him: *Wherefore hast thou smitten thine ass? unless she had turned from me surely now I had slain thee and saved her alive.* Then Balaam said to the angel: *I have sinned, for I knew not that thou stoodest in the way against me.* Behold, Philothea, Balaam is the cause of the evil, yet he strikes and beats his poor ass, that could not prevent it. It is often the same with us; for example, this woman sees her husband or child sick, and presently betakes herself to fasting, haircloth, and the discipline, as David did on the like occasion. Alas! my dear friend, you beat the poor ass, you afflict your body, but it cannot remedy the evil, nor is it on that account that God's sword is drawn against you. Correct your heart, which has idolized this husband, and which has suffered a thousand vices in this child, and destined it to pride, vanity, and ambition. Again, this man perceives himself frequently to relapse in a shameful manner into the sin of impurity; an inward remorse comes sword in hand against his conscience, to pierce it through with a holy fear; and presently his heart coming to itself, he says, Ah! wicked flesh, ah! treacherous body, thou hast betrayed me: and immediately he lays great blows on his flesh, with immoderate fasting, excessive disciplining, and unsupportable hair-shirts. O poor soul, if thy flesh could speak, as Balaam's ass did, she would say to thee, Why, O wretch, dost thou strike me? It is against thee, O my soul, that God arms his vengeance; it is thou that art the criminal; why dost thou lead me into bad company? why dost thou employ mine eyes, my hands and my lips in wantonness? why dost thou trouble me with impure imaginations? Cherish thou good thoughts, and I shall have no evil motions; keep company

[1] Numb. xxii. 28.

with the modest, and I shall not be provoked to lust. It is thou, alas! that throwest me into the fire, and yet thou wouldst not have me burn; thou castest smoke into my eyes, and yet wouldst not have them inflamed. And God, without doubt, says to you in these cases: Beat, break, rend, and crush your hearts principally, for it is against them that my anger is excited. As, to cure the itch, it is not so necessary to wash or bathe the body, as it is to purify the blood and refresh the liver: so to cure our vices, it may be good to mortify the flesh, but it is above all necessary to purify our affections, and to renew our hearts effectually. But, as a universal rule, never undertake corporal austerities, but with the advice of your spiritual guide.

Chapter XXIV

Of Conversation and Solitude

TO seek and to avoid conversation are two blameable extremes in the devotion of those who live in the world, which is that kind of devotion of which I am speaking to you. To shun all conversations savours of disdain and contempt of our neighbour; and to seek them is a mark of sloth and idleness. We must love our neighbour as ourself, and to show that we love him, we must not flee his company; and to testify that we love ourselves we must abide in ourselves, when we are by ourselves. *Think first of thyself*, says St. Bernard, *and then of others.* If then nothing press you to go abroad into company, or to receive company at home, stay in yourself, and entertain yourself with your own heart; but if company visit you, or any just cause invite you into company, go in God's name, Philothea, and meet your neighbour heartily and kindly.

We call those conversations evil which are held with some evil intention, or when the company is vicious, indiscreet, and dissolute; and such as these we must avoid, as much as bees shun a swarm of wasps or hornets. For, as when persons have been bitten by mad dogs, their sweat, their breath, and their very spittle, become infectious, especially for children, and those of delicate constitution; so we cannot keep company with vicious and dissolute persons, without hazard and danger, especially to those whose devotion is as yet but young and tender.

There are some conversations useless for any other purpose than recreation, which are only held for the sake of diversion from our serious occupations. To these we must not be too much addicted, although we may allow them to occupy the leisure destined for recreation.

Other conversations have civility for their object, such are mutual visits, and certain assemblies made to do honour to our neighbour. With respect to these, as we need not be scrupulous in the practice of them, so neither must we be altogether uncivil in shunning them; but modestly comply with our duty respecting them, so as equally to avoid both ill-breeding and levity.

There remain profitable conversations, such as those of devout and virtuous persons. It will always be of great benefit to you, Philothea, to converse frequently with such persons as these. The vine planted among olive-trees, bears grapes which are oily and have the taste of olives; so the soul which is often in the company of virtuous people cannot but partake of their qualities. Drones alone cannot make honey, but make it with the help of the bees, so it is of great advantage to us in the exercise of devotion to converse with devout souls.

In all conversations sincerity, simplicity, meekness, and modesty are always to be preferred. There are people who make no gesture or motion, but with so much affectation as to weary every one; and as he who can never walk without counting his steps, nor speak but by singing, would be troublesome to the rest of mankind, so they who affect an artificial carriage, and do nothing but with an air, are very disagreeable in conversation; and in this sort of people there is always some presumption. Moderate cheerfulness should ordinarily predominate in our conversation. St. Romuald and St. Anthony are highly commended, that, notwithstanding all their austerities, they had always both their countenances and their conversation adorned with cheerfulness, gaiety, and courtesy. *Rejoice with them that do rejoice.*[1] And again I say to you with the Apostle, *Rejoice in the Lord alway, and again I say rejoice. Let your moderation be known unto all men.*[2] In order for you to rejoice in our Lord, the subject of your joy must not only be lawful, but also becoming; and this I say, because there are some things lawful which yet are not becoming; and in order that your moderation may be known to all men, keep yourself free from insolence, which is always reprehensible. To cause one of the company to fall down, to blacken another's face, to prick or pinch a third, to take advantage of the weak intellect of another, are rude and insolent jokes and amusements.

[1] Rom. xii. 15.
[2] Phil. iv. 4.

But still, besides that mental solitude to which you may retreat, even amidst the largest companies, as I have already observed, you ought also to love local and real solitude; not that I expect you to go into the desert, as St. Mary of Egypt, St. Paul, St. Anthony, St. Arsenius, and the other ancient solitaries did, but to be for some time alone in your chamber or garden, or in some other place where, undisturbed, you may withdraw your spirit into itself, and recreate your soul with pious meditations, holy thoughts, or by a little spiritual reading. After the example of the great Bishop of Nazianzum who, speaking of himself, says: "I walked all alone, about sunset, and passed the time upon the sea shore; for I am accustomed to use this recreation to refresh myself, and to shake off a little my ordinary cares:" and afterwards he relates the pious reflections he made, which I have already mentioned elsewhere. After the example also of St. Ambrose, of whom St. Augustine relates that often going into his chamber (for he never denied entrance to any one) he found him reading, and that after having stayed awhile, for fear of interrupting him, he departed again without saying a word, thinking that the little time that remained to this great pastor for recruiting his spirit, after the hurry of so many affairs as he had upon his hands, ought not to be taken from him. So when the Apostles one day told our Lord how they had preached, and how much they had done, He said to them, *Come ye apart into a desert place, and rest awhile.*[2]

CHAPTER XXV

Of Decency in Attire

ST. PAUL desires that devout women (and the same may be said of men) should be attired *in decent apparel, adorning themselves with shamefacedness and sobriety.*[1] Now the decency of apparel and other ornaments depends on the material, the fashion, and the cleanliness of them. As to the cleanliness, it should be almost always perfect in our apparel, on which, as much as possible, we should not suffer any kind of filth or dirt. Exterior cleanliness represents in some measure internal purity. God himself requires corporal purity in those who approach His altars, and have the principal charge of devotion.

As to the material and fashion of our dress, propriety depends upon circumstances of time, age, quality, company and occasion. People are ordinarily better dressed on holidays, and this in proportion to the solemnity of the feast which is celebrated. In times of penance, as in Lent, their ornaments are laid aside. At marriages they put on wedding garments; at funerals they use mourning; when near the prince they dress themselves in their best attire, which

[1] 1 Tim. ii. 9.

[2] Mark vi. 21.

they cast off when they are only amongst their own domestics.

The married woman may and ought to adorn herself when she is with her husband, and he desires it; but if she should do so when she is at a distance from him, it will be asked, whose eyes she desires to please with that particular care? A greater liberty in point of ornaments is allowed to maidens, because they may lawfully desire to appear agreeable to many, although with no other intent than to gain one by holy marriage. Neither is it esteemed amiss that widows who purpose to marry should adorn themselves in some measure, provided they betray no levity; for having already been mistresses of families and passed through the griefs of widowhood, they are considered to be of a more mature and settled mind. But as for those that are widows indeed, not only in body, but in heart also, no other ornament becomes them but humility, modesty, and devotion; for if they wish to make men in love with them, they are not widows indeed, and if they have no such desire, why do they carry about with them the instruments of love? The host who no longer wishes to receive guests, should pull down the sign from his house. Old people are always ridiculous when they attempt to make themselves gay; it is a folly which is only supportable in youth.

Be neat, Philothea; let there be nothing slovenly about you, or ill put on. It is a kind of contempt of those with whom we converse to come into their company improperly dressed; but avoid carefully all affectation, vanity, singularity, or levity in your dress. Keep yourself always, as much as possible, on the side of plainness and modesty, which, without doubt, are the greatest ornament of beauty, and the best excuse for the want of it.

St. Peter[1] admonishes young women in particular not to wear their hair much curled and plaited. Men who are so weak as to indulge in such fopperies, are justly ridiculed for their effeminacy; and vain women are counted but weak in their chastity; at least, if they have any, it is not to be discovered

[1] 1 Epist. iii. 3.

amidst so many toys and fopperies. They say they think no evil in these things; but I repeat, as I have said elsewhere, that the devil always does. For my part, I would have my devout people, whether men or women, the best clad of the company, but the least pompous and affected; I would have them adorned, as it is said in the Proverbs, with grace, propriety, and dignity. St. Louis says in one word, that each one should dress according to his condition; so that the wise and the good may have no reason to say you do too much, nor young people to say you do too little. But in case young people will not content themselves with what is proper, we must conform to the judgment of the wise.

CHAPTER XXVI

Of Discourse; and first, how we must speak of God

AS physicians judge of the health or sickness of a man by looking at his tongue, so our words are true indications of the quality of our souls. *By thy words*, says our Saviour, *thou shalt be justified, and by thy words thou shalt be condemned.*[1] We move our hand readily to the pain that we feel, and our tongue to the love we entertain.

If then, Philothea, you love God much, you will often speak of God in your familiar discourses with those of your household, your friends, and your neighbours. *For the mouth of the righteous is ever used in wisdom, and his tongue will be talking of judgment.*[2] As bees, with their little mouths, meddle with nothing but honey, so should your tongue be always sweetened with its God, and find no greater pleasure than in feeling the sweet praises and blessings of His name flowing between your lips; as they say St. Francis used to suck and lick his lips after pronouncing the holy name of

[1] Matt. xii. 37.

[2] Ps. xxxvii. 30.

the Lord, to draw as it were from thence the greatest sweetness in the world.

But speak always of God as of God; that is, reverently and devoutly; not making a parade, nor preaching, but with a spirit of meekness, charity, and humility, distilling as much as you can, as it is said of the Spouse in the Canticles,[3] the delicious honey of devotion, and of things Divine, drop by drop, sometimes into the ears of one and sometimes of another, praying to God in the secret of your soul that it would please Him to make this holy dew sink into the hearts of those who hear you.

Above all things, this angelic office must be done meekly and gently; not by way of correction, but by way of inspiration: for it is surprising how powerfully gentleness and an amiable manner of proposing good things attract the heart.

Never, therefore, speak of God or devotion for form's sake or for talk's sake, but always with attention and reverence. I give you this advice that you may avoid that remarkable vanity which is found in many who make profession of devotion, who, on all occasions, speak holy and fervent words out of habit, without ever thinking of what they say; and imagine themselves to be such as their words indicate, which is not the case.

Chapter XXVII

Of Modesty in our Words, and the respect we owe to Persons

IF *any offend not in word he is a perfect man.*[4] Be careful then never to let slip an improper word; for although you speak it not with an ill intention, yet those who hear it may receive it otherwise. An evil word falling into a weak heart

[3] Cant. iv. 11. [4] Jam. iii. 2.

spreads and dilates itself like a drop of oil falling on linen: nay, it sometimes seizes on the heart in such a manner as to fill it with a thousand unclean thoughts and temptations; for as the poison of the body enters by the mouth, so the poison of the heart enters by the ear, and the tongue that communicates it is a murderer. For although perhaps the poison which it has cast forth has not wrought its effect, because it found the hearts of the hearers guarded with some antidote; yet it was not for want of its malice that they were not killed. Let no man therefore tell me that he has no such thought; for our Lord, the searcher of hearts, has said, that *out of the abundance of the heart the mouth speaketh*. And if we have no evil thought, yet the devil has, and always secretly makes use of those immodest words to pierce the heart of some one. They who have eaten the herb *angelica*, have always sweet and agreeable breath, so they who have honour and chastity, which is the angelical virtue, in their hearts, have their words always pure, courteous, and modest. As for indecent and obscene things, the Apostle will not have them even named amongst us; assuring us that nothing so much corrupts good manners as evil communications.

When immodest words are uttered under a disguise, with affectation and subtlety, they are infinitely more poisonous; for as the sharper a dart is, the more easily it enters into our bodies, so the more pointed an evil word is, the deeper it penetrates into our hearts; and they who esteem themselves men of gallantry for speaking such words, do not know why people meet to converse; for they should be like a swarm of bees, convened together to make the honey of some sweet and virtuous entertainment, and not, like a nest of wasps assembled together to suck in corruption. If some fool should address you with indecorous words, shew him that your ears are offended, either by turning yourself immediately away, or by such other mark of resentment as your discretion may direct.

To be a scoffer is one of the worst conditions a mind can be in: God detests this vice greatly, and has heretofore inflicted strange punishments on account of it. Nothing is so contrary to charity or devotion as scorn and contempt of our neighbour. But as derision or mockery are never without scoffing, therefore it is a very great sin; so that divines are right in saying that mockery is the worst kind of offence a man can be guilty of against his neighbour by words; for other offences may be committed with some esteem for the party offended, but this is committed with scorn and contempt.

But as for certain sportive words, spoken by one to another, with a modest gaiety and cheerfulness, they belong to the virtue called *eutrapelia* by the Greeks, which we may call *good conversation;* and by these we take a lawful and friendly recreation from such slight occasions as human imperfections furnish us with. Only we must be careful not to pass from this allowable mirth to scoffing; for scoffing provokes to laughter in the way of scorn and contempt of our neighbour; whereas innocent mirth and drollery excite laughter by a simple liberty and familiar freedom, joined to the sprightly wit of some ingenious conceit. St. Louis, when the Religious offered to speak to him after dinner of high and sublime matters, told them: *it is not now time for grave reasoning, but for recreating ourselves with some mirthful conceits; let every man say innocently, what he has a mind.* This he said out of consideration for the nobles who were present, to receive marks of kindness from the king. But let us, Philothea, so pass our time of recreation as not to lose a blessed eternity by our devotion.

Chapter XXVIII

Of Rash Judgments

JUDGE *not, and ye shall not be judged*, says the Saviour of our souls; *condemn not, and ye shall not be condemned.*[1] No, says the apostle, *Judge nothing before the time until the Lord come, who both will bring to light the hidden things of darkness, and will make manifest the counsels of the heart.*[2] O how displeasing are rash judgments to God! The judgments of the children of men are rash, because they are not judges of one another, and, in judging, they usurp the office of our Lord. They are rash, because the principal malice of sin depends on the intent of the heart, which is an impenetrable secret to us. They are rash, because every one has enough to do to judge himself, without taking upon him to judge his neighbour. In order not to be judged hereafter, it is equally necessary that we should refrain from judging others, and that we should be careful to judge ourselves. For as our Lord forbids the one, so the Apostle enjoins the other, saying, that *if we would judge ourselves, we should not be judged.*[3] But, O good God! we act quite the contrary; for that which is forbidden we cease not to do, judging our neighbour on every occasion, and that which we are commanded, viz., to judge ourselves, we never do.

We must apply remedies against rash judgments, according to their different causes. There are some hearts naturally sour, bitter, and harsh, which make every thing that they receive equally bitter and sour; *turning judgment*, as the prophet Amos[4] says, *into gall*, never judging their neighbour but with all rigour and harshness. Such have great need to fall into the hands of a good spiritual physician; for this bitterness of heart being natural to them, it is hard to overcome, and though it be not in itself a sin, but an imperfection only, yet it is dangerous, because it introduces rash judgment and detraction into the soul and causes them to remain there. Some judge rashly, not through harshness, but through pride, imagining that in the same proportion as they depress the honour of others they raise their own: arrogant and presumptuous spirits, who so admire themselves and place themselves so high in their own esteem that they look on all the rest of mankind as

[1] Luke vi. 37. [2] 1 Cor. iv. 5. [3] 1 Cor. xi. 31.

[4] Amos vi. 12.

little and mean. *I am not as other men are*,[5] said the foolish Pharisee. Others have not this manifest pride, but have a certain complacency in considering the evil qualities of other men, because they make themselves and make others appreciate more keenly the contrary good qualities with which they think themselves endowed. And this complacency is so secret and imperceptible, that people, unless very sharp sighted, do not see it, and even they who are infected with it do not see it if it is not pointed out to them. Others, to excuse themselves to themselves, and to assuage the remorse of their own conscience, very willingly judge others to be guilty of the same kind of vice to which they themselves are addicted, or of some other as great; thinking that the more sinners there are, the less blameable is their own sin. Many are in the habit of rash judgment, merely for the pleasure they take in philosophizing and discussing people's characters and peculiarities by way of mental exercise; and if, unhappily, they sometimes stumble on the truth in their judgment, their rashness and their pleasure in such judgments increase to so violent an excess as to render it in a manner impossible ever to effect their cure. Others judge by passion, and always think well of what they love, and ill of what they hate; excepting in one case only, not less wonderful than true, in which the excess of love incites them to pass an ill judgment on that which they love; a monstrous effect proceeding from an impure, imperfect, unquiet, and diseased love, which is *jealousy*, which every one knows, on a simple look, on the least smile, condemns the person beloved of disloyalty or adultery. In fine, fear, ambition, and other such weaknesses of the mind, frequently contribute towards the breeding of suspicion and rash judgment.

But what remedy is there? They who drink the juice of the Ethiopian herb called *ophiusa*, imagine that they everywhere see serpents and other frightful things; so they who have swallowed down pride, envy, ambition, and hatred, think everything they see evil and blameable. The former, to be healed, must

[5] Luke xviii. 11.

drink palm wine; and I prescribe the same remedy to the latter; drink as much as you can of the sacred wine of charity, and it will deliver you from those noxious humours that beget rash judgments. Charity is afraid to meet evil, so much the less does she go to seek after it; but whenever she does meet it, she turns her face aside, and pretends to take no notice. She shuts her eyes at first sound of it before she sees it, and afterwards believes, with a holy simplicity, that it was not evil, but only some shadow or apparition of evil; and if she cannot help sometimes recognising it to be really evil, she presently turns from it, and endeavours to forget its shape. Charity is the sovereign remedy for all evils, but especially for this. All things appear yellow to the eyes of the icteric and of those who are afflicted with jaundice; they say that to be cured of this disease they must wear celandine under the soles of their feet. The sin of rash judgment is indeed a spiritual jaundice, and makes all things appear evil to the eyes of those who are infected with it. He that would be cured mu apply the remedies, not to his eyes, nor to his understanding, but to his affections, which are the feet of the soul. If your affections are mild, your judgment will be mild also; if your affections are charitable, your judgment will be also charitable. I shall here present you with three admirable examples: Isaac had said that Rebecca was his sister; Abimelech saw him playing with her, that is to say, caressing her in a tender manner,[6] and immediately he concluded she was his wife; a malicious eye would rather have judged her to have been his harlot, or, if she were his sister, that he had been incestuous; but Abimelech adopted the most charitable opinion he could infer from such an occurrence. We must always do the like, Philothea, ever judging as much as possible in favour of our neighbour; and if one action could bear a hundred faces, we should always look on that which is the fairest.

The Blessed Virgin was with child,[7] and St. Joseph plainly perceived it; but on the other hand, as he saw her quite holy, pure and an-

[6] Gen. xxvi. 8. [7] Matt. i. 18.

gelical, he could not believe that she had become pregnant in a sinful way; so he resolved by leaving her privately, to leave the judgment of her case to God; though the reason was very strong to make him conceive an ill opinion of his Virgin Spouse, yet he would not judge her by it; and why? because says the Spirit of God, *he was a just man.* A just man, when he can no longer excuse either the action, or the intention of him whom otherwise he sees to be virtuous, nevertheless will not judge him; but puts it out of his mind, and leaves the judgment of it to God. Thus our blessed Saviour on the cross,[8] not being able altogether to excuse the sin of those who crucified Him, yet at least extenuated the malice of it by alleging their ignorance. When we cannot excuse the sin, let us at least render it worthy of compassion, attributing it to the most favourable cause which it can have, such as ignorance or infirmity.

But may we never then judge our neighbour? No, without doubt, never. It is God, Philothea, who judges malefactors in public justice. It is true He uses the voice of magistrates to make Himself intelligible to our ears; they are His interpreters, and ought to pronounce nothing but what they have learnt of Him, as His oracles; if they do otherwise, following their own passions, then it is they indeed who judge, and who consequently shall be judged; for it is forbidden to men, as men, to judge others.

To see or know a thing is not to judge it; for judgment, at least according to the Scripture meaning, presupposes some difficulty, great or small, true or apparent, which is to be decided. It is therefore it says, *That he who believeth not, is judged already,*[9] because there is no doubt of his damnation. Is it not then a wrong thing to doubt of our neighbour? No, for we are not forbidden to doubt but to judge. But it is not allowed either to doubt or suspect at random, but only so far as reason and argument may constrain us to doubt, otherwise our doubts and suspicions will be rash.

If some evil eye had seen Jacob when he kissed Rachel by the well, or had seen Re-

[8] Luke xxxi. 24.

[9] John iii. 1.

becca receive bracelets and ear-rings from Eliezer, a man unknown in that country, he would no doubt have thought ill of these two patterns of chastity, but without reason or good ground; for when an action is of itself indifferent, it is a rash suspicion to draw an ill consequence from it, unless many circumstances give strength to the argument. It is also a rash judgment to draw an argument from an action, in order to blame the person; but this I shall explain more clearly hereafter.

In fine, those who take good care of their consciences are not very subject to rash judgments. For, as the bees when they see mists or cloudy weather keep in their hives, and make their honey, so the thoughts of good souls do not go in search of perplexities, nor among the cloudy actions of their neighbours; but, to avoid meeting with them, withdraw themselves, and make good resolutions for their own amendment.

It is the part of an unprofitable soul to amuse herself with examining into the lives of other men; I except those who have charge of others, whether in the family or the State, for a good part of their conscience consists in looking to and watching over that of others; let them discharge their duty with love; and having done so, let them keep and watch themselves with regard to this subject.

Chapter XXIX

Of Detraction

RASH judgment begets uneasiness, contempt of our neighbour, pride, self-complacency, and a hundred other most pernicious effects; among which detraction holds the first place as the true plague of conversation. O that I had one of the burning coals of the holy altar to touch the lips of men, that their iniquities might be taken away, and their sin cleansed, in imitation of the seraph who purified the mouth of Isaiah![1] He who could deliver the world from detraction would free it from a great part of the sins of iniquity.

Whosoever robs his neighbour of his good name, besides the sin he commits, is bound to make reparation in different ways, according to the different kinds of detraction; for no man can enter into heaven with the goods of another; and amongst all exterior goods, a good name is the best. Detraction is a kind of murder; for we have three lives, the spiritual, which consists in the grace of God; the corporal, which depends on the soul; and the civil, which consists in our good name; sin deprives us of the first, death takes away the second, and detraction robs us of the third. But the detractor, by one blow of his tongue, commonly commits three murders; he kills his own soul, and the soul of him who listens, and by a spiritual homicide takes away the civil life of the person whom he slanders; for as St. Bernard says, both he who detracts, and he who hearkens to the detractor, they have each the devil about them; the one has him in his tongue, and the other in his ear. David, speaking of detractors, says: *They have whet their tongues like a serpent.*[2] Now the serpent's tongue, as Aristotle says, is forked, and has two points; so is that of the detractor, who at one stroke stings and poisons the ear of the hearer, and the reputation of him of whom he speaks.

I earnestly conjure you then, dear Philothea, never to slander any one, either directly or indirectly; take heed of imputing false crimes and sins to your neighbour, and do not expose those which are unknown, nor aggravate those which are manifest, nor put an evil meaning on his good works, nor dissemble them maliciously, nor explain them away; for in all these ways you will greatly offend God; but most of all by false accusations, and denying the truth to the prejudice of your neighbour; for it is a double sin to lie and to hurt your neighbour at one and the same time.

They who preface detraction by protestations of respect, or intermingle little compliments and jokes, are the

[1] Isa. vi.

[2] Ps. cxxxix.

most subtle and venomous of all detractors. "I protest," say they, "I love him; and that in other respects he is a worthy man; but yet the truth must be told, he did ill to commit such a treacherous action;" "she is a very virtuous girl, but alas! she was surprised," and such like little embellishments. Do you not perceive the artifice? The archer draws the arrow as near to himself as he can, but it is only that he may shoot it with the greater force; so these detractors seem to draw the detraction towards themselves, only to discharge it the harder, that it may pierce into the hearts of their hearers the deeper. The detraction which is uttered in the shape of a jest is still more cruel than all the rest. For, as hemlock is not of itself a very strong poison, but rather a poison which may be easily remedied, yet when taken with wine is incurable; so a detraction, which of itself might, as they say, pass lightly in at one ear and out at the other, yet sticks fast in the brain of the hearers when it is couched under some subtle and merry jest. "*The venom of asps is under their lips*," says David. The bite of the asp is almost imperceptible, and its venom at first produces titillation, by means of which the heart and the bowels expand themselves, and receive the poison, against which there is afterwards no remedy.

Say not that such a one is a drunkard, though you have seen him drunk; nor that he is an adulterer, because he has been surprised in that sin; for a single act does not necessarily imply a habit. The sun stood still once in favour of the victory of Joshua, and was darkened another time in favour of our Saviour's victory, yet no one will therefore say that the sun is either immovable or dark. Noah was once drunk, and Lot another time, yet neither the one nor the other was a drunkard; nor was St. Peter bloody-minded for having once shed blood, nor a blasphemer though he once blasphemed. To bear the name of a vice or a virtue, one must have made some progress in it, it must be habitual. It is then a misrepresention to say, such a man is passionate, or a thief, because we have seen him once in a passion or guilty of stealing. Although a man has been a long time vicious, yet we are in danger of belying him if we call him vicious. Simon the leper called Magdalen a sinner, because she had been so long before; yet he lied, for she was then no longer a sinner, but a most holy penitent, and therefore our Saviour took her cause into his protection. The vain Pharisee took the humble publican for a great sinner, or even perhaps an unjust man, an adulterer, an extortioner, but was greatly deceived, for even at that very time he was justified.[1] Ah! since the goodness of God is so immense, that one moment suffices to pray for and receive His grace, what assurance can we have, that he who was yesterday a sinner, is so to-day? The day that is past ought not to judge the present day, nor the present day to judge that which is past: it is only the last day that judges all. We can then never say a man is wicked, without danger of lying; all that we can say, if we must speak, is, that he did such a bad action, or lived ill at such a time, or that he does ill at present; but we must never draw consequences from yesterday to this day, nor from this day to yesterday, much less to to-morrow.

But, though we must be extremely cautious not to speak ill of our neighbour, yet we must avoid the contrary extreme, into which some fall, who, to avoid the sin of detraction commend and speak well of vice. If a person is indeed a detractor, say not in his excuse, that he is frank and thoughtless; if a person is notoriously vain, say not that he is genteel and elegant; never call dangerous familiarities by the name of simplicity and innocence; nor varnish disobedience with the name of zeal; nor arrogance with the name of freedom: nor lasciviousness with the name of friendship. No, dear Philothea, we must not in order to avoid the vice of detraction, favour, flatter, or cherish other vices; but we must roundly and freely call evil evil, and blame that which is blameable; for in doing this we glorify God, provided we observe the following conditions.

To speak commendably against the vices of another

1 Luke xviii.

it is necessary that the profit, either of him of whom we speak, or of them to whom we speak requires it. For instance, when the indiscreet familiarities of such or such persons, which are manifestly dangerous, are related in the company of girls, or the liberties taken by this or that person, in their words or gestures, which are plainly improper ; if I do not freely blame the evil, but rather excuse it, those tender souls who hear it, may take occasion to give themselves some such like liberties. Their profit then requires that I should freely reprehend these liberties upon the spot, except I could put off this good office to be done better, and with less prejudice to the persons spoken of, on some other occasion. Besides this, it is also necessary that it should belong to me to speak on the subject, as that I am one of the chief of the company, and that if I did not speak, it would look as though I approved of the vice. But if I be one of the least, I ought not to take upon me to make the censure. But, above all it is necessary that I should be exactly just in my words, so as not to say a single word too much. For example : if I blame the familiarity of this young man, and that young woman, because it is indiscreet and dangerous, Philothea, I must hold the balance so even, as not to exaggerate the matter by a single grain. Should there be only a slight appearance, I will not call it any thing more ; if nothing else but a mere indiscretion, I will not call it anything worse; should there be neither indiscretion, nor real appearance of evil, but only that some malicious spirit may take from it a pretext to speak ill, I will either say nothing whatever, or I will say that and no more. My tongue, whilst I am speaking of my neighbour, is in my mouth like a razor in the hand of a surgeon, who wishes to cut between the nerves and the tendons. The cut I give must be so accurate that I say neither more nor less than the truth. In fine it must be our principal care in blaming any vice, to spare as much as possible the person in whom it is found.

It is true, we may speak freely of infamous, public, and notorious sinners, provided it be in the spirit of charity and compassion, and not with arrogance and presumption, nor with complacency in the sin of others, which is always the part of a mean abject heart. Amongst all these, must be excepted the declared enemies of God and His church, such as the sects of heretics and schismatics and their ringleaders, since it is charity to cry out against the wolf when he is among the sheep. We must decry them as much as we can wherever we see occasion.

Every one takes the liberty to censure princes, and to speak ill of whole nations, according to the different affections they bear them. Philothea, do not commit this fault; for besides the offence to God, it may bring you into a thousand quarrels.

When you hear any one spoken ill of, make the accusation doubtful, if you can do it justly; if you cannot, excuse the intention of the person accused; if that cannot be done, express compassion for him, divert the discourse, remembering yourself, and putting the company in mind, that they who do not fall owe all the thanks to God; recall the detractor to himself with meekness, and declare some good action of the party offended, if you know of any.

Chapter XXX

Further Counsels on Discourse

LET your speech be meek, frank, sincere open, simple and truthful. Guard yourself from equivocations, artifices, and dissimulations; for although it may not be advisable to say all sorts of truths at all times, yet it is never allowable to speak contrary to the truth. Accustom yourself, therefore, never to tell a lie deliberately, either by way of excuse or otherwise; remembering that God is the God of Truth. Should you tell a lie unawares, and you can correct it on the spot by some explanation or retractation, do so; an honest excuse has always more grace and power to bear one harmless than a lie.

Though one may sometimes discreetly and prudently disguise and cover the truth by some sleight of words, yet it must never be done but when the glory and service of God manifestly require it: in any other case such artifices are dangerous; for, as the Holy Scripture says, *The Holy Spirit will have nothing to do with the deceitful.*[1] No artifice is so good and desirable as plain dealing; wordly prudence and carnal artifice belong to the children of this world: but the children of God walk in a straight way, and their heart is without guile. *He that walketh uprightly*, says the wise man,[2] *walketh surely.* Lying, double-dealing, and dissimulation are always signs of a weak and mean spirit.

St. Augustin has said, in the fourth book of his Confessions, "That his soul and that of his friend were but one soul; and that he abhorred this life after the death of his friend, because he was not willing to live by halves: and that yet for the same cause he was unwilling to die, that his friend might not wholly die." These words seemed to him afterwards too artificial and affected, so that he recalled them, and censured them in his book of Retractions, and called them a folly. See, Philothea, the tenderness of this holy and beautiful soul with respect to the least affectation in his words.

Fidelity, plainness, and sincerity of speech, are great ornaments of the Christian life. *I will take heed*, says holy David,[3] *to my ways, that I offend not in my tongue;* and again,[4] *Set a watch, O Lord, before my mouth, and keep the door of my lips.* It is a counsel of St. Louis not to contradict any one in discourse, unless it were either sinful, or very hurtful to acquiesce. This is to avoid all contentions and disputes. But should it be necessary to contradict any one, or oppose our own opinion to that of another, we must do it with such mildness and dexterity as not to exasperate his spirit, and all the more so since nothing is ever gained by harshness.

1 Wisd. i. 5. 2 Prov. x 9.

3 Ps. xxxix. i. 4 Ps. cxli. 3.

To speak little, so much recommended by wise men of old, is not to be understood to mean that we should utter but few words, but that we should not speak many unprofitable words; for in the matter of speaking one does not regard quantity so much as quality. But, in my opinion, we ought to avoid both extremes; for to affect too much the reserved and severe, and to refuse to share in the familiar chat which goes on in conversation, looks either as if one had want of confidence in the company or a disdain for it; and on the other hand, to be always babbling and gossipping, so as to afford neither leisure nor opportunity to others to speak, is a mark of shallowness and levity.

St. Louis condemned whispering and talking aside in company, and particularly at table, lest it should give others occasion to suspect that some evil was spoken of them. "He who is at table," said he, "in good company, and has something to say that is merry and pleasant, ought to speak it so that everybody may hear him; if it is a thing of importance, he ought not to talk about it at all."

Chapter XXXI

Of Pastimes and Recreations: and first, of such as are lawful and commendable

It is necessary sometimes to relax our minds as well as our bodies by some kind of recreation. St. John the Evangelist, as Cassian relates, was one day found by a huntsman with a partridge on his hand, which he was caressing for his recreation. The huntsman asked how such a man as he could spend his time in so poor and mean an occupation? St. John replied: Why dost thou not carry thy bow always bent? For fear, answered the huntsman, that if it were always bent, it would loose its spring and become useless. Be not surprised, then, replied the apostle, that I should sometimes remit a little of the close application and attention of my spirit and enjoy a little recreation, that I may afterwards employ myself more fervently in divine contemplation. It is doubtless a vice to be so rigorous, rough, and austere, as neither to be willing to take any recreation ourselves, nor allow it to others.

To take the air, to walk, to entertain ourselves with cheerful and friendly conversation, to play on the lute or any other instrument, to sing to music, or go a hunting, are recreations so innocent, that for the proper use of them, there needs but that common prudence, which gives to everything its due order, time, place, and measure.

Those games, in which the gain serves as a prize or recompense for the dexterity and industry of the body or of the mind, such as tennis, football, pall-mall, running at the ring, chess, and backgammon, are recreations in themselves innocent and allowable; it is only necessary to guard against excess, either in the time one spends in them, or in the sum one plays for; for if one spends too much time in them, they are no longer an amusement, but an occupation; one refreshes neither the mind nor the body, but on the contrary stupifies and oppresses them. After playing five or six hours at chess, the mind is altogether fatigued and exhausted. To play long at tennis is not a recreation but a fatigue to the body. Or if the stake played for is too great, the affections of the players become disordered; besides, it is unjust to hazard so much upon kinds of skill and industry of so little importance as those which are exercised at play. But, above all, Philothea, take especial care not to set your affections upon these amusements; for how innocent soever any recreation may be, it is a vice to set our heart upon it. I do not say that you must take no pleasure in your sport whilst at play, for then it would be no recreation; but I say, you must not fix your affection on it, nor let it take up too much time, nor be too eager after it.

Chapter XXXII

Of Prohibited Games

THE games of dice, cards, and the like, in which the game depends principally on hazard, are not only dangerous recreations, as dances are, but are absolutely and in their own nature bad and reprehensible; hence they have been forbidden by the laws, both civil and ecclesiastical. You will say perhaps, what great harm is there in them? Success in these games does not depend on reason, but on chance, which often falls upon him whose ability and industry deserve nothing; and reason is offended at such a result. But you will say, the players have agreed to these conditions. That is a good argument to show that the winner does no wrong to the losers, but it does not prove that the agreement is a rational one, or the game either; for the gain which ought to be the recompence of industry, is made the reward of chance, which deserves no reward whatever, since it no way depends upon us. Besides, although these games bear the name of recreations, and are played under that pretext, yet they are by no means recreations, but violent occupations. For is it not an occupation when the mind is kept on the stretch by an unremitted attention, and agitated by perpetual disquiet, fear and anxiety? Can there be any state of mind more painful, gloomy and melancholy than that of gamesters? You must not speak whilst they are at play, you must not laugh, you must not cough, for fear of giving offence. In fact, there is no pleasure in play, except in winning; and is not that pleasure iniquitous, which can only be obtained at the cost of loss and vexation to one's companion. Surely such satisfaction is infamous. For these three reasons gaming is prohibited.

St. Louis, on hearing that the Count of Anjou, his brother, and Monsieur Gautier de Nemours, were gaming, arose out of his sick-bed, went staggering to their chamber, and taking the tables, the dice, and part of the money, cast them out at the window into the sea, and was very angry with them. The holy and chaste damsel Sara, speaking to God, of her innocence, says,[1] *Thou knowest, O Lord, that I have never joined myself with players.*

[1] Tob. iii.

Chapter XXXIII

Of Balls and Pastimes which are lawful, but dangerous

BALLS and dances are things in their own nature indifferent, yet according to the ordinary manner in which they are conducted, they tend and incline very much to the side of evil, and are consequently full of danger and risk. Being generally carried on by night in darkness and obscurity, it is very easy for vicious circumstances to obtain admittance, in a subject which is of itself so susceptible of evil. They occasion late hours, after which the morning of the next day is lost, and consequently the opportunity of serving God therein. In a word, it is always folly to exchange the day for the night, light for darkness, and good works for follies? At a ball every one strives who shall outdo the rest in vanity, and vanity so disposes the heart to evil affections, and to dangerous attachments, that such things are the usual consequences of dances.

I say to you of dances, Philothea, what physicians say of mushrooms, that the best of them are good for nothing; so I tell you the best balls are hardly good. If, nevertheless, you must eat mushrooms, be sure they are well prepared. If upon some occasions, which you cannot well avoid, you must go to a ball, see that your dancing is well prepared. But you will ask me how must it be prepared? I answer, with modesty, dignity, and a good intention. Eat them sparingly and seldom, says the physician of mushrooms, for be they ever so well dressed, the quantity makes them poisonous: dance but little, and very seldom, I say, Philothea, otherwise you put yourself in danger of acquiring a liking for it.

Mushrooms, according to Pliny, being spongy and porous, easily attract infection to themselves from the things that are about them; so that being near serpents and toads they imbibe their poison. Balls, dances, and other nocturnal assemblies, ordinarily attract the reigning vices and sins of the neighbourhood, namely, quarrels, envy, scoffing, and wanton loves; and as these exercises open the pores of the bodies of those who use them, so they also open the pores of their hearts. So that should some serpent breathe into their ears some loose word or flattery or temptation, or should some basilisk cast impure looks, or wanton glances of love, the heart easily allows itself to imbibe them and be poisoned. O Philothea, these idle recreations are ordinarily dangerous; they dissipate the spirit of devotion, enfeeble the mind, chill charity, and excite a thousand evil affections in the soul, and therefore they are not to be used but with the greatest caution.

But physicians say that above all after mushrooms we must drink good wine; and I say, that after dancing it is necessary to refresh our souls with some good and holy considerations, to prevent the dangerous impressions which the vain pleasure taken in dancing may have left in our minds. But what considerations?

1. Consider, that at the same time that you were at the ball, many souls were burning in the flames of hell, for sins they had committed at dances, or occasioned by dances. 2. That many Religious, and devout persons were at that very time before God, singing His praises, and contemplating His beauty. Ah! how much more happily was their time employed than yours! 3. That while you were dancing, may souls departed out of this world in great anguish, and that thousands of men and women then suffered great pains in their beds, in hospitals, in the streets, by gout, stone, and fever. Alas! they have no rest, and will you have no

compassion for them? do you not call to mind that you will one day groan as they did, whilst others will dance as you did? 4. That our blessed Saviour, the Blessed Virgin, the angels and saints, beheld you at the ball. Ah! how greatly did they pity you, seeing your heart pleased with such nonsense, and taken up with such a toy. 5. Alas! while you were there, time was passing away, and death was approaching nearer; see how he mocks you, and summons you to his dance, in which your groans for your sins shall serve for the music, and where you shall make but one step from this life to the next. The dance of death is the true pastime of mortals, since by it we pass in a moment from time to eternity, to everlasting happiness or never-ending woe. I have set down these brief considerations for you; but God will suggest to you many more to the like effect, if you fear Him.

Chapter XXXIV

At what time we may Play or Dance

FOR playing and dancing to be lawful, we must use them by way of recreation, not out of any strong affection for them; for a short time, not till we are wearied or stupified; and but seldom, for to practise them habitually is to turn a recreation into an occupation. But on what occasions may we play and dance? Proper occasions for dancing or for innocent games are frequent, those for the forbidden games are rare, because they are much more open to censure and to danger. But, in a word, dance and play, in accordance with the conditions which I have noted, when your own prudence and discretion may direct you to do so in compliance with the request of the company in which you are engaged; for compliance which springs from charity, makes indifferent things good, and dangerous things allowable; it even takes away the harm from those things which are in some measure evil; and therefore games of hazard, which otherwise would be reprehensible, are not so, if we use them sometimes out of this proper compliance.

I was pleased to read, in the Life of St. Charles Borromeo, that he complied with the Swiss in certain things, in which otherwise he was very strict; and that St. Ignatius of Loyola, being invited to play did not refuse. As to St. Elizabeth of Hungary, she played and danced sometimes, when she was present at assemblies of recreation, without any prejudice to her devotion; for devotion was so deeply rooted in her soul, that as the rocks about the Lake of Rieti grow larger by the beating of the waves, so her devotion increased among the pomps and vanities to which her condition exposed her. Great fires are increased by the wind, but small ones are extinguished if we do not screen them from it.

CHAPTER XXXV

That we must be Faithful, both on great and small Occasions

THE sacred Spouse in the Canticles, says that his Spouse has *ravished his heart with one of her eyes, and one of the hairs of her neck.*[1] Now among all the exterior parts of the human body, none is more noble, either for its skilful construction or for its activity than the eye, and none more mean than the hair. Wherefore the divine Spouse would give us to understand that not only the great works of devout persons are pleasing to Him, but also the least and most trivial; and that to serve Him acceptably we must take care to serve Him well, not only in great and high things, but

[1] Chap. iv. 9.

in those that are small and low; since by the one as by the other we may *ravish His heart with love.*

Prepare yourself, then, O Philothea, to suffer many great afflictions, even martyrdom itself, for our Lord; resolve to surrender to Him whatever is most dear to you, if it shall please Him to take it; father, mother, brother, husband, wife, children; even your eyes, or your life; for you ought to prepare your heart for all these sacrifices. But as long as Divine Providence does not send you afflictions so great and painful, that is, does not require your eyes, give him at least your hair. I mean, suffer meekly those small injuries, those little inconveniences, those inconsiderable losses which daily befall you; for by means of such little occasions as these, managed with love and affection, you will gain His heart entirely, and make it all your own. These little daily charities, this headache or toothache, this cold, this ill-humour of husband or wife, this breaking of a glass, this slight or rudeness, this loss of a pair of gloves, of a ring, or of a handkerchief; this little self-denial we make in going early to bed, and rising in good time for prayer or for Holy Communion; that little bashfulness we have in doing certain acts of devotion in public; in short, all these trivial sufferings, being accepted and embraced with love, are highly pleasing to the Divine Goodness, who in return for a cup of cold water only, has promised an ocean of all felicity to his faithful ones. And since these occasions present themselves every moment, to manage them well is a great means to heap up a store of spiritual riches.

When I saw in the life of St. Catherine of Sienna so much rapture and elevation of spirit, so many wise sayings, and even sermons uttered by her, I did not doubt that with this eye of contemplation she had ravished the heart of her heavenly Spouse. But I was no less pleased when I found her in her father's kitchen, humbly turning the spit, blowing the fire, dressing the meat, kneading the bread, and doing the meanest offices of the house, with a courage full of love and affection towards her God. And I esteem no less the little and humble meditation she made amongst these mean and abject employments, than the ecstacies and raptures she so often had, which, perhaps, were only given her in recompense of this humility and abjection. This was her meditation: she imagined that whilst she was dressing meat for her father, she was preparing it for our Saviour, like another St. Martha, and that her mother held the place of the blessed Virgin, and her brothers that of the Apostles: she excited herself in this manner to serve in spirit the whole court of heaven, employing herself in these low services with great delight, because she knew that such was the will of God. I have mentioned this example, Philothea, that you may know of what importance it is to direct all your actions, be they ever so mean, to the service of His Divine Majesty.

To this end I counsel you as strongly as I can to imitate the virtuous woman, whom the great Solomon so highly praises: *She girdeth her loins with strength* (as he says); *she openeth her mouth with wisdom*: that is, she is occupied in high, noble, and important things, and yet disdains not *to lay her hands to the spindle, and her hands hold the distaff.*[1] Gird your loins with strength, exercise yourself in prayer and meditation, in frequenting the sacraments, in exciting souls to the love of God, and inspring good thoughts into their hearts, and in a word, in the performance of great and important works, according to your vocation; but never forget your distaff and your spindle; that is to say, take care to practise those low and humble virtues, which grow like flowers at the foot of the cross, such as serving the poor, visiting the sick, taking care of your family, and attending to all your domestic concerns, with that profitable diligence which will leave you no time to be idle: and with all these occupations, mingle such considerations as those I have just related of St. Catherine.

Great occasions of serving God present themselves but seldom, but little ones frequently. *Now he that is faithful in that which is least*, says our Saviour, *shall be set over that which is much.*[2] Do all things then in the name of God, and you

1 Prov. xxxi. 2 Matt. xxv. 23.

will do all things well: whether you eat, or whether you drink, or whether you sleep, or whether you recreate yourself, or whether you turn the spit, doing all these things because it is God's will that you should do them, then you will profit much in the sight of God.

Chapter XXXVI

That we must be Just and Reasonable

IT is reason that makes us men, and yet it is a rare thing to find men truly reasonable, because self-love usually leads us astray from reason, drawing us insensibly into a thousand small, yet dangerous injustices and wrongs; which, like the little foxes spoken of in the Canticles, spoil the vines; for because they are little, we take no notice of them; but because they are many in number, they fail not to do us much harm.

These things of which I am about to speak, are they not unjust and unreasonable? We condemn every little thing in our neighbours, and excuse ourselves in things that are great; we want to sell very dear and to buy very cheap; we desire that justice should be exercised in another man's house, but mercy and connivance in our own; we would have everything we say taken in good part, but we are sensitive and touchy about what others say to us; we would have our neighbour sell us his property, at the price we offer; but is it not more reasonable that he should keep his goods and leave us our money? We take it ill that he will not accommodate us; but has he not more reason to be offended that we should desire to incommode him.

If we love one particular exercise, we despise all others; and set ourselves against everything that is not according to our own taste. If there be any of our inferiors who has not a prepossessing appearance, or to whom we have once taken a dislike, whatever he does we take it ill, we never cease to mortify him, and find fault with all he does. On the contrary, if any one has an agreeable manner which pleases us, he can no nothing which we are not willing to excuse. There are some virtuous children whom their parents can scarcely bear to see, because of some bodily imperfection; and there are others who are vicious, but because of some personal graces they are favourites. On all occasions we prefer the rich to the poor, although neither of better condition, nor so virtuous; we even prefer people because they are better clad. We exact our own dues strictly, but would have others lenient in demanding theirs; we are punctilious in maintaining our own rank, but would have others humble and condescending; we soon find fault with our neighbour, but none must find fault with us; what we do for others seems always very great, but what others do for us seems as nothing. In a word, we are like the partridges in Paphlagonia, which have two hearts; for we have one heart kind, gracious, and courteous towards ourselves, and another hard, severe, and exacting towards our neighbour. We have two weights, one to weigh to our advantage, and the other to weigh to the detriment of our neighbour. *But*, says the Scripture,[1] *with flattering lips and with a double heart do they speak;* that is to say, they have two hearts; and to have *divers weights*, a greater, to receive with, and a less, to deliver out withal, *is an abomination unto the Lord*.[2]

Philothea, be fair and just in all your actions: put yourself always in your neighbour's place, and put him in yours, and so you will judge rightly; imagine yourself the seller when you are buying, and the buyer when you are selling, and you will sell and buy justly. These injustices are trifling, and do not require us to make restitution, inasmuch as they only consist in taking rigorous advantage of the conditions in our own favour, yet we are bound to amend them, for they are great defects in reason and

1 Ps. xi. 3.
2 Prov. xx. 10, 23.

charity, and little better than cheating. Believe me, one loses nothing by being generous, noble, and courteous, with a heart royal, just, and reasonable. Therefore, Philothea, remember frequently to examine whether your heart is such towards your neighbour, as you would have his be towards you, were you in his place; for this is the touchstone of true reason. Trajan, being blamed by his confidants, for making the imperial majesty, as they thought, too accessible, said: "Ought I not then to be such an emperor towards private men, as I would desire an emperor to be towards me, were I myself a private man."

CHAPTER XXXVII

Of Desires

EVERY one knows that we must keep ourselves from the desire of vicious things, since the desire of evil is of itself evil; but I go further, Philothea, and tell you that you must not desire dangerous things, such as balls, plays, or such like diversions, nor covet honours and offices, nor aspire to visions and ecstacies, for there is a great deal of danger, and vanity, and delusion in such things. Desire not things which are at a great distance, that is to say, which cannot happen for a long time, as many do, who by this means dissipate their thoughts and weary their hearts unprofitably, and are in danger of becoming unsettled. If a young man earnestly desires to be settled in some office before the proper time, what does all his anxiety avail him? If a married woman desires to be a nun, to what purpose is it? If I desire to buy my neighbour's property before he is willing to sell it, am I not wasting my time in this desire? If, when I am sick, I desire to preach, to celebrate the holy Eucharist, to visit others that are sick, and do things which only those who are in health can do, are not all these desires vain, since it is out of my power to put them in execution? Yet in the mean time these unprofitable desires occupy the place of others which I ought to have --to be patient, resigned, self-denying, obedient, and meek under my sufferings—which are what God would have me practise at that time; but we are generally like people who long for cherries in autumn and grapes in the spring.

I by no means approve of persons who are engaged in some duty or calling wasting their time in desiring some other kind of life than that in which they are already engaged; nor exercises incompatible with their present condition; for this dissipates the heart, and makes it unfit for its proper duties. If I desire to practise the solitude of a Carthusian, I lose my time; and this desire occupies the place of that which I ought to have, viz., to employ myself well in my present office. I would not even have any one desire to have greater talent or judgment, for these desires answer no purpose, and occupy the place of that which every one ought to have, of cultivating what he has, be it little or great. Nor would I have any one desire means to serve God which he has not, but rather that he should faithfully employ those which he has. Now, this is to be understood only of desires which occupy the heart; for, as to simple wishes, they do no harm if they are not too frequent.

Do not desire crosses, but in proportion to the patience with which you have borne those which have been already sent you; for it is a mistake to desire martyrdom, and not to have the courage to bear an injury. The enemy often suggests a great desire of things that are absent, and which will never happen to us, that so he may divert our mind from present objects, from which, trivial as they are, we might obtain great profit. We fight with the monsters of Africa in imagination, and in the mean time, for want of attention, we suffer ourselves to be stung by every insignificant reptile that lies in our way. Do not desire temptations, for that would be rashness; but accustom your heart to wait for them courageously, and to defend yourself against them when they come.

A variety of food, especially if taken in any considerable quantity, overloads the stomach, and if it be weak, ruins it: so do not overcharge your soul, either with a multitude of worldly desires, which will ruin it, or even with those which are spiritual, for they will overload it. When the soul is purified from bad humours, she feels a craving after spiritual things, and, like one famished, she longs after a thousand kinds of exercises of piety, mortification, penance, humility, charity, and prayer. It is a good sign of health, Philothea, to have a keen appetite; but you must consider whether you can well digest all that you would eat. Amongst so many desires, choose then, by the advice of your spiritual father, such as you can practise at present, and turn them to the best advantage: afterwards God will send you others, which you must also practise in their proper season; and thus you will never lose your time in unprofitable desires. I do not say that you must reject any kind of good desires, but that you must take them in order; those which cannot be executed now should be locked up in some corner of the heart till their time come; and in the meantime practise those which are seasonable. This advice I give not only to spiritual persons, but also to worldly people; for without attending to it, there would be no living without confusion and anxiety.

CHAPTER XXXVIII

Instructions for Married People

MATRIMONY *is a great mystery.*[1] It is honourable to all, in all, and in every thing, that is, in all its parts; to all, because even virgins ought to honour it with humility; in all, be-

[1] Eph. v. 32.

cause it is equally holy in the rich and poor; in all its parts, because its origin, its end, its advantages, its form, and its matter, are all holy. It is the nursery of Christianity which replenishes the earth with faithful souls, to complete the number of the elect in heaven; so that the conservation of marriage is of the last importance to the commonwealth, for it is the origin and source of all its streams.

Would to God that his most beloved Son were invited to all marriages, as He was to that of Cana; then the wine of consolations and benedictions would never be wanting; for the reason why there is commonly a scarcity of it at the beginning, is, because Adonis is invited instead of Jesus Christ, and Venus instead ofhis Blessed Mother. He that would make marriage happy, ought in his espousals to represent to himself the sanctity and dignity of this sacrament. But alas! instead of this, there are a thousand disorders committed in diversions, feasting, and immodest discourse; it is no wonder, then, if disorders result in the married life. Above all things, I exhort married people to that mutual love which the Holy Ghost so much recommends in the Scripture. O you who are married, it is nothing to tell you to love each other with a natural love, for the turtle doves do that; nor to say love one another with a human love, for the heathens do so; but I say to you, after the great Apostle, *Husbands, love your wives even as Christ also loved the Church. And you wives, love your husbands, as the Church loveth her Saviour.*[2] It was God who brought Eve to our first father Adam, and gave him her to wife; it is also God, O my friends, who with His invisible hand, has tied the knot of the holy bond of your marriage, and given you to one another; why do you not then cherish each other with a love holy, consecrated and divine.

The first effect of this love is indissoluble union of your hearts. Two pieces of fir glued together, if the glue be good, cleave so fast one to the other, that you may sooner break the pieces in any other place than that where they are joined. But God joins the husband to the wife

[2] Eph. v.

with His own blood; for which cause this union is so strong, that the soul must sooner separate from the body than the husband from the wife. But the union which is meant is not principally of the body, but of the heart, of the affection, and of the love.

The second effect of this love ought to be the inviolable fidelity of each to the other. Seals were anciently graven upon rings worn on the fingers, as the Scripture itself testifies. This explains the meaning of the ceremony which takes place in marriage. The church, by the hand of the priest, blesses a ring, and giving it first to the man, testifies that she puts a seal upon his heart by this sacrament, that henceforward neither the name nor the love of any other woman may enter therein, so long as she shall live who has been given to him; afterwards the bridegroom puts the ring on the hand of the bride, that she may understand that her heart also must never admit an affection for any other man, so long as he shall live upon earth whom our Lord here gives to her for a husband.

The third fruit of marriage is the lawful procreation and education of children. It is a great honour to you that are married, that God, designing to multiply souls, which may bless and praise Him to all eternity, makes you cooperate with Him in so noble a work, by the production of the bodies into which He infuses, like heavenly drops, immortal souls as He creates them, for He does create them when infusing them into the body.

Preserve, then, O husbands, a tender, constant, and cordial love for your wives: for the woman was taken from that side of the first man which was nearest his heart, to the end she might be loved by him cordially and tenderly. The weaknesses and infirmities of your wives, whether in body or mind, ought never to provoke you to any kind of disdain, but rather to a sweet and affectionate compassion; since God has created them such, to the end that, depending upon you, you should receive from them more honour and respect, and that you should have them in such a manner for your companions, that nevertheless you should be their heads and superiors

And you, O wives, love the husbands whom God has given you tenderly and cordially, but with a respectful love, and full of reverence; for therefore, indeed, did God create them of a sex more vigorous and predominant; and was pleased to ordain, that the woman should depend upon the man, being a bone of his bone, and flesh of his flesh; and that she should be made of a rib taken from under his arm, to show that she ought to be under the hand and guidance of her husband. And all Holy Scripture strictly recommends to you this subjection, which, at the same time, it renders pleasant, not only by prescribing that you should accommodate yourselves to it with love, but also by commanding your husbands to exercise it with great affection, tenderness, and gentleness. *Husbands* (says St. Peter),[3] *dwell with your wives according to knowledge, giving honour unto the wife as unto the weaker vessel.*

But while I exhort you to advance more and more in this mutual love which you owe to one another, beware lest it degenerate into any kind of jealousy; for it often happens, that as the worm is bred in the apple which is most delicate and ripe, so jealousy grows in that love of married people which is the most ardent and violent, which, nevertheless, it spoils and corrupts, breeding by insensible degrees, strifes, dissensions, and divorces. But jealousy never comes where the friendship on both sides is grounded on solid virtue; and therefore, where it enters, it is an infallible mark that the love is in some degree sensual and gross, and has fallen upon a subject where it has met with but an imperfect and inconstant virtue, liable to distrust. It is then a foolish ostentation of friendship, to try to exalt it by jealousy; for jealousy is indeed a sign of the greatness and grossness of the friendship, but never of its goodness, purity, and perfection; since the perfection of friendship presupposes an assurance of the virtue of those whom we love, and jealousy presupposes a doubt of it.

If you desire, O husbands, that your wives should be faithful to you, let them learn the lesson from your

[3] 1 Peter iii. 7.

example. "With what face," says St. Gregory Nazianzen, "can you exact modesty of your wives when you yourselves live immodestly? How can you require of them that which you give them not? Would you have them chaste, behave yourselves chastely towards them. And, as St. Paul says, *Let every man know how to possess his vessel in sanctification.* But if, on the contrary, you yourselves teach them not to be virtuous, it is no wonder that you are disgraced by their fall. But you, O wives, whose honour is inseparably joined with purity and modesty, be zealous to preserve this your glory, and suffer no kind of loose behaviour to tarnish the whiteness of your reputation." Fear all kind of assaults, be they ever so small; never suffer any flattery to come near you; whoever offers to praise your beauty or your grace ought to be suspected; for he who praises the ware which he cannot buy, is strongly tempted to steal it; but if to your praise he adds the dispraise of your husband, he offers you a great insult; for it is evident that he not only has a mind to ruin you, but accounts you already half ruined, since the bargain is half made with the second merchant, when one is dissatisfied with the first.

Ladies formerly, as well as now, were accustomed to wear a number of pearls in their ears; Pliny says, for the pleasure of the jingling which they make in touching one another; but I, who know that Isaac, the great friend of God, sent ear-rings as the first earnest of his love to the chaste Rebecca, believe that this symbolical ornament signifies that the first part which a husband should take possession of in his wife, and which his wife should faithfully keep for him, is her ears; to the end that no other language or sound should enter there, but the sweet and pleasant music of chaste and pure words, which are the oriental pearls of the gospel: for we must always remember that souls are poisoned by the ear, as the body is by the mouth.

Love and fidelity joined together, beget always familiarity and confidence: and therefore the saints have used many reciprocal caresses in their marriage, caresses truly amorous yet pure, tender yet sincere. Thus, Isaac and Rebecca, the most chaste married couple of ancient times, were seen through a window caressing one another,[4] in such a manner that though there was no immodesty, Abimelech was convinced that they could be no other than man and wife. The great St. Louis, equally rigorous to his own flesh, and tender in the love of his wife, was almost blamed for the abundance of such caresses; though indeed he rather deserved praise for being able to bring his martial and courageous spirit to stoop to these little offices, requisite to the conservation of conjugal love; for although these little demonstrations of pure and frank affection do not bind hearts, yet they bring them near to one another, and serve for an agreeable zest to mutual intercourse.

St. Monica, being with child of the great St. Augustine, dedicated him by frequent oblations to the Christian religion and to the service and glory of God, as he himself witnesses, saying, *that he had already tasted the salt of God in his mother's womb.* This is a great lesson for Christian women, to offer up to his Divine Majesty their offspring even before they come into the world; for God, who accepts the offerings of an humble and willing heart, at that time commonly seconds the affections of mothers; witness Samuel, St. Thomas Aquinas, St. Andrew of Fiesola, and divers others. The mother of St. Bernard, a mother worthy of such a son, as soon as her children were born, used to take them in her arms, and offer them up to Jesus Christ; and from thenceforth loved them with respect, as consecrated things intrusted to her by God; which succeeded so happily that in the end the whole seven became very holy. But when children are come into the world, and begin to have the use of reason, both their fathers and mothers ought to take great pains to imprint the fear of God on their hearts. The good queen Blanche performed this office fervently towards the king St. Louis, her son; for she often said to him, I had much rather, my dear child, see you die before my eyes, than see you commit a single mortal sin;—which remained so deeply engraved

[4] Gen. xxvi. 8.

in his soul, that as he himself related, not one day of his life passed in which he did not remember it, and take all possible care to observe this divine teaching. Families and generations in our language are called *houses*, and even the Hebrews called the generation of children the building up of a *house*, for it is in this sense it is said that God *made houses*[5] for the midwives of Egypt. Now, this is to show that to raise a house or family does not consist in storing up a quantity of worldly goods, but in rearing up children in the fear of God, and in virtue, in which no pains or labour ought to be spared, for children are the crown of their parents. Thus St. Monica, with so much fervour and constancy, fought against the evil inclinations of her son, St. Augustine, that having followed him by sea and land, she made him more happily the child of her tears by the conversion of his soul, than he had been of her blood by the generation of his body.

St. Paul leaves to wives the care of the household as their portion; for which reason, many think with truth, that their devotion is more profitable to the family than that of the husband, who, not residing so ordinarily among the domestics, cannot of consequence so easily frame them to virtue. On this consideration Solomon, in his Proverbs,[6] makes the happiness of the whole household to depend on the care and industry of the virtuous woman whom he describes.

It is said in Genesis,[7] that Isaac, seeing his wife Rebecca barren, prayed to the Lord for her, or, according to the Hebrew, prayed to the Lord over against her, because one prayed on the one side of the oratory, and the other on the other; so the prayer of the husband made in this manner was heard. Such union as this of the husband and wife in holy devotion, is the greatest and most fruitful of all; and to this they ought mutually to encourage and to draw each other. There are fruits, such as the quince, which because of the harshness of their juice, are not agreeable except when preserved; there are others which, because of their tenderness cannot be long kept,

[5] Ex. i. 21.

[6] Chap. xxxi.

[7] Chap. xxv. 21.

unless they are preserved in like manner, such as cherries and apricots. So wives ought to wish their husbands to be preserved with the sugar of devotion; for a man without devotion is a kind of animal, severe, harsh, and rough; and husbands ought to wish that their wives should be devout; because without devotion a woman is very frail, and subject to fall from, or to fade in, virtue. St. Paul says, *that the unbelieving husband is sanctified by the believing wife, and the unbelieving wife by the believing husband;* because in this strict alliance of marriage, the one may easily draw the other to virtue; but what a blessing is it, when the man and the wife, being both believers, sanctify each other in the true fear of God.

As to the rest: the mutual forbearance with one another should be so great, that they should never be both angry with each other at the same time so that there should never be dissension or dispute between them. Bees cannot stay in a place where there are echoes or reboundings of voices; nor can the Holy Ghost remain in a house where there are clamour, strife, contradictions and altercations. St. Gregory Nazianzen witnesses that in his time married people made a feast on the anniversary day of their wedding. For my part, I should approve of the introduction of this custom, provided it were not attended with worldly and sensual recreations; but that the husband and wife should confess and communicate on that day, and recommend to God with a more than ordinary fervour the happy progress of their marriage; renewing their good resolutions to sanctify it more and more by mutual love and fidelity, and taking new breath, as it were, in our Lord, for the better supporting the duties of their vocation.

Chapter XXXIX

Counsels for Widows

SAINT PAUL instructs all prelates in the person of Timothy, saying: *Honour widows which are widows indeed.*[1] Now to be a widow indeed, these things are necessary.

1. That the widow be not only a widow in body but in heart also; that is, that she be resolved with an inviolable resolution to remain in the state of a chaste widowhood; for those who are only widows till an opportunity presents itself of being married again, are only widows as to the body, but are already remarried as far as the desire of the heart is concerned. But if she that is a widow indeed, in order to confirm herself in the state of widowhood, will consecrate herself to God by a vow, she will add a great ornament to her widowhood, and give a great security to her resolution, for then she will not suffer so much as the least thought of marriage to occupy her heart for a single moment; so that this sacred vow will serve as a strong barrier between her soul and all projects contrary to her resolution. St. Augustine strongly recommends this vow to the Christian widow; and the ancient and learned Origen goes much farther, for he exhorts married women to vow and dedicate themselves to a chaste widowhood, in case their husbands die before them; to the end that, amidst the pleasures of marriage, they may also, by means of this anticipated promise, enjoy the merit of a chaste widowhood. A vow makes the good works done in pursuance of it more acceptable to God, strengthens our resolution to do them, and gives to God not only the good works which are, as it were, the fruits of our good will, but dedicates to Him the will itself, which is, as it were, the tree of all our actions. By simple chastity we lend our body to God, re-

[1] 1 Tim. v. 3.

taining, notwithstanding, the liberty to indulge in sensual pleasures at some future time; but by a vow of chastity we make an absolute and irrevocable gift of our body to God, without reserving to ourselves any power of recalling it, and thus happily render ourselves bond-slaves to Him, whose bondage is better than all royalty. Now I highly approve the counsel of these two great persons, but I should wish that those souls which are so happy as to desire to follow it, should do it prudently, holily, and gravely, having first well examined their resolutions, invoked the light of heaven, and taken the counsel of some wise and devout director; by this means all will be done with more fruit.

2. Moreover, this renunciation of second marriage must be done with the simple intent of turning all the affections of the soul, whole and undivided, towards God, and joining the whole heart with that of His divine Majesty; for if the desire to leave her children rich, or any other worldly motive, keep the widow in her state of widowhood, she may perhaps have praise for it, but certainly not before God; for in the eyes of God nothing can truly merit praise but what is done for His sake.

3. Moreover, the widow that would be a widow indeed, must voluntarily separate and restrain herself from worldly satisfactions. *For she that liveth in pleasures is dead while she liveth.*[2] To desire to be a widow, and to be nevertheless pleased with being courted, flattered, and caressed; to be fond of balls, dancing, and feasting; to indulge in perfumes, dress, and affectation; is to be a widow who liveth as to the body, but is dead as to the soul. What does it signify, I pray you, whether the sign of the inn of Adonis, or profane love, be composed of white feathers, in the fashion of a plume, or of crape spread like a net around the face? Yes, it is often an artifice of vanity to make the weeds set off the whiteness of the skin; for the widow having experience of the fashions by which women can please men best, casts the more dangerous baits before their minds. The widow, then, who lives in these fond delights, is dead while she liveth, and is, pro-

[2] 1 Tim. v. 6.

perly speaking, a mere image of widowhood.

The time of pruning is come, the voice of the turtle is heard in our land, says the Canticle.[3] The pruning of worldly superfluities is necessary to all who desire to live devoutly, but it is especially necessary for the true widow, who like a chaste turtle comes fresh from weeping, bewailing, and lamenting the loss of her husband. When Naomi returned from Moab to Bethlehem, the women of the town who had known her when she was first married, said one to another, *Is this Naomi? But she said unto them, Call me not Naomi*, for Naomi signifies gracious and beautiful, *but call me Mara*, bitter, *for the Lord hath dealt very bitterly with me;*[4] this she said on account of having lost her husband. Even so the devout widow never desires to be esteemed either beautiful or gracious, contenting herself with being such as God wishes her to be, that is to say, humble and lowly in her own eyes.

Lamps that are fed with aromatic oil give out a sweeter smell when their flame is put out; so widows whose love has been pure in their marriage, send forth a sweeter perfume of virtue and chastity, when their light, namely, their husband, is extinguished by death. To love her husband as long as he lives, is an ordinary thing among women; but to love him so well as that after his death she will hear of no other, is a degree of love which belongs only to those who are widows indeed. To hope in God, whilst her husband serves for a support, is a thing not so rare; but to hope in God, when she is destitute of this support, is worthy of great praise. Wherefore it is easier to know in widowhood the perfection of the virtues which a woman had in the time of her marriage.

The widow who has children, standing in need of her prudence and care, and principally in what relates to their souls and their establishment in life, neither can nor ought by any means to abandon them; for the apostle Paul says clearly, that they are obliged to take care of their children, that they may give them that which they

[3] ii. 12. In the Authorized Version, "the time of the singing of birds is come."
[4] Ruth i. 20

received from their parents.[5] And besides, *if any provide not for his own, and specially for those of his own house, he is worse than an iufidel.*[6] But if her children be in such a state as to stand in no need of her guidance, then should the widow gather together all her affections and thoughts, to apply them more purely to her own advancement in the love of God.

I counsel the true widow, unless some absolute necessity oblige her in conscience to engage in external troubles, such as lawsuits, to avoid them altogether, and to follow that method in managing her affairs which is the most peaceable and quiet, although it may not seem the most advantageous. For the advantages to be reaped from worldly troubles must be very great, to bear any comparison with the happiness of a holy tranquillity. To say nothing of the fact that disputes and lawsuits distract the heart, and often open a gate to the enemies of chastity; while to please those whose favour they stand in need of, they are put upon such behaviour as is neither suitable to devotion, nor pleasing to God.

Let prayer be the widow's continual exercise; for seeing she ought now to have no other love but for God, she ought scarce to have words for any other but for God. For as the iron which, by the presence of the diamond, is hindered from following the attraction of the loadstone, springs towards it as soon as the diamond is removed: so the heart of the widow, which could not well give itself up so entirely to God, nor follow the attraction of His divine love, during the life of her husband, ought immediately after his death to run ardently after the sweet odour of the heavenly perfumes: *Because of the savour of Thy good ointments, Thy name is as ointment poured forth, therefore do the virgins love thee,*[7] as if she said, in imitation of the heavenly Spouse: O Lord, now that I am all my own, receive me that I may be all Thine: *draw me, we will run after Thee.*[8]

The virtues proper for the exercise of a holy widow, are perfect modesty, the renunciation of honours, ranks, assemblies, titles, and all such vanities; serving the

[5] 1 Tim. v. 2. [6] 1 Tim. v. 8.

[7] Cant. i. 3. [8] Cant. i. 4.

poor and the sick; comforting the afflicted; instructing girls in a devout life; and making herself a perfect pattern of all virtues to young women. Necessity and plainness should be the two ornaments of her dress; humility and charity the ornaments of her actions; courtesy and mildness the ornaments of her tongue; modesty and purity the ornaments of her eyes; and Jesus Christ crucified the only love of her heart. In fine, the true widow is in the church a little March violet, who sends forth an incomparable sweetness by the odour of her devotion, and keeps herself almost always concealed under the broad leaves of her lowliness, while her dark colour testifies her mortification. She grows in cool and uncultivated places, not willing to be importuned with the conversation of worldly people, the better to preserve the freshness of her heart against all the heats which the desire of riches, of honours, or even of love might bring upon her. *She is happier* (says the holy apostle), *if she so abide.*

I have many other things to say upon this subject; but I shall have said all when I have said let the widow who is tender of the honour of her condition, read attentively the excellent epistles which the great St. Jerome has written to Furia, to Salvia, and to all those other ladies who were so happy as to be the spiritual daughters of so great a father; for nothing can be added to that which he says to them, except this admonition only—that the true widow ought never to blame nor censure those who pass to a second, or even to a third or fourth marriage; for in some cases God so disposes of them for His greater glory; and that she must always have before her eyes this doctrine of the ancients, that neither widowhood nor virginity have any place or rank in heaven but that which is assigned them for their humility.

[9] 1 Cor. vii. 40.

Chapter XL

A Word to Virgins

O VIRGINS, I have only three words to say to you, for the rest you will find elsewhere. If you contemplate a temporal marriage, be careful to keep your first love for your first husband. In my opinion, it is a great deception to present, instead of an entire and sincere heart, a heart worn, spoiled, and tired out in love. But if your good fortune call you to pure and virginal spiritual espousals, and you desire to preserve your virginity for ever, O then keep your love with all possible diligence for that divine Spouse, who, being purity itself, loves nothing so much as purity; and to whom are due the first fruits of all things, but principally the first fruits of our love. St. Jerome's epistles will furnish you with all counsels necessary for you; and seeing your condition obliges you to obedience, choose a guide, under whose direction you may more holily dedicate your heart and body to His divine Majesty.

PART THE FOURTH

CONTAINING NECESSARY COUNSELS AGAINST THE MORE ORDINARY TEMPTATIONS

Chapter I

That we must not concern ourselves about what the World will say

AS soon as worldly people perceive that you desire to lead a devout life, they will discharge at you a thousand arrows of mockery and detraction. The more malicious will attribute your change to hypocrisy, bigotry, and artifice. They will say that the world has frowned upon you, and that it is because it has rejected you that you have recourse to God. Your friends will hasten to make a thousand remonstrances which they imagine to be very prudent and kind. They will say, you will fall into some melancholy humour; you will lose your credit in the world; you will make yourself insupportable; you will grow old before your time; your domestic affairs will suffer; you must live in the world as the world does; you may very well be saved without so many mysteries; and a thousand like impertinences.

Dear Philothea, all this is but foolish and wretched babbling? These people have no real care either for your health or for your affairs. *If ye were of the world*, says our Saviour,[1] *the world would love its own: but because ye are not of the*

[1] John xv. 19.

world therefore the world hateth you. We have seen gentlemen and ladies pass the whole night, nay many nights together, at chess or cards, and can there be any state of mind more painful, more melancholy and more gloomy than theirs? and yet the world does not say a word, and their friends never trouble themselves about that; but if we spend an hour in meditation, or rise in the morning a little earlier than ordinary to prepare for communion, every one runs to fetch the doctor to cure us of hypochondria and low spirits. They will pass a month of nights in dancing and no one will complain, but after going to the midnight service on Christmas Eve, every one coughs and complains the next morning. Who does not see that the world is an unjust judge, gracious and favourable to its own children, but harsh and severe towards the children of God?

We can never stand well with the world without losing our souls with it. We can never satisfy it, it is too capricious. *John came neither eating nor drinking*, says our Saviour,[2] *and ye say he hath a devil: the Son of Man is come eating, and ye say, Behold a gluttonous man, and a wine-bibber.* It is the truth, Philothea; if we relax and indulge in mirth, or play, or dancing with the world, the world will be scandalized at us; and if we do not, it will accuse us of hypocrisy and sourness. If we dress well, the world will attribute it to some bad motive; if we neglect our dress, it will impute it to meanness. Our mirth will be termed dissoluteness; and our mortification sullenness; and as it thus looks upon us with an evil eye, we never can please it. It aggravates our imperfections into sins, and our venial sins into mortal, and our sins of frailty into sins of malice. Whereas *Charity*, says St. Paul, *is kind*, the world is malicious; whereas *charity thinketh no evil*, the world, on the contrary, always thinks evil, and when it cannot condemn our actions, it will accuse our intentions. Whether the sheep have horns or not, whether they are white or black, the wolf will not fail to devour them if he can.

Do what we may, the world will still wage war

[2] St. Luke vii. 33.

against us. If we are long at confession, it will wonder how we can have so much to say: if we stay but a short time, it will say we have not confessed all. It will spy out all our motions, and for one little word of anger, it will protest that our temper is insupportable; the care of our affairs will appear covetousness, and our meekness folly. But as for the children of the world, their anger is called generosity; their avarice good husbandry; their familiarities honourable intercourse;—the spiders always spoil the work of the bees.

Let us disregard this blind world, Philothea; let it cry as long as it pleases, like an owl, to disturb the birds of the day. Let us be steadfast in our designs, and constant in our resolutions. Our perseverance will prove whether we have, in good earnest, sacrificed ourselves to God, and dedicated ourselves to a devout life. Comets and planets appear almost equally luminous; but comets are only fiery exhalations which soon pass away, while planets remain in perpetual brightness. So hypocrisy and true virtue are much alike in appearance, but it is easy to distinguish one from the other, because hypocrisy cannot last long, but is quickly dissipated like smoke, while true virtue is always firm and constant.

It contributes much to the security of devotion at the beginning, to suffer reproaches and calumny on its account; we thereby avoid the danger of pride and vanity, which sometimes destroy the fruits of devotion, as the midwives of Egypt, by the order of the infernal Pharaoh, killed the male children of the Israelites on the very day of their birth. We are crucified to the world, and the world ought to be crucified to us; it looks upon us as fools, let us look upon it as mad.

CHAPTER II

That we must be of Good Courage

LIGHT, though beautiful and pleasant to our eyes, nevertheless dazzles them after we have been long in the dark. Before we become familiar with the inhabitants of any country, be they ever so courteous and gracious, we find ourselves somewhat strange amongst them. It may probably happen, Philothea, that this change of life may cause you some feelings of repugnance; that this wide and general farewell which you have taken of the follies and vanities of the world, may make some impressions of sadness and discouragement on your mind. If this should be the case, have a little patience, I pray, for it will come to nothing. It is nothing but a little strangeness, occasioned by novelty; when it is passed away you will experience ten thousand consolations.

It may perhaps be painful to you a first to relinquish that praise which fools and flatterers gave to your vanities ; but would you for the sake of it forfeit that eternal glory with which God will assuredly recompense you? The vain amusements and pastimes in which you have hitherto employed your time, will again present themselves to allure your heart, and cause it to return to them ; but will you renounce eternal happiness for such deceitful follies? Believe me, if you persevere, you will soon receive consolations so delicious and agreeable as shall oblige you to confess that the world had nothing but gall in comparison of this honey, and that one day of devotion is better than a thousand years of worldly life.

But you perceive that the mountain of Christian perfection is exceedingly high : Ah! say you, how can I ever reach its summit? Courage, Philothea. When the young bees begin to assume their form we call them *nymphs :* as yet they are unable to fly to the flowers, or the mountains, or the neighbouring hills, to gather honey; but, little by little, feeding on the honey which the old ones have prepared, their wings appear, and they acquire strength enough to fly and seek their food all over the country. It is true we are as yet but *nymphs*, or little *bees*, in devotion, and cannot yet rise to the height of our design, which is no less than to reach the top of Christian perfection; but if we begin to take shape, through our desires and resolutions, our wings will soon begin to grow, and we shall one day become spiritual bees, and be able to fly; in the meantime let us feed upon the honey of the many good instructions which devout persons of old times have left us, and pray to God to give us wings like a dove, that we may not only be enabled to fly during the time of this present life, but also may rest in the eternity of the life to come.

CHAPTER III

Of the Nature of Temptations, and of the difference there is between being Tempted and yielding to it

IMAGINE to yourself, Philothea, a young princess greatly beloved by her spouse, to whom some libertine sends a base confidant with infamous proposals: *First*, this confidant states to the princess his master's proposals; *secondly*, the princess is pleased or displeased with the proposals; *thirdly*, either she consents or she refuses. In the same manner Satan, the world, and the flesh, seeing a soul espoused to the Son of God, send her temptations and suggestions, by which, 1, sin is proposed to her; 2, she is either pleased or displeased with the suggestion; 3, she either consents or refuses. These are, in brief, the three steps of descent into sin, temptation, delectation, and consent. And though these three acts are not so plainly seen in all kinds of sins, yet are they clearly to be recognised in all the greater sins.

Though a temptation, to any sin whatsoever, should last during life, it would never render us displeasing to the divine Majesty, provided we took no pleasure in it, and did not yield our consent to it. The reason is, because in temptation we do not act, but endure, and as in this we take no pleasure, so we cannot incur any guilt. St. Paul suffered a long time the temptations of the flesh, and yet so far was he from being displeasing to God on that account, that God, on the contrary, was glorified thereby. The blessed Angela de Foligno felt such cruel temptations of the flesh, that she moves us to pity by her account of them. Great also were the temptations endured by St. Francis and St. Benedict, causing one to cast himself upon thorns, and the other into snow, to mitigate them; and yet they lost nothing of God's favour, but increased therein.

You must then be courageous, Philothea, amidst temptations, and never suppose yourself overcome so long as they displease you; observing well the difference between being tempted and consenting to temptation. We may feel temptations, though they displease us, but we can never consent to them unless they please us, since the being pleased with them is ordinarily the step by which we arrive at consent. Let then the enemies of our salvation lay as many baits and allurements in our way as they please; let them stay always at the door of our heart, in order to get admittance; let them make us as many proposals as they will; still, so long as we continue steadfast in taking no pleasure in the temptation, it is utterly impossible that we should offend God; any more than the husband of the princess of whom I spoke could be displeased with her, for the infamous message sent to her, if she took no pleasure whatever in it. Yet, in this case, there is this difference between the princess and the soul, that the princess having heard the wicked proposition, may, if she please, drive away the messenger, and never suffer him to appear in her presence any more; but it is not always in the power of the soul not to feel the temptation, though it is always in her power not to consent to it; for which reason, although the temptation should last ever so long a time, yet it cannot hurt us as long as it is disagreeable to us.

But, with respect to the delectation which may follow temptation, it is to be observed that, as there are two parts in the soul, the inferior and the superior, and that the inferior does not always follow the superior, but acts independently of it, it frequently happens that the inferior part takes delight in the temptation without the consent, nay, against the will of the superior. This is that strife and warfare which the Apostle St. Paul describes, when he says, that *the flesh lusteth against the spirit*, and that there is *a law in the members warring against the the law of the mind.*[1]

Have you never seen, Philothea, a great wood fire covered with ashes? Should one come ten or twelve hours after in search of fire there, there is but a spark in the midst of the hearth, and that scarcely to be found; yet there it is, since there it is found, and with it one may kindle again all the other coals which lay extinguished round it. It is just so with charity, which is our spiritual life, in the midst of great and violent temptations; for the temptation, causing delectation in the inferior part, covers the whole soul as it were with ashes, and reduces the love of God to a spark; for it appears no more, except in the midst of the heart, at the very bottom of the spirit; and even there it scarcely seems perceptible, and one has difficulty in finding it; yet there it is in reality, since, notwithstanding all the trouble and disorder we feel in our soul and our body, we still retain a resolution never to consent to the sin nor to the temptation; and the delectation, which pleases the outward man displeases the inward, so that although it surrounds the will, yet it is not within it; by which we see that such delectation is contrary to the will, and being so it cannot be sin.

[1] Gal. v. 17 and Rom. vii. 23.

CHAPTER IV

An Example on this Subject

IT is so important that you should understand this matter perfectly, that I shall not hesitate to explain it more at large.

The history of the conflict of St. Catherine of Sienna with temptation will illustrate the subject; it is as follows: The wicked spirit had permission from God to assault the purity of this holy virgin with all his power, provided always that he did not touch her. He presented, then, all kinds of impure suggestions to her heart; and assuming, with his companions, human forms, he represented scenes of impurity before her eyes, accompanying them with impure words and solicitations. And although all these things were exterior, nevertheless, by means of the senses, they penetrated deep into the heart of the virgin, which as she herself confessed, was even brimful of them; so that nothing remained in her, except the pure superior will, which was not shaken by this storm of wickedness and carnal delectation. This temptation continued for a long time, till one day our Saviour appearing to her, she said to Him: Where wert Thou, my sweet Saviour, when my heart was full of so great darkness and uncleanness? To which He answered: I was in your heart, my daughter. But how, replied she, couldest Thou dwell in my heart, where there was so much impurity? Dost Thou dwell in such unclean places? To which our Lord replied: Tell me, did these foul thoughts of your heart give you pleasure or sadness, bitterness or delight? The most extreme bitterness and sadness, said she. Who was it then, replied our Saviour, that put this great bitterness and sadness into your heart, but I, who remained concealed within the midst of your soul? Believe me, daughter, had not I been present, these thoughts which surrounded your will, but could not conquer it, would doubtless have entered in, would have been received with pleasure by your will, and would have brought death to your soul; but I, being in your heart, infused that displeasure and resistance into it which enabled it to reject the temptation as much as it could: but not being able to do it as much as it would, it conceived the greater displeasure and hatred both against the temptation and against itself; and thus, these troubles have proved occasions of great merit and great gain to you, and a great increase of your strength and virtue.

See, Philothea, how this fire was covered with ashes, and how the temptation and delectation had even entered the heart, and surrounded the will, which alone, assisted by our Saviour, made resistance by its aversion, displeasure, and detestation of the evil suggested to it, constantly refusing her consent to the sin which besieged her on every side. Ah! what distress for a soul that loves God, not so much as to know whether He is within her or not, and whether the divine love, for which she fights, is altogether extinguished in her or not? But it is the very flower of perfection of heavenly love for the lover to suffer and fight for love, not knowing whether he possesses that love for which and by which he fights.

Chapter V

Encouragement to a Soul which is under Temptation

THESE violent assaults and extraordinary temptations, Philothea, are never permitted by God, but against those souls whom He desires to elevate to the highest degree of divine love; yet it does not follow that after such trials they will be certain to attain it; for it has often happened that those who have been constant under such violent assaults have, for want of faithfully corresponding to the divine favour, been afterwards overcome by very small temptations. This I tell you, that if it should ever happen to you to be assaulted by great temptations, you may know that God confers an extraordinary favour on you, and thereby declares His will to make you great in His sight and that nevertheless you may be always humble and fearful, not assuring yourself that you will be able to conquer small temptations, after you have prevailed against great ones, by any other means than a constant fidelity towards his Divine Majesty.

Whatever temptations then may hereafter befall you, or with whatever delectations they may be accompanied, so long as your will refuses her consent, not only to the temptation, but also to the delectation, do not give yourself the least trouble, for God is not offended. As when a man has fainted and shows no sign of life, we lay our hand on his heart, and if we feel any motion, however slight, we judge him to be alive, and that by the application of some restorative he may be made to recover his strength and senses; so it sometimes happens that through the violence of a temptation, our soul seems to have fallen into a total exhaustion of its powers, so that it has no longer any spiritual life or motion, as if it were in a swoon; but if we desire to know how it is with her, let us lay our hand upon our heart and ascertain whether the heart, that is the will, still retains its spiritual motion, that is to say, whether it has done its duty in refusing to consent and to yield to the temptation and delectation; for so long as this motion of refusal remains in our heart, we may rest assured that charity, the life of our soul, remains in us, and that Jesus Christ our Saviour is there present, although concealed; so that by means of the continual exercise of prayer, the sacraments, and confidence in God, our strength will come again to us, and we shall live a vigorous and happy life.

Chapter VI

How Temptation and Delectation may become Sinful

THE princess of whom we have before spoken, could not help the dishonourable suit which was made to her, because, as we have supposed, it was made against her will; but had she, on the contrary, given occasion to the suit by any lightness of manner, or any desire to excite love in him who sought her, then, beyond doubt, she would not be free from the blame of this dishonourable suit, and however she might play the prude, she would certainly deserve both blame and punishment. Thus, it sometimes happens that temptation alone involves us in sin, because we ourselves are the cause of it. For example, if I know that when I play I fall easily into violent passion, and that the passion leads me into blasphemy; and that, therefore, gaming is a temptation to me to commit those sins; in that case, I sin every time I play, and I am accountable for all the temptations which befall me in gaming. In like manner, if I know that certain conversations will expose me to the danger of falling into sin, and yet willingly expose myself to them, I am undoubtedly guilty of all the temptations I meet with on such occasions.

When the delectation which proceeds from the temptation can be avoided, it is always a sin to admit it, a greater or less sin, in proportion as the pleasure we take, or the consent we give to it, is of longer or shorter duration. If the young princess, of whom we have spoken, had not only heard the dishonourable proposals addressed to her, but also had taken pleasure in them, and suffered her mind to dwell with satisfaction on the subject, she would have been very much in fault; for then though she does not consent to the actual sin proposed, yet she spiritually consents to the sin by the satisfaction she takes in it. It is always a sin to yield the heart as well as the body, to a sin, nay, this sin depends so much on the consent of the heart, that without it the consent of the body would not be a sin.

Therefore, when you are tempted to any sin, consider whether you have not willingly given occasion to your being tempted, for then the temptation itself puts you in a state of sin, because you have flung yourself into the danger. This is to be understood when you could without any great difficulty have avoided the occasion, and foresaw, or ought to have foreseen, that temptation would occur; but if you have not given any occasion to the temptation, it cannot in any way be imputed to you as a sin.

When the delectation which follows temptation might have been avoided, and yet has not been avoided, there is always some kind of sin, more or less, according to the time one has dwelt upon it, or according to the pleasure one has taken in it. A woman who has given no occasion to her being courted, but yet takes pleasure therein, is to be blamed, if the pleasure she takes arises from the courtship. But if, for example, the gallant who addresses her play excellently well upon the lute, and she takes pleasure, not in his courtship, but in the harmony and sweetness of his lute, this would be no sin, though she ought not to continue to indulge in this pleasure, for fear it should lead to her taking pleasure in his courtship. In like manner, if any one should propose to me some ingenious stratagem to take revenge of my enemy, and I neither delight in, nor give any consent to the proposed revenge, but only am pleased with the subtilty of the artful stratagem, I certainly do not sin therein, still I ought not to continue long amusing myself with this pleasure, for fear lest by degrees it should lead me to take some delight in the revenge itself.

One is sometimes surprised by some feeling of delectation, which immediately follows the temptation, before we are well aware of it. This, at most, can only be a light venial sin; but it becomes greater if, after we have perceived the evil which has befallen us, we negligently continue for some time, dallying with the delectation, hesitating whether we should admit or reject it; and the sin still becomes greater if, after being sensible of the delectation, we dwell upon it through downright negligence, without being determined to reject it; but when we voluntarily, and with full deliberation, resolve to please ourselves in such delectations, this deliberate purpose is of itself a great sin, provided the object in which we take delight be also a great sin. It is a great crime in a woman to be willing to entertain improper affections, although she never designs to yield herself up really to her lovers.

Chapter VII

Remedies against Great Temptations

As soon as you perceive yourself tempted, do as the children do in the country, when they see a wolf or a bear; for they run at once into the arms of their father or mother, or at least they call out to them for help and protection. Do you run in the same way to God, and cry to Him for pity and help. It is the remedy which our Lord points out to us. *Pray that ye enter not into temptation.*[1] If you find that the temptation nevertheless still continues, or even increases, hasten in spirit and embrace the holy cross, as if you saw our Saviour Jesus Christ crucified before you; protest that you will never consent to the temptation; entreat His help against it and continue still refusing your consent, as long as the temptation shall continue.

But in making these protestations and refusals of consent, do not look the temptation in the face, but look only on our Lord; for if you look at the temptation, especially whilst it is strong, it may shake your courage. Divert your thoughts to some good and laudable occupations, for such occupations entering into your mind and engaging your attention, will drive away the evil temptations and suggestions.

But the great remedy against all temptation, whether great or small, is to lay open one's heart, and communicate its suggestions, feelings and affections to one's director; for you must observe, that the first condition the wicked one makes with a soul which he desires to seduce, is to keep silence; as those who aim at seducing wives or maidens, forbid them above all things to communicate their proposals to their parents or husbands.

But if, after all this, the temptation should still obstinately continue to harass and persecute us, we have nothing to do on our part but to con-

[1] Matt. xxvi. 41.

tinue as obstinately to protest that we will not consent; for as maidens can never be married, so long as they answer "No," so the soul, although she may be ever so long tempted, can never be overcome so long as she says "No."

Never dispute with your enemy, nor answer him a single word, except that wherewith our Saviour confounded him, *Get thee behind Me, Satan, thou shalt worship the Lord thy God, and Him only shalt thou serve.* And as a chaste wife should never answer the wicked wretch who makes her a dishonourable proposal, nor look him in the face, but quit him abruptly, and at the same instant turn her heart towards her husband, and renew the vow of fidelity which she has made to him; so the devout soul who sees herself assaulted by temptation, ought to lose no time in disputation, but simply turn herself towards Jesus Christ her Spouse, and renew her vow of fidelity to Him, and her desire to remain solely and entirely His for ever.

Chapter VIII

That we must resist Small Temptations

ALTHOUGH we must fight against great temptations with an invincible courage, and the victory we gain over them is extremely advantageous, it may happen, nevertheless, that we may profit more in fighting manfully against small ones; for as great temptations are great in quality, so the lesser are great in quantity, for which reason the victory over the lesser may be equal to that over the greater. Wolves and bears are without doubt more dangerous than flies, yet they do not attack us so often, nor give us so much trouble, nor exercise our patience so much. It is an easy thing to abstain from murder, but it is a very difficult thing to restrain all the little sallies of anger, for which occasions are continually occurring. It is very easy for a man or a woman to refrain from adultery, but not so easy to refrain from glances of the eyes, from giving or taking favours, or from speaking or hearkening to flattering words. It is easy not to admit a rival to one's husband or wife, as to the body, but not as to the heart; easy to refrain from defiling the marriage-bed, but difficult to abstain from everything which is prejudicial to conjugal affection; easy not to steal another man's goods, but difficult not to covet them; easy not to bear false witness in a court of justice, but not easy never to tell a lie; easy not to get drunk, but not easy to be perfectly temperate; easy not to wish another man's death, but difficult not to desire what would be inconvenient to him; easy not to slander him, but difficult to abstain from despising him. In a word, these lesser temptations of anger, suspicion, jealousy, envy, flirtation, levity, vanity, insincerity, affectation, craftiness, and impure thoughts, are continually trying even those who are the most devout and resolute. We must therefore, my dear Philothea, prepare ourselves for this warfare with great care and diligence, and rest assured that as many victories as we gain over these lesser enemies, so many precious stones will be put into the crown of glory which God is preparing for us in heaven. Wherefore, I say, that while we are ever ready to fight courageously against great temptations when they come, we must in the meantime diligently defend ourselves against those which seem feeble and trivial.

Chapter IX

How to resist Small Temptations

NOW as to those lesser temptations of vanity, suspicion, impatience, jealousy, envy, and the like, which like flies and gnats continually dance before our eyes, and sometimes sting us upon the cheek, or the nose; as it is impossible to be altogether freed from being teased by them, the best defence we can make is not to trouble ourselves much about them; for although they may tease us, yet they can never hurt us, as long as we are firmly resolved to serve God.

Despise then these petty assaults, do not condescend even to think on what they would suggest. Let them buzz about your ears as much as they like, and dance here and there about you, and pay no more attention to them than you would to flies, and when they offer to sting you, and you see them settling upon your heart, do nothing but simply brush them away, without contending against them or disputing with them; and perform some actions of a contrary nature to the temptation, especially acts of the love of God. But if you will be led by me, you will not set your mind on opposing by the contrary virtue, the temptation which you feel for that would be to dispute with it; but after having performed an act of the contrary virtue, provided you have had leisure to observe the nature of the temptation, then simply turn your heart towards Jesus Christ crucified, and by an act of love embrace in spirit His sacred feet. This is the best means to overcome the enemy, as well in little as in great temptations; for as the love of God contains within itself the perfection of all the virtues, even more excellently than the virtues themselves, it is the most sovereign remedy against all vices; and by accustoming your mind in all temptations to have recourse to this universal refuge, you need not even examine by what kind of temptation it is troubled, but simply feeling itself troubled, it will fly to this great remedy; which, moreover, is so terrible to the evil spirit that when he perceives that his temptations incite us to such acts of divine love, he ceases to tempt us. Thus much may suffice concerning small and frequent temptations; any one who spent his time in going more into details about them, would give himself a great deal of trouble to little purpose.

Chapter X

How to fortify our Hearts against Temptations

CONSIDER from time to time what passions are most predominant in your soul, and having discovered them, adopt a manner of life the very opposite to them in thoughts, and words, and deeds. If, for example, you find yourself inclined to vanity, think often on the miseries of human life, what inquietude these vanities will raise in your conscience at the day of your death, how unworthy they are of a generous heart; that they are nothing but empty toys, fit only for the amusement of children. Speak often against vanity, and although it be against the grain do not cease to cry it down heartily, for by this means you will engage yourself even in honour, to the opposite side. And by dint of talking against a thing we bring ourselves to hate it, though at first we had an affection for it. Do works of abjection and of humility, as much as possible, though with ever so much reluctance; since by this means you so get a habit of humility, and enfeeble your vanity, that when temptation comes, you will have less inclination to favour it, and more strength to resist it.

If you are inclined to covetousness, think often of the folly of a sin which makes us slaves to that which was made to serve us; that at death we must part with all, and leave it in the hands of those who perhaps may squander it away, or to whom it may be a cause of ruin and damnation. Speak aloud against avarice, and in praise of contempt of the world. Force yourself to give frequent alms, and to let slip some occasions of gain.

Should you be inclined to give or receive flirtations, often think how very dangerous this kind of amusement is, as well to yourself as others; how unworthy a thing is it to profane by employing it in idle pastime the noblest affection of our soul, and how worthy of blame is such an extreme levity of mind. Speak often in praise of purity and simplicity of heart, and let your actions, to the utmost of your power, be conformable to your words, by avoiding levities and dalliances.

In short, in time of peace, namely, when temptations to the sin to which you are most inclined, do not molest you, make frequent acts of the contrary virtue; and if the occasions to practise it do not present themselves, endeavour to find them; for by this means you will strengthen your heart against future temptations.

CHAPTER XI

Of Inquietude

AS inquietude is not a single temptation, but a source from whence many temptations flow upon us, it is therefore necessary that I should say something concerning it. Inquietude or sadness, then, is nothing else but the grief of mind which we feel on account of some evil which affects us against our will, whether the evil be exterior, as poverty, sickness, contempt; or interior, as ignorance, dryness, repugnance, temptation. When the soul then perceives that she has some such evil, she is displeased at having it, and that is inquietude; she is anxious to be freed from it, and to have the means of getting rid of it; and so far she is right, for every one naturally desires good, and flees from what it takes to be evil. If the soul seeks the means of deliverance from her evil, for the love of God, she will seek it with patience, meekness, humility, and tranquillity, expecting her deliverance more from the goodness and providence of God than from her own industry or diligence; but if she seeks her deliverance from self-love, then she will be eager and hot in quest of the means, as if the success depended more on herself than on God. I do not say that she thinks so, but that she acts as if she thought so. And if she does not immediately find what she desires, she falls into great disquietude, and impatience which do not remove the evil, but aggravate it; and so the soul becomes oppressed with such extreme anguish and distress, with so great loss of courage and strength, as to imagine her evil beyond a remedy. Behold, then, how the sadness, which in the beginning was reasonable, begets inquietude, and inquietude produces an increase of sadness, which is extremely dangerous.

Inquietude is the greatest evil which can befall the soul, sin only excepted. For as the seditious and intestine commotions of any commonwealth lay it waste and prevent it from being able to resist a foreign invasion, so our heart, being disturbed and disquieted within, loses the strength to maintain the virtues it had acquired, and the means to resist the temptations of the enemy, who then uses his utmost efforts to fish, as they say, in troubled waters.

Inquietude proceeds from an inordinate desire to be delivered from the evil we feel, or to acquire the good we hope for; and yet there is nothing which more increases the evil, and which removes the good further off, than inquietude and eagerness. Birds remain prisoners in the nets, because when they find themselves caught, they flutter and beat about to get loose again, and by that means entangle themselves the more. Whenever, then, you are desirous to be freed from evil, or to attain some good, before all things settle your mind in repose and tranquillity, calm your judgment and will; and then gently and quietly pursue your desire, taking in regular order the means which are most suitable. When I say gently and quietly, I do not mean negligently, but without hurry, trouble, or inquietude; otherwise instead of obtaining the effect desired, you will mar all, and embarrass yourself more and more.

My soul is alway in my hand, yet do I not forget Thy law, said David.[1] Examine frequently in the day, or at

1 Ps. cxix. 109.

least in the morning and evening, whether you have your soul in your hands, or whether some passion or inquietude has not snatched it from you. Consider whether you have your heart at command, or whether it be not escaped out of your hands, to engage itself in some disorderly affection of love, hatred, envy, covetousness, fear, uneasiness or joy; and if it should be gone astray seek after it before you do anything else, and bring it quietly back to the presence of God, replacing all your affections and desires under the obedience and direction of His divine will; for as they who are afraid of losing anything which is precious, hold it fast in their hands, so, in imitation of this great King, we ought always to say, O my God, my soul is in danger, and therefore I carry it always in my hands, and in this manner I have not forgotten Thy holy law.

Do not let your desires, be they ever so trivial and unimportant, disquiet you, lest afterwards those that are greater and of more importance find your heart more disposed to trouble and disorder. When you perceive inquietude occur, recommend yourself to God, and resolve to do nothing which your desires ask until you are restored to tranquillity, unless it be something that cannot be deferred, and then restrain the flow of your desire with a gentle and steady effort, tempering and moderating it as much as possible, and do that which is to be done, not according to your desire, but your reason.

If you can discover the cause of your inquietude to your spiritual director, or at least to some faithful and devout friend, doubt not but you will find ease immediately; for the communicating of the grief of the heart has the same effect on the soul, as bleeding has on the body of a man in a fever; and this is the best of all remedies. Accordingly the holy king St. Louis gave this counsel to his son: "If thou hast any uneasiness in thy heart, tell it presently to thy spiritual guide, or to some good person, and then thou shalt be enabled to bear the evil very lightly through the comfort he will give thee."

CHAPTER XII

Of Sadness

GODLY *sorrow,* says St. Paul, *worketh repentance to salvation,*[1] *but the sorrow of the world worketh death.* Sadness then may be good or evil, according to the different effects which it produces in us. It is true it produces more evil than good effects, for it only produces two that are good, compassion and repentance; but six which are evil, namely, anxiety, sloth, indignation, jealousy, envy, and impatience, which made the wise man say, *sadness kills many, and there is no profit in it,*[2] because for two good streams which flow from the source of sadness there are six very bad ones.

The enemy makes use of sadness to tempt the good; for as he tries to make the wicked rejoice in their sins, so he strives to make the good sad in their good works; and as he can only induce people to commit evil, by making it appear agreeable, so he can only divert them from good, by making it appear disagreeable. The evil one is pleased with sadness and melancholy, because he is sad and melancholy, and will be so to all eternity; wherefore he desires that every one shall be like himself.

The sadness which is evil, troubles and disquiets the soul, causes unreasonable fears, gives a distaste to prayer, stupifies and oppresses the brain, robs the mind of counsel, resolution, judgment, and courage, and destroys her strength. In a word it is like a severe winter, which cuts off all the beauty of the country, and destroys all the living creatures; for it takes away all sweetness from the soul, and renders her disabled and powerless in all her faculties. If you should at any time be seized with this evil sadness, Philothea, apply the following remedies.

[1] 2 Cor. vii. 10.
[2] Eccles. xxx. 25.

Is any among you sad,[3] *let him pray.* Prayer is a sovereign remedy, for it lifts up the spirit to God, who is our only joy and consolation. But in praying, let your affections and words, whether interior or exterior, be such as tend to trust and love of God, such as, *O God of mercy, O all-good God, O gentle Saviour, O God of my heart, my joy, my hope, my dear Spouse, the well-beloved of my soul,* and the like.

Oppose vigorously any inclinations to sadness, and although it may seem that all you do at that time is done coldly, without relish, and languidly, nevertheless do not fail to do it; for the enemy seeks by sadness to make us weary of good works; and when he sees that we cease not to do them, and that being done in spite of opposition they are the more meritorious, he will cease to trouble us.

Sing spiritual canticles, for the work of the evil one has often been arrested by this means; witness the evil spirit wherewith Saul was afflicted, whose violence was repressed by such music. It is also desirable to employ ourselves in exterior works, and to vary them as much as possible, in order to divert the soul from the melancholy object, and to purify and warm the spirits, sadness being a passion of a cold and dry complexion.

Perform external actions of fervour, although you do them without relish; such as (in spirit) embracing Christ upon the cross, kissing His feet and His hands, lifting up your eyes and your hands to heaven, raising your voice to God in words of love and confidence, like these: *My beloved is mine, and I am his. A bundle of myrrh is my well-beloved unto me, he shall dwell between my breasts.*[4] *Mine eyes wait upon Thee, O Lord, saying, O when wilt Thou comfort me?*[5] O Jesus, be thou a Jesus to me. Live Jesus, and my soul shall live. *Who shall separate me from the love of God?*"[6] &c.

Discover all the feelings, affections, and suggestions which proceed from your sadness, humbly and faithfully, to your spiritual guide. Seek the conversation of de-

[3] St. James v. 13.

[4] Cant. ii. 16, i. 13.
[5] Ps. cxix. 82.
[6] Rom. viii. 35.

vout persons, and frequent their company during this time as much as you can. And last of all, resign yourself into the hands of God, preparing yourself to suffer this troublesome sadness with patience, as a just punishment of your vain joys, and doubt not that God, after you have been tried, will deliver you from this evil.

Chapter XIII

Of Spiritual and Sensible Consolations, and how we ought to behave in them

GOD continues the existence of this great world in a state of perpetual vicissitude, by which day is always succeeded by night, spring by summer, summer by autumn, autumn by winter, and winter again by spring. One day seldom perfectly resembles another; some are cloudy, others rainy; some dry, others windy; a variety which greatly contributes to the beauty of the universe. It is the same with man, who, according to the saying of the ancients, is an epitome of the world, for he never remains long in the same state; his life flows upon the earth like the waters, floating and undulating in a perpetual diversity of motion, which sometimes lifts him up by hope, sometimes casts him down by fear, sometimes inclines him to the right hand by consolation, sometimes to the left by affliction; and not one of his days, nor even one of his hours, is in every respect like another.

All this is a great warning to us. Amidst so great an inequality of occurrences, we should endeavour to preserve an inviolable equality of heart; and, although all things turn and change around us, we should remain constantly immovable, ever looking and aspiring and aiming towards God. Let the ship take what course it will, let it sail towards the east, west, north, or south, by whatsoever wind it may be driven, yet its compass always points towards the fair polar-star. Let everything turn upside down, not only around us, but even within us; let our soul be sad or joyful, in sweetness or bitterness, in peace or trouble, in light or darkness, in temptation or repose, in pleasure or disgust, in dryness or tenderness, let the sun scorch us or the dew refresh us. Ah! still let the needle of our heart, our spirit, our superior will, which is our compass, incessantly tend towards the love of God its Creator, its Saviour; in a word, its only and Sovereign Good. *Whether we live or die*, says the Apostle,[1] *we are the Lord's*. And, *Who shall be able to separate us from the love of God?*[2] No, nothing should ever separate us from this love; neither tribulation, nor anguish, nor death, nor life, nor present grief, nor fear of future accidents, nor the artifices of evil spirits, nor the height of consolations, nor the depth of afflictions, nor tenderness, nor dryness, ought ever to separate us from this holy charity, which is rooted in Jesus Christ.

[1] Rom. xiv. 8. [2] Rom. viii. 39.

This absolute resolution never to forsake God, nor to abandon His sweet love, serves as a counterpoise to our souls, to keep them in a holy equilibrium amidst the inequality of the vicissitudes of this life; for as bees, surprised by a gale in the fields, take up little pebbles to help them to retain their balance in the air, and not be so easily carried away by the wind; so our soul, having by a firm resolution strongly embraced the precious love of God, continues constant in the midst of the inconstancy and vicissitudes of consolations and afflictions, whether spiritual or temporal, exterior or interior.

But, besides this general instruction, some particular rules are needed on this subject.

1. I say then that devotion does not always consist in sensible sweetness, delight, consolation, or tenderness of heart, which move us to sighs and tears, and gives us a certain agreeable and savoury satisfaction in spiritual exercises. No, dear Philothea, all this is not identical with devotion; for there are many souls who experience these tendernesses and consola-

tions, and nevertheless do not cease to be very vicious, and consequently have no true love of God, much less any true devotion. Saul whilst persecuting poor David to death, who was fleeing before him in the wilderness of Engedi, entered alone into a cavern, where David and his people lay concealed; David, who on this occasion might have killed him a thousand times, spared his life, and would not so much as put him in bodily fear; but having suffered him to go out quietly, he afterwards called after him to demonstrate to him his innocency, and to convince him that he had been at his mercy. Now, upon this, what is there that Saul did not do to show that his heart was mollified towards David? He called him his son, he wept aloud, he praised him, he acknowledged his goodness, he prayed to God for him, he foretold his future greatness, and he recommended his own family to his care. What greater show could be made of sweetness and tenderness of heart? Nevertheless, his heart was not changed; since he did not cease to persecute David as cruelly as before. In like manner, there are some persons, who, on considering the goodness of God, and the passion of the Saviour, feel great emotions of heart; which cause them to pour forth ardent sighs, tears, prayers, and acts of thanksgiving, so that one would think their hearts were possessed with an extraordinary degree of devotion. But when it is put to the test, we see that as the passing showers of a hot summer, which fall in great drops on the earth, but do not sink into it, serve for nothing but to produce mushrooms; so these tears and emotions falling on a vicious heart, and not penetrating it, are altogether unprofitable; for notwithstanding all this apparent devotion, these poor souls will not part with a farthing of the ill-gotten riches they possess; nor renounce one of their perverse affections; nor suffer the least inconvenience for the service of the Saviour, over whose sufferings they have been weeping; so that the pious emotions which they had were no better than spiritual mushrooms. Such things are not only not true devotion, but very often they are great deceptions of the enemy, who by amusing souls with these false consolations makes them rest contented therewith, and prevents them from searching any further after true and solid devotion, which consists in a constant, resolute, prompt, and active will to do whatever we know will be pleasing to God.

A child will weep tenderly when he sees his mother touched with a lancet to let blood; but if his mother for whom he is weeping, should at the same time demand the apple which he has in his hand, he would not part with them. Such is for the most part the nature of our tender devotions; when contemplating the stroke of the lance which pierced the heart of Jesus Christ upon the cross, we weep bitterly. Ah! Philothea, it is very right to weep over the death and bitter passion of our blessed Redeemer; but why then do we not give him the apple which we have in our hands, which he so earnestly asks for? namely our heart, the only apple of love which our dear Saviour requires of us? Why do we not resign to Him all those little affections, delights, and complacencies, which He wants to pluck out of our hands, but cannot, because they are the sugar-plums of which we are more fond than of His heavenly grace? Ah! these are the friendships of little children, tender indeed, but weak, capricious, and without results. Devotion does not consist in these emotions and sensible affections; which sometimes proceed from a soft nature, susceptible of any impression we have a mind to give it; and sometimes come from the enemy, who stirs up our imaginations only to delude us.

2. Yet these tender and loving emotions are sometimes good and profitable, for they excite the appetite of the soul, strengthen the spirit, and add to the promptitude of devotion a holy gaiety and cheerfulness, which make our actions lovely and agreeable even externally. It is this relish for the things of God which made David cry out: *O Lord, how sweet are Thy words unto my throat! yea, sweeter than honey unto my mouth.*[3] Assuredly, the least consolation of devotion that we receive is in every respect preferable to the greatest delights of the world.

3 Ps. cxix. 103.

The milk of the heavenly Spouse is sweeter to the soul than the wine of the most delicious pleasures of earth. He who has once tasted it, esteems all other consolations no better than gall and wormwood: for as they who keep the herb *scitique* in their mouth, imbibe so excessive a sweetness from it that they neither feel hunger nor thirst; so they to whom God has given this heavenly manna of spiritual sweetness and consolation can neither desire nor relish the consolations of the world, so far at least as to take delight in them and fix their affections on them. They are little foretastes of those immortal delights which God gives to the souls that seek him; they are the sweets which he gives to his little children to allure them; they are the cordial waters wherewith he strengthens them, and they are sometimes the earnest of eternal felicities. It is said that Alexander the Great, sailing on the open ocean, discovered Arabia Felix, by perceiving the fragrant odours which the wind brought to him from thence, and thereupon encouraged both himself and his companions; so we oftentimes receive on this sea of our mortal life those sweet odours and delights which give us a foretaste of the delights of the heavenly country to which we tend and aspire.

3. But you will perhaps ask me, since there are sensible consolations which are good, and come from God, and others unprofitable, dangerous, and even pernicious, which proceed either from nature, or from the enemy; how shall I be able to distinguish the one from the other, and know those that are evil or unprofitable from those that are good? It is a general doctrine, dear Philothea, with regard to the affections and passions of our souls, that we must know them by their fruits. Our hearts are the trees; the affections and passions are the branches; and their works or actions are the fruits. The heart is good which has good affections and passions, and those affections and passions are good which produce in us good effects and holy actions. If these sweetnesses, tendernesses, and consolations, make us more humble, patient, tractable, charitable, and compassionate towards our neighbour; more fervent

in mortifying our concupiscences and evil inclinations; more constant in our religious exercises; more pliant and submissive to those whom we ought to obey; more sincere and upright in our lives, then doubtless, Philothea, they proceed from God. But if these consolations have no sweetness but for ourselves; if they make us curious, harsh, quarrelsome, impatient, obstinate, haughty, presumptuous, and rigorous towards our neighbour; if we already imagine ourselves to be little saints, and disdain to be any longer subject to direction or correction, they are beyond all doubt false and pernicious consolations, for a good tree can only bring forth good fruit.

4. Whenever we experience any of these sweetnesses and consolations, we must humble ourselves exceedingly before God, and beware of saying, because of them, *O how good am I!* No, Philothea, these consolations are not proofs of our goodness, for as I have already said, devotion does not consist in them: but let us say, *O how how good is God to such as hope in Him, to the soul that seeks Him!* He who has sugar in his mouth cannot say that his mouth is sweet, but that the sugar is sweet; so, although this spiritual sweetness is excellent, and though God, who gives it, is most good, yet it does not follow that he who receives it is good. 2. Let us acknowledge ourselves to be as yet but little children who have need of milk, and that these sugar-plums are given us because our tender and feeble spirit has need of baits and allurements to entice us to the love of God. 3. But afterwards, speaking generally and of ordinary cases, let us humbly accept of these graces and favours, and esteem them very highly, not so much on their own account, as because it is the hand of God which puts them into our hearts; as a mother does who, the more to please her child, puts the sugar-plums into his mouth with her own hand, one by one: for if the child has understanding, he sets a greater value on the tenderness and caresses of his mother than on the sweetness of the sugar-plums; and thus, Philothea, it is a great thing to have these sweetnesses, but the sweetness of these sweet-

nesses is to know that God with His loving and paternal hand puts them, as it were, into our mouth, our heart, our soul, our spirit. 4. Having thus received them humbly, let us use them carefully, according to the intention of Him who gives them. And to what end, do you think, does God give us these sweet consolations? To make us sweet towards every one, and excite us to love Him. The mother gives sugar-plums to her child to make him kiss her; let us then kiss our blessed Saviour, who gives us these sweet things; but to kiss Him is to obey Him, keep His commandments, do His will, and follow His desires; in short, to embrace Him with a tender obedience and fidelity. Whenever, therefore, we receive any spiritual consolation, we must that day be more diligent in doing good, and in humbling ourselves. 5. Besides all this, we must from time to time renounce these sweetnesses, tendernesses, and consolations, withdrawing our heart from them, and protesting that while we humbly accept them and love them, because God sends them, and they excite us to love Him, yet it is not these we seek, but God Himself, and His holy love; not the consolations, but the Consoler; not their sweetness, but the sweet Saviour; not their tenderness, but Him who is the delight of heaven and earth. It is in this manner we ought to dispose ourselves to presevere in the holy love of God, although throughout our whole life we were never to meet with any consolation; and be ready to say, as well upon Calvary as upon Tabor: *O Lord, it is good for me to be with Thee*, whether Thou be upon the Cross, or in Thy glory. 6. To conclude, I admonish you, that should you experience any great abundance of such consolations, tenderness, tears, and sweetnesses, you must confer faithfully with your spiritual director, that you may learn how to moderate and behave yourself under them; for it is written, *Hast thou found honey! Eat so much as is sufficient for thee.*[4]

[4] Prov. xxv. 16.

Chapter XIV

Of Spiritual Dryness

DO as I have now directed you, dear Philothea, when visited by consolations. But this fine weather will not always continue; but sometimes you will find yourself so absolutely destitute of all feeling of devotion, that your soul will seem to you to be a fruitless, barren desert, in which there is no trace of a pathway to find her God, nor any water of grace to refresh her, because of the dryness which seems to lay her entirely waste. Alas! how much does a poor soul in such a state deserve compassion, and especially when this dryness is very great; for then, like David, she feeds herself with tears day and night, while *her enemies that trouble her cast her in the teeth, saying*, Ah, poor wretch, *where is now thy God?* By what path shalt thou be able to find Him? Who can ever restore to thee the joy of His holy grace?[1]

What should you do then, Philothea? Examine the source from which this evil comes; for we ourselves are often the cause of our spiritual dryness. 1. As a mother refuses to give sugar to her child subject to worms, so God withholds consolations from us, when we take a vain complacency in them, and are subject to the worms of self-conceit and presumption. *O my God, it is good for me that I have been in trouble;* yes, *for before I was troubled I went wrong.*[2] 2. When we neglect to gather the sweets and delights of the love of God, at the proper season, he removes them from us in punishment of our sloth. The Israelites who neglected to gather the manna betimes in the morning, could gather none after sunrise, for it was then all melted away. 3. We are sometimes laid in the bed of sensual contentments and perishing consolations, as the sacred spouse was in the Canticles:[3] the Spouse of our

[1] Ps. xlii. 12, 13.

[2] Ps. cxviii. 71, 67.

[3] Cant. v.

soul knocks at the door of our heart, and invites us to return to our spiritual exercises; but we haggle with Him because it grieves us to quit these vain amusements and to separate ourselves from these false satisfactions; wherefore He departs, and permits us to slumber on. Afterwards, when we desire to seek Him, it is with great difficulty we find Him; and it is no more than we have justly deserved; since we have been so unfaithful and disloyal as to have refused the participation of His love, to enjoy the consolations of the world. Ah! if you still have the flour of Egypt, you will not have the manna of heaven. Bees detest all artificial colours; and the sweetnesses of the Holy Spirit are incompatible with the counterfeit delights of the world.

4. The double-dealing and subtlety which we use in our spiritual communications with our director, may also produce dryness and barrenness, for since you lie to the Holy Ghost, it is no wonder He should refuse you his consolations. You will not be sincere and ingenuous like a little child, you shall not then have the sugar-plums of little children.

5. If you have glutted yourself with worldly satisfactions, it is no wonder that you have no taste for spiritual delights. Doves that are already filled (says the old proverb) find cherries bitter. *He hath filled the hungry with good things*, says the Blessed Virgin,[4] *and the rich he hath sent empty away.* They who are filled with worldly pleasures are incapable of spiritual-delights.

6. If you have been careful to preserve the fruits of the consolations which you have received, you shall receive new ones; for to him that hath, more shall be given; but he who has not kept what was given him, but has lost it through his own fault, he shall be deprived even of that which he had not; that is to say, he shall be deprived of those graces which were prepared for him. Rain enlivens plants which have foliage, but those which have not, it deprives even of life, for it rots them altogether.

From such causes as these we lose the consolations of

[4] Luke ii. 33.

devotion and fall into dryness and barrenness of spirit. Let us then examine our consciences whether we can find any such faults in ourselves; but observe, Philothea, that this examination is not to be made with inquietude and too much curiosity; but having faithfully considered our conduct if we find the cause of the evil in ourselves, let us thank God for the discovery; for the evil is half cured when the cause of it is known; but if, on the contrary, you can find nothing in particular which seems to have occasioned this dryness, do not spend time in a more minute examination, but with all simplicity do what I now advise you.

First, humble yourself very much before God, with a deep sense of your own nothingness and misery. Alas! O Lord, what am I when left to myself, but a dry ground, which, being cracked in every direction, shows its thirst for rain from heaven; and in the meantime it is dispersed by the wind, and reduced to dust. 2. Call upon God, and beg comfort of Him. *Give me, O Lord, the comfort of Thy help again. Father, if it be possible, let this cup pass from me.*[5] Away, O thou barren north wind, that witherest my soul; and come, O gentle gale of consolations, and blow upon my garden, that its good affections may diffuse around the odour of sweetness.[6] 3. Go to your confessor, and open to him fully your heart. Let him see clearly all the windings of your soul, follow the advice he shall give you with the utmost simplicity and humility, for God, who is well pleased with obedience, frequently renders profitable the counsels we take from others, but especially from those who are the guides of our soul, even when they afford no great prospect of success; as He made the waters of Jordan healthful to Naaman, which Elisha had ordered him to use, without any appearance of human reason.[7] But, after all this, there is nothing so profitable, so fruitful in such conditions of spiritual dryness and barrenness, as not to suffer our affections to be too strongly fixed upon the desire of being delivered from them. I do

[5] Ps. li. 12. Luke xxii. 42.
[6] Cant. iv. 16.
[7] 2 Kings v. 14.

not say that we ought not simply to wish for deliverance, but that we should not set our heart upon it, but rather yield ourselves up to the pure mercy of God's special providence, that He may make use of us amidst these thorns as long as He pleases. Let us say: *O Father, if it be possible let this cup pass from me:* but let us add courageously, *yet not my will but Thine be done.* And here let us stop with as much tranquillity as possible; for God beholding us in this holy indifference, will comfort us with many graces and favours; as when He saw Abraham resolved to deprive himself of his son Isaac, He was satisfied with seeing him in this disposition of pure resignation, and comforted him with a most delightful vision and the most consolatory benedictions. We ought then, under all kinds of afflictions, whether corporal or spiritual, and amidst all distractions or subtractions of sensible devotion which happen to us, to say from the bottom of our heart, with profound submission, *The Lord gave me consolations, and the Lord has taken them away; blessed be name of the Lord.*[8] For if we continue in this humility, He will restore us His delightful favours as He did to Job, who constantly used such words in all his desolations.

Finally, Philothea, in all our spiritual drynesses and barrennesses, let us never lose courage, but waiting with patience for the return of consolation, earnestly pursue our course. Let us not omit any of our exercises of devotion, but if possible, let us multiply our good works; and not being able to present liquid sweetmeats to our dear Spouse, let us offer him dry ones; for it is all one to him, if only the heart which offers them is perfectly fixed in the resolution of loving him. When the spring is fair, the bees produce more honey, and fewer young ones; for the fine weather favouring them, they are so occupied in their harvest amongst the flowers, that they forget the production of their young; but when the spring is cold and dull, they produce more young ones, and less honey, for not being able to go abroad to gather honey, they employ themselves at home to increase

[8] Job i. 21.

and multiply their race. Thus it happens frequently, O Philothea, that the soul, finding herself in the fair spring of spiritual consolations, amuses herself so much in gathering and sucking them, that in the abundance of these sweet delights, she produces fewer good works; whilst on the contrary, in the midst of spiritual dryness, the more destitute she finds herself of the consolations of devotion, the more she multiplies her good works, and abounds in the interior generation of the true virtues of patience, humility, self-contempt, resignation, and renunciation of self-love.

It is a great mistake of many, especially of women, to believe that the service we do to God, without relish, tenderness of heart, or sensible satisfaction, is less agreeable to His Divine Majesty; on the contrary, our actions are like roses, which when fresh have more beauty, but have more strength and sweetness when dried; even so, though our works done with tenderness of heart are more agreeable to ourselves, (to ourselves, I say, who regard only our own delight,) yet, when performed in time of dryness, they possess more sweetness, and are more precious in the sight of God. Yes, dear Philothea, in times of dryness our will makes us serve God, as it were, by main force; and consequently, it must needs be more vigorous and constant than in times of consolation.

It is no such great matter to serve a prince in the quietness of a time of peace, and amongst the delights of the court; but to serve him amidst the hardships of war, in troubles and persecutions, is a true mark of constancy and fidelity. B. Angela de Foligno says, that the prayer which is most acceptable to God is that which we make by force and constraint, the prayer to which we apply ourselves not for any relish we find in it, nor by inclination, but purely to please God; to which our will carries us against our inclinations, violently forcing its way through the midst of the dryness and repugnance which oppose it. I say the same of all sorts of good works, whether interior or exterior; for the more contradictions we find in doing them, whether exterior or interior, the higher they are esteemed in the sight of God. The less there is of our own interest in the pursuit of virtues ,the brighter does the purity of divine love shine forth in them. A child readily kisses its mother when she gives him sugar ; but it is a sign of great love, if he kisses her after she has given him wormwood or any other bitter potion.

CHAPTER XV

A Confirmation and Illustration of what has been said by a notable Example

TO make the whole of this instruction more plain, I will here relate an excellent passage from the history of St. Bernard as I found it in a learned and judicious writer. It ordinarily happens, says he, to almost all who are beginning to serve God, and are not as yet experienced in the subtractions of grace nor in spiritual vicissitudes, that when they miss the sweetness of sensible devotion, and the agreeable light which invites them to run forward in the way of God, they at once lose breath, and fall into discouragement and sadness of heart. Persons skilful in the religious life assign for it this reason, viz., that our reasonable nature cannot continue long without some kind of delight, either heavenly or earthly. Now as souls which are raised above themselves by the taste of spiritual pleasure, easily renounce visible objects, so when, by the divine disposition, spiritual joy is withdrawn from them, finding themselves at the same time deprived of corporal consolations, and not being as yet accustomed to wait with patience for the return of the true sun, it seems to them as if they belong neither to heaven nor earth, and that they will remain buried in a perpetual night ; so that like little infants who are being weaned, they languish and moan, and become annoying and troublesome to every one, and especially to themselves. This is what happened in one of St. Bernard's journeys, to Geoffry of Peronne, one of the company, who had been lately dedicated to the service of God. This person, being suddenly seized with spiritual dryness, deprived of consolation, and possessed with interior darkness, began to call to mind his worldly friends, his kindred, and the riches he had lately forsaken. This produced so strong a temptation, that he was not able to prevent his behaviour from revealing it. One of his greatest confidants perceived it, and having taken an opportunity, he accosted him with mildness, and said to him privately: What means this Geoffry? How is it that you are so unwontedly pensive and melancholy? Ah, brother! answered Geoffry, with a deep sigh, I shall never more be joyful so long as I live. The other moved with pity by these words, went presently with brotherly zeal, and told all this to their common father, St. Bernard, who perceiving the danger, went into a neighbouring church to pray to God for him: whilst Geoffry in the mean time being overwhelmed with sadness, rested his head on a stone and fell asleep. Shortly after each of them arose, the one from prayer, having obtained the favour he asked, and the other from sleep, but with so serene and smiling countenance, that his friend, surprised at so great and sudden a change, could not refrain from reproaching him in a good-natured manner with the answer he had a little before given him. Geoffry replied: If I told you before, that I should never more be joyful, I now assure you that I shall never more be sorrowful.

Such was the issue of the temptation of this devout person. But observe in this narrative, dear Philothea, 1. That God commonly gives some foretaste of heavenly delight to those who enter into His service, in order to withdraw them from earthly pleasures, and encourage them to the pursuit of divine love; as a mother, who, to entice her little infant to her breast, puts honey upon her teat. 2. That nevertheless this good God also sometimes, in His wise dispensations, withholds from us the milk and the honey of consolation, that, by weaning us in this manner, we may learn to feed on the more dry and solid bread of a vigorous devotion, exercised under the trial of distaste and temptation. 3. That sometimes violent storms of temptation arise amidst these drynesses and sterilities of soul, and then we must resolutely fight against the temptations, for they come not from God; but we must patiently suffer the drynesses, since God has ordained them for our exercise. 4. That we must never lose courage amidst those interior pains and conflicts, nor say with the good Geoffry, *I shall never more be joyful;* for in the midst of night, we must await the return of day; and, on the other hand, in the fairest spiritual weather, we must not say, I shall never more be sorrowful: for as the wise man says, *In the day of prosperity, we must not be unmindful of affliction.*[1] We must hope in the midst of afflictions, and fear in the midst of prosperity; and in both we must always humble ourselves. 5. That it is a sovereign remedy to discover our evil to some spiritual friend, who can give us comfort.

[1] Ecclus. xi. 25.—VULGATE.

In fine, to conclude this very necessary caution, I observe that as in all other things so in this, our good God and our spiritual enemy have contrary designs. God seeks by these things to conduct us to a perfect purity of heart, to an entire renunciation of self-interest in what relates to His service, and to a perfect self-denial: but the evil one endeavours to make us lose courage, to make us return to sensual pleasures, to make us troublesome to ourselves and to our neighbours, in order to depreciate and disgrace holy devotion. But, provided you observe the instructions I have given you, you will greatly advance in the way of perfection under the discipline of these interior afflictions, of which I must still say a few more words before I conclude.

Sometimes spiritual distaste and sterility and dryness proceed from indisposition of body; as when, through an excess of watching, labour, or fasting, we find ourselves oppressed by lassitude, drowsiness, weariness, and such like infirmities; which, though they arise from the body, do not fail to incommode the spirit through the intimate connexion that exists between them. Now, on such occasions, we must always remember to perform some acts of virtue with the whole energy of our spirit and superior will. For although our whole soul seems to be asleep, and overwhelmed with drowsiness and fatigue, yet the actions of our spirit cease not to be very acceptable to God; and we may say at such times with the sacred Spouse[2] *I sleep, but my heart waketh.* And, as I have observed before, if there be less relish in thus performing our spiritual exercise, yet there is more merit and virtue. But the remedy on such occasions is to recruit the strength and vigour of our body by some kind of lawful relaxation. So St. Francis ordained that his religious should use such moderation in their labours, as not to oppress the fervour of their spirits.

[2] Cant. v. 2.

This glorious father himself was once assaulted and agitated by so deep a melancholy of spirit, that he could not help showing it in his behaviour; for if he was disposed to converse with his religious, he was unable; if he withdrew himself from them he was worse; abstinence and corporal mortification oppressed him, and prayer gave him no relief. He continued two years in this way, so that he seemed to be quite abandoned by God; but at length, after he had humbly suffered this violent storm, our Saviour, in an instant, restored him to a happy tranquillity. If, therefore, the greatest servants of God are subject to these shocks, how can we, who are among the least of them, be astonished if they sometimes happen to us?

PART THE FIFTH

CONTAINING EXERCISES AND INSTRUCTIONS FOR RENEWING THE SOUL, AND CONFIRMING HER IN DEVOTION

CHAPTER I

We ought every Year to Renew our Good Resolutions by the following Exercises

THE first point of these exercises consists in recognising fully their importance. Human nature easily falls from its good affections, by reason of the frailty and evil inclinations of the flesh, which load the soul, and draw her always downwards, unless she often raises herself upwards by the force of resolution; just like the birds which fall suddenly to the ground if they do not multiply the strokes of their wings, to keep themselves in flight. In order to this, dear Philothea, you must very often reiterate and renew the good resolutions you have made to serve God; lest, by neglecting to do so, you should fall back into your first state, or rather into a worse; for spiritual falls always cast us down to a lower level than that from which we mounted up to devotion.

As there is no watch, be it ever so good, but must be daily wound up, and now and then taken to pieces to remove the rust and dust, and mend or repair what may be worn or out of order, so he who has a proper care for his dear soul ought to wind it up daily to God by the foregoing exercises, and often to look if it goes truly, and to set it right, and at least once a year take it to pieces and examine its works, *i.e.*, all its affections and passions in detail, in order that any defects may be repaired; and as the watchmaker anoints the wheels, the springs, and all the movements with some delicate oil, that the motions of the wheels may be more easy, and the whole of the watch less subject to rust; so a devout person, after thus taking to pieces his heart, in order to renew it, should anoint it with the sacraments of confession and the Holy Eucharist. This exercise will repair your strength, impaired by time, rekindle your heart, reanimate your good resolutions, and make your virtues bloom again. The primitive Christians did so on the anniversary day of the baptism of our Lord, when, as St. Gregory Nazianzen relates, they used to renew the professions and protestations which they had made in baptism. Do you the same, my dear Philothea, undertaking it willingly and performing it very earnestly. Having then chosen a convenient time, according to the advice of your ghostly father, and withdrawn yourself a little into solitude, both spiritual and actual, make one, or two, or three meditations on the following points, according to the method I have prescribed in the Second Part.

Chapter II

Considerations on the Favour which God does us in calling us to His Service, considered according to the Protestations contained in the First Part

CONSIDER the articles of your protestation. The first was that you forsook, cast away, detested, and renounced for ever all mortal sin; the second that you dedicated and consecrated your soul, your heart, and your body, with all their powers and faculties, to the love and service of God; the third, that if it should happen to you to fall into any sin, you would immediately rise again by the help of God's excellent grace. Are not these your resolutions just, noble, and generous? Consider well in your soul, then, how holy and reasonable and desirable this protestation is.

2. Consider to whom you made this protestation; you made it to God. If our deliberate word given to men binds us strictly, how much more when given to God? *When Thou saidst seek ye My face, my heart said unto Thee, Thy face, Lord, will I seek.*[1]

Consider in whose presence you made this protestation; it was in the presence of the whole court of Heaven. Yes, that blessed company beheld you with emotions of joy and approval; they saw, with unspeakable love, your heart prostrate at the feet of your Saviour, consecrating itself to His service. As there was a particular joy on that occasion in the heavenly Jerusalem, so there will be now a commemoration of the same, if with a sincere heart you renew your resolutions.

4. Consider how you were led to make your protestation. Ah! how good and gracious was God to you at that time? O tell me sincerely were you not invited to it by the sweet attractions of the Holy Ghost? The cords by which God drew your little bark to this haven of safety, were composed of love and charity? How He allured you by the divine sweetness of His grace in sacraments, in spiritual reading, and in prayer. Ah! dear Philothea, you were asleep and God watched over you: He thought over your soul thoughts of peace, and meditated in your favour meditations of love.

5. Consider when God led you to these holy resolutions; it was in the flower of your age. Ah! what a happiness to learn so soon what we cannot know soon enough. St. Augustine, having been called at the age of thirty years, exclaimed: *O eternal Beauty! how late have I known Thee? Alas! I saw Thee, but did not regard Thee;* and you may well say, O

[1] Ps. xxvii. 8.

eternal sweetness! why did I not taste Thee sooner? Alas! you did not then deserve it. Therefore, acknowledging the favour God has done you in attracting you to Himself in your youth, say with David,[2] *Thou hast taught me, O my God, from my youth up until now, therefore will I tell of Thy wondrous works.* But if this has happened in your old age, ah! Philothea, what grace, that after having thus misspent your former years, God should call you before your death, and stop the course of your misery at the time when, if it had continued, you must have been miserable for eternity.

6. Consider the effects of this vocation, and, comparing what you now are with what you were, you will doubtless find in yourself great changes for the better. Do you not esteem it a happiness to know how to converse with God by prayer; to be inflamed with a desire to love Him; to have calmed and pacified many passions which used to disquiet you; to have avoided many sins and perplexities of conscience; and, lastly, to have communicated so much oftener than you would have done, uniting yourself to the sovereign source of eternal grace. Ah! how great are these favours! We must weigh them, Philothea, with the weights of the sanctuary; it is God's right hand which has done all this: *The right hand of the Lord*, says David,[3] *hath the pre-eminence, the right hand of the Lord bringeth mighty things to pass; I shall not die, but live, and declare the works of the Lord.*

After all these considerations, which, as you see, supply abundance of pious affections, conclude simply with an act of thanksgiving, and fervent prayer that you may make profit by them, and so retire with humility and great confidence in God, deferring to make resolutions till after the second article of this exercise.

[2] Ps. xvii. 47.

[3] Ps. cxviii. 16, 17.

Chapter III

On the Examination of the Soul on her progress in the Devout Life

As the second point of the exercise is somewhat long, I would say to you that in order to practise it, it is not necessary to perform it all at once, but at different times, taking what regards your conduct towards God, for one time; what relates to yourself, for another; what concerns your neighbour, for a third; and the consideration of your passions for the fourth. It is not necessary, nor is it expedient that you should perform it on your knees, except at the beginning, in placing yourself in the presence of God, and at the end, in offering your affections. The other points of the examination you may make profitably whilst walking about, or still more profitably in bed, provided you can preserve yourself against drowsiness, and keep thoroughly awake; but then to do this, you must have read them attentively beforehand. It is necessary, however, to go through the whole of the second point in three days and two nights at furthest, taking such time in each day and night as you are able; for if this exercise be gone through at times too far distant from each other, it will lose its force, and the impressions it will make will be too feeble.

After each point of the examination, you must take notice in what you come short, in what you have done wrong, and what are the principal irregularities you have discovered, that you may declare them to your confessor, in order to obtain counsel, and acquire resolution and spiritual strength to overcome them. Although on the days on which you perform this and the other exercises, it is not necessary to make an absolute retreat, yet you must do so in some measure, especially towards the evening, that you may go sooner to bed, and take that repose of body and mind which is necessary for consideration. You must also during the day time make frequent aspirations to God ; moreover, all this must be done with a heart inflamed with the love of God, and the desire of attaining perfection.

In order then to begin this examination properly.

1. Place yourself in the presence of God.

2. Invoke the Holy Ghost, begging for light and insight that you may gain a perfect knowledge of yourself, with St. Augustine who cried out to God, in the spirit of humility, "O Lord, make me to know Thee, and to know myself;" and with St. Francis, who asked of God, "Lord, who art Thou, and who am I?" Protest that you do not desire to discover your advancement in order to rejoice in yourself, but to rejoice in God : nor to glorify yourself in it, but to glorify and praise God for it.

Protest likewise that if you find, as you fear you shall, that you have made but little advancement, or even that you have gone backward, you will not be by any means dejected, nor chilled by any sort of discouragement or faintheartedness; but, on the contrary, you will encourage and animate yourself the more, and will humble yourself, and apply yourself with the assistance of divine grace, to amend your faults.

Then consider quietly, and calmly how you have behaved to the present hour, towards God, towards your neighbour, and towards yourself.

Chapter IV

An Examination of the State of the Soul toward God

HOW stands your heart with respect to mortal sin? Are you firmly resolved never to commit it, on any account whatsoever? Have you continued in this resolution from the time of your protestation till the present moment? In this resolution consists the foundation of the spiritual life.

How is your heart disposed with regard to the commandments of God. Do you find them good, pleasant, and agreeable? Ah! my daughter, he whose taste is in good order and whose stomach is healthy, loves good meats, and rejects bad.

How is your heart affected with regard to venial sins? We cannot keep ourselves so pure as not to fall now and then into such sins; but is there none to which you have a particular inclination; or, which would be still worse, is there none to which you bear an affection and love?

How is your heart affected with respect to spiritual exercises? Do you love them? Do you esteem them? Or do you find them irksome? Have you a distaste for them? To which of them do you find yourself more or less inclined? In hearing the word of God, in reading it, in discoursing of it, in meditating, in aspiring to God, in going to confession, in receiving spiritual advice, in preparing yourself for communion, in communicating, in restraining your affections; in all this what is there that goes against your heart? and if you find anything to which your heart has less inclination, examine whence this dislike arises, what is the cause of it.

How stands your heart towards God himself? Does it take pleasure in the remembrance of God? Does this remembrance leave an agreeable sweetness behind it? *Ah!* said David, *I remembered God and was delighted.* Do you find a certain readiness in your heart to love God, and a particular satisfaction in exercising this love? Does your heart delight in reflecting on the immensity of God, on His goodness, on His sweetness? If the remembrance of God comes to you amidst the occupations and vanities of the world, does it make itself room? Does it seize upon your heart? Does it seem to you that your heart turns in that direction, and, as it were, runs to meet her God? Certainly there are such souls to be found.

A wife, when her husband returns home from a far country, as soon as she sees his approach or hears his voice, although she be ever so busy and detained from him by some strong reasons, yet her heart is not withheld from him, but quits all other thoughts to think of her husband who is returned. It is the same with souls which greatly love God; let them be ever so busy, when the remembrance of God comes near them, they lose almost the thought of all things else, for joy to see that dear remembrance returned, and this is an extremely good sign.

How is your heart affected towards Jesus Christ, God and man? Is your delight about him? Bees please themselves about their honey, and wasps about corrupted things, so good souls find their contentment about Jesus Christ, and feel an extreme tenderness of love towards Him, but the wicked please themselves about vanities.

As to your tongue: how do you speak of God? Does it please you to speak well of him, according to your condition and ability? Do you love to sing His praises?

As to your works: consider whether you have at heart the exterior glory of God, and are emulous of doing something for His honour; for such as love God, love, like David, the adorning of His house.

Can you find that you have forsaken any affection, or renounced anything for the sake of God? for it is a good sign of love, to deprive ourselves of anything in favour of Him whom we love. What, then, have you hitherto forsaken for the love of God?

Chapter V

An Examination of the State of the Soul towards itself

HOW do you love yourself? Do you love yourself too much as regards this world? If so, you desire to live always here, and are very solicitous to establish yourself on this earth; but if you love yourself as regards heaven, you will desire, or at least be content, to depart from hence whenever it shall please our Lord.

Do you keep due order in the love of yourself? For it is the disorderly love of ourselves which ruins us. Now a well-ordered love requires that we should love the soul better than the body; that we should be more solicitous to acquire virtue than anything else; that we should set a higher estimation on the favour of heaven than on the honour of this low and perishable world. A well-ordered heart will oftener say within itself, *What will the angels say* if I think of such a thing? than, *What will men say?*

What kind of love have you for your own heart? Is it irksome to you to serve it in its sickness? Alas! you owe it this care to assist and procure assistance for it when passions torment it, and to lay aside all things else for this.

What do you esteem yourself before God? Doubtless nothing. It is no great humility in a fly to esteem itself nothing in comparison of a mountain; nor for a drop of water to hold itself nothing in comparison of the sea; nor for a spark of fire to hold itself nothing in respect of the sun; but humility consists in not esteeming yourselves above others, and in not desiring to be over estimated by others. How do you stand in this respect?

As to your tongue: do you sometimes boast of yourself about one thing or other? Do you flatter yourself when you speak about yourself?

As to works: do you indulge in pleasures contrary to your health? I mean in vain or unprofitable pleasures, late hours, and the like.

Chapter VI

An Examination of the State of the Soul towards our Neighbour

THE love of husband and wife ought to be sweet and calm, strong and constant, and this principally because God ordains and wills it. I say the same of the love of our children, and our near relations, and also of our friends, every one according to his degree.

But to speak in general, how is your heart affected towards your neighbour? Do you love him from your heart and for the love of God? To ascertain this clearly, you must have in mind certain troublesome and intractable people, for it is towards such that we exercise the love of God towards our neighbour; and still more with regard to such as injure us, either by their actions or words. Examine well whether your heart is free in respect to them, or whether you do not find a great repugnancy to love them.

Are you apt to speak ill of your neighbour, and especially of those who do not love you? Do you refrain from doing evil to your neighbour, either directly or indirectly? Provided you are reasonable, you will easily see how it stands with you.

Chapter VII

An Examination of the Affections of our Soul

I HAVE thus drawn out at length these points, in the examination of which lies the knowledge of the spiritual advancement which we have made; as for the examination of sins, that is for the confessions of those who do not think seriously of advancing.

Yet you must not labour upon any of these points further than to consider calmly in what state your heart has been touching them since your protestation, and what considerable faults against it you have committed.

But to abridge the whole, we must reduce the examination to a search into our passions ; and if it be troublesome to consider every point so much in detail as has been said, we may examine ourselves as to what we have been, and how we have behaved ourselves :—

In our love towards God, towards our neighbour, and towards ourselves.

In our hatred towards our own sins and towards those of others, for we must desire the extirpation both of the one and the other.

In our desires relating to riches, pleasures, and honours.

In our fear of the dangers of sin, and in that of the loss of our worldly goods, for we are apt to fear the one too much and the other too little.

In our hope, placed too much perhaps on the world and creatures, and too little on God and things eternal.

In sadness, whether it is excessive and for foolish things, or joy, whether it is excessive and for unworthy things.

In fine, what affections entangle our heart, what passions possess it, in what it has principally been led astray.

For by the passions of the soul we may judge its state, by examining them one after the other; and as a performer on the lute, by touching all the strings, finds which are out of tune, and tunes them by winding them up or letting them down; so if, after having examined the passions of love, hatred, desire, hope, sadness, and joy in our soul, we find them out of tune for that harmony which we desire to play, which is the glory of God, we should tune them by means of His grace, and the counsel of our ghostly father.

CHAPTER VIII

Affections to be exercised after this Examination

AFTER having quietly considered each point of examination, and seen how you stand with respect to it, you must afterwards proceed to the affections in this manner.

1. Return thanks to God for any amendment you may have found in your life since your Protestation, and acknowledge that it has been His mercy alone that has wrought it in and for you.

2. Humble yourself greatly before God, acknowledging that if you have not advanced much it has been through your own fault, because you have not faithfully, courageously, and constantly corresponded with the inspirations, lights, and motions which he has given you in prayer, and at other times.

3. Promise that you will eternally praise Him for the graces exercised in your favour, to withdraw you from your evil inclinations to this little amendment.

4. Ask pardon for the unfaithfulness and disloyalty with which you have corresponded with His grace.

5. Offer Him your heart, to the end that he may make Himself the entire master of it.

6. Beseech Him to make you entirely faithful to Him.

CHAPTER IX

Considerations proper for the Renewal of your Good Purposes

AFTER having made your examination, and conferred with some worthy director concerning your defects, and the proper remedies for them, take one of the following considerations every day by way of meditation, employing in it the time of your mental prayer, observing always the same method with regard to the preparations and the affections as you used in the meditations of the first part, placing yourself first in the presence of God, imploring His grace to establish you firmly in His holy love and service.

CHAPTER X

The first Consideration: of the Excellence of the Soul

CONSIDER the worth and excellence of your immortal soul, endued with an understanding which knows not only this visible world, but knows also that there are angels in paradise; knows that there is a Sovereign, good and ineffable God; knows that there is an eternity; and knows besides how to live aright in this visible world, so as to associate herself with the angels in paradise, and to enjoy God eternally.

Moreover your soul has a will capable of loving God, and incapable of hating him in himself. Look at your heart, how noble it is, and how as bees can never stay upon any corrupt thing, but only alight upon the flowers, so your heart can find rest in God alone, and no creature can satisfy it. Recall fearlessly to your remembrance the dearest and strongest affections which have heretofore possessed your heart, and judge in truth, whether in the midst of them it was not full of inquietude, and molested by tormenting thoughts, and importunate cares, amidst which your poor heart was miserable.

Alas! our hearts running after creatures, pursues them eagerly, thinking they will satisfy its desires: but as soon as it has overtaken them, it finds its satisfaction still afar off, God not being willing that our heart should find any resting place, any more than the dove which went out of Noah's ark, to the end it may return to himself from whom it proceeded. Ah! how beautiful our heart is in its nature! why do we detain it against its will in the service of creatures?

O beautiful soul! thus ought you to say, thou art capable of knowing and loving God, why wilt thou trifle away thy time about anything less than God? Since thou mayest aspire to eternity, why dost thou concern thyself about transitory moments? It was one of the regrets of the prodigal son, that while he might have fared deliciously at his father's table he was feeding at that of swine. Since, O my soul, thou art capable of God, woe to thee if thou content thyself with anything less than God.

Rouse your soul vigorously with this consideration; put her in mind that she is eternal, and worthy of eternity; encourage her with these thoughts.

CHAPTER XI

The second Consideration: of the Excellence of Virtue

CONSIDER that nothing but virtue and devotion can make your soul content in this world. See how beautiful they are, and draw a comparison between the virtues and their contrary vices. What sweetness in patience, compared with revenge? In meekness, compared with anger and vexation? In humility, compared with arrogance and ambition? In liberality, compared with covetousness. In charity, in comparison with envy? In sobriety, compared with revellings? Virtues have this admirable quality, that they delight the soul with an incomparable sweetness and satisfaction after we have exercised them; whereas vices leave the soul exceedingly wearied and disordered. Why then do we not endeavour to acquire these sweetnesses?

With respect to the vices, he who has but a few of them is uneasy, and he who has more of them is the more dissatisfied; but as for virtues, he who has but a few, has already some contentment, which increases as the virtues themselves increase.

O devout life! how lovely, how sweet, how agreeable, and delightful art thou! thou soothest our tribulations, and givest sweetness to our consolations; without thee wealth is an evil, and pleasures are full of restlessness, trouble, and deceit. Ah! he who knows thee well, may say with the Samaritan woman, *Lord, give me this water;* an aspiration very frequent with the holy mother Theresa, and St. Catherine of Genoa, although upon different occasions.

CHAPTER XII

The Third Consideration: on the Example of the Saints

CONSIDER the example of the saints in every condition of life; what have they not done to love God, and devote themselves to Him? Look at the martyrs invincible in their resolutions; what torments have they not suffered in maintaining them. But above all, behold these fair and blooming virgins, whiter than the lilies in purity, more red than the rose in charity; some at twelve, others at thirteen, fifteen, twenty, and twenty-five years of age, have endured a thousand kinds of martyrdom, rather than renounce their resolution, not only as regards the profession of their faith, but also as regards their protestation of devotion; some dying rather than forsake the state of virginity; others rather than desist from serving the afflicted, comforting the tormented, and burying the dead. Ah! what constancy has the weaker sex shown in such circumstances?

Consider the holy confessors, with what firmness have they despised the world; how invincible have they shown themselves in their resolutions, from which nothing could ever divert them; they have embraced them without reserve, and maintained them without exception. What admirable things does St. Augustine relate of his mother Monica, with what constancy did she pursue her purpose of serving God, both in marriage and widowhood; and St. Jerome also of his dear daughter Paula, in the midst of so many oppositions, in the midst of such a variety of accidents! What is there that we might not do after such excellent patterns? They were what we are; they did it for love of the same God, and for the acquisition of the same virtues; why should not we then do as much, according to our condition and vocation, for our cherished resolution and holy protestation.

CHAPTER XIII

The fourth Consideration: of the Love of Jesus Christ towards us

CONSIDER the incomparable love wherewith Jesus Christ our Lord has suffered so much in this world, and especially in the garden of Olives, and on Mount Calvary. This love beheld you; and by all these pains and sufferings obtained of God the Father good resolutions and protestations for your heart; and by the same means obtained also all that is necessary to maintain, nourish, strengthen and fulfil them. O resolution, how precious art thou, being the daughter of such a mother as the passion of my Saviour! O how ought my soul to cherish thee, since thou hast been so dear to my Jesus! Ah! Saviour of my soul, Thou didst die to purchase for me these resolutions; grant me Thy grace to die rather than part with them.

Observe, my Philothea, it is certain that the heart of our dear Jesus beheld your heart from the tree of the cross, and loved it, and by this love obtained for it all the good things you will ever have, and among them your resolutions. Yes, Philothea, we may all say with the prophet Jeremiah: *O Lord, before I had a being, thou didst behold me, and calledst me by my name:*[1] since the divine goodness did actually prepare for us all the general and particular means of our salvation, and consequently our good resolutions. As a pregnant woman prepares the cradle, the linen, and swathing clothes, and even a nurse for the child she hopes to bring forth, although it is not yet in the world, so our Saviour, designing to bring you forth to salvation, and make you His child, prepared upon the tree of the cross all that was necessary for you, your spiritual cradle, your linen, and swathing clothes, your nurse, and all that was needed for your happiness; such are all those means, all those attractions, all those graces whereby He leads your soul, and would bring it to perfection.

Ah! my God, how deeply ought we to imprint this on our memory? Is it possible that I have been loved, and so tenderly loved by my Saviour, as that he could think of me in particular, even in all these little occurrences by which he has drawn me to Himself! How then ought we to love, cherish, and convert them all to our profit? O how sweet to think that the tender heart of God thought upon Philothea, loved her, and procured her a thousand means of salvation, as much as if there had been no other soul in the world to think on: as the sun shining upon one place of the earth, enlightens it no less than if it shined on no other; so thought and cared our Lord for all His dear children, in such a way that He thought on each of them as though He had forgotten all the rest. *He loved me,*

[1] Jer. i. 5

said St. Paul, *and gave Himself for me;* as if He had said for me alone, as if He had done nothing for the rest. O Philothea, this ought to be engraved on your soul, in order to cherish and nourish your resolution, which has been so precious to the heart of our Saviour.

CHAPTER XIV

The fifth Consideration: of the eternal love of God towards us

CONSIDER the eternal love which God has borne towards you; for before our Lord Jesus Christ, as man, suffered on the cross for you, His Divine Majesty contemplated you in His Sovereign goodness, and loved you exceedingly. But when did He begin to love you? Even when He began to be God. But when did He begin to be God? Never: for He has always been God without beginning and without end; so He has always loved you from eternity; and in consequence of this love, has prepared for you those graces and favours which He has given you. Hence, speaking to you as much as to any other, by the prophet Jeremiah,[1] He says: *I have loved thee with an everlasting love, therefore with loving-kindness have I drawn thee:* and amongst other things He caused thee to make firm resolutions to serve Him.

O God, what resolutions are these which God has thought on, meditated, designed from all eternity! Ah, how dear and precious ought they be to us! What ought we not to suffer rather than give up a tittle of them! no, not if all the world should perish, for the whole world is not worth one soul, and a soul is worth nothing without good resolutions.

[1] Chap. xxxi. 3.

Chapter XV

General Affections on the preceding Considerations, and the conclusion of these Exercises

O DEAR resolutions! you are the fair tree of life which my God has planted with His own hand in the midst of my heart, which my Saviour desires to water with His blood, and make it fruitful. Rather a thousand deaths than suffer any wind to pluck thee up. No; neither vanity, nor delights, nor riches, nor tribulations, shall ever withdraw me from my design.

Alas! O Lord, it is thou thyself who hast planted and eternally preserved in thy Fatherly bosom, this fair tree for the garden of my heart. Alas! how many souls are there who have not been favoured in this manner, and how then can I ever sufficiently humble myself beneath thy mercy?

O fair and holy resolutions! if I keep you, you will keep me; if you live in my soul, my soul will live in you; live then for ever, O resolutions, you are eternal in the mercy of God, live eternally in me, and let me never forsake you.

After these affections you must particularize the means necessary to maintain your dear resolutions, and protest that you will be faithful in making good use of them; such as diligence in prayer, in the sacrament, in good works, in the amendment of your faults discovered in self-examination, in avoiding the occasions of evil, and in following the counsels which shall be given you.

Then, as if with renewed breath and strength, make a thousand protestations that you will persevere in your resolutions; and as if you held your heart, your soul, and your will in your hands, dedicate them, consecrate them, sacrifice them, and immolate them to God, protesting that you will never take them back again, but leave them in the hand of His Divine Majesty, to follow in all things and always His holy ordinances.

Pray to God to renew you entirely, and that He would give His blessing to, and strengthen, this your renewed protestation.

In this emotion of heart, go to your ghostly father, and accuse yourself of the principal faults which you may have remarked since your general confession, and receiving absolution, pronounce your protestation before him and sign it in the same manner as the first time; and in conclusion, unite your renewed heart to its Saviour, in the most holy sacrament of the Eucharist.

CHAPTER XVI

Of our Sentiments after this Exercise

ON the day you have made this renewal, and the following days, you ought frequently to repeat with heart and mouth those glowing words of St. Paul, of St. Augustine, of St. Catherine of Genoa, and of others. "No, I am no more my own; whether I live, or whether I die, I am my Saviour's. It is no longer *I* and *mine;* my *me* is Jesus, and my *mine* is His. O world, thou art always thyself, and I have hitherto been always myself; but from henceforth I shall be myself no more." No, we shall be no more ourselves, for we shall have our heart changed, and the world, that has so often deceived us, will be deceived in us; for perceiving our change only by little and little, it will think us still Esau, but it will find us to be Jacob.

All these exercises ought to dwell in the heart, and when we finish our consideration and meditation, we ought to turn gently and softly towards our ordinary affairs and intercourse, lest the liquor of our resolutions should be suddenly spilt; for it must soak and penetrate through all parts of the soul, but without effort either to the mind or the body.

Chapter XVII

An Answer to two Objections which may be made to this Introduction

THE world perhaps will tell you, Philothea, that these exercises and advices are so numerous, that he who would practise them, must apply himself to nothing else. Alas! Philothea, should we do nothing else, we should do enough, since we should do all that we ought to do in this world. But do you not see the fallacy? If it were necessary to perform all these exercises every day, they would then indeed occupy us entirely: but it is not requisite to perform them except in their proper time and place. How many civil laws there are in the Digest and the Code which must all be observed, but only as they occur, it is not necessary to observe them all every day. David, a king charged with the most difficult affairs, performed many more exercises than I have prescribed to you. St. Louis, a prince admirable both in war and peacc, and who administered justice and transacted business with unequalled care, heard two masses every day, said vespers and compline with his chaplain; made his meditation; visited hospitals; confessed, and took the discipline every Friday; heard sermons frequently, and often held spiritual conferences: yet with all this, he never lost a single occasion of promoting the public good; and his court was more splendid and flourishing than it ever had been in the time of his predecessors. Perform then boldly these exercises as I have marked them out for you, and God will give you sufficient leisure and strength to do all the rest of your affairs, yes though he should make the sun stand still for you, as he did for Joshua. We always do enough, when God works with us.

The world will perhaps say, that I assume almost

throughout the whole work, that my Philothea has the gift of mental prayer, and yet every one has it not; so that this introduction will not serve for all. It is true that I have thus assumed it, and it is no less true that every one has it not; but it is also true that almost every one, even the most dull, may have it, provided they have good guides, and are willing to take as much pains to obtain it as it deserves. But should there be some who have not this gift in any proportion whatsoever, which I think can very rarely be the case, a wise spiritual director will easily make them supply that defect, by the attention which he will teach them to give to reading, or hearing others read, the considerations included in the meditations.

Chapter XVIII

The three final and principal Counsels of this Introduction

ON the first day of every month, after your meditation, repeat the protestation in the first part:[1] and frequently protest your determination to observe it; saying with David, *I will never forget Thy commandments, for with them Thou hast quickened me.*[2] When you feel your soul in any disorder, take in hand your protestation, and humbly kneeling, recite it with your whole heart, and you will feel great relief and comfort.

Make open profession of your desire to be devout; mind I do not say of being devout, but of your desire to be devout; and do not be ashamed to practise those usual and necessary actions which conduct the soul to the love of God. Acknowledge frankly that you practise meditation; that you would rather die than commit a mortal sin; that you are resolved to frequent the sacraments, and to follow the counsels of your director, though it is often desirable

[1] See page 53. [2] Ps. cxix. 93.

not to name him; for this candid profession that we desire to serve God, and to consecrate ourselves entirely to His love, is very acceptable to His divine majesty, who would not have us be ashamed either of Him or of His cross. Besides, it forestalls many remonstrances which the world would make against such a course, and obliges us in honour to act according to what we profess. The philosophers professed themselves philosophers that they might be left at liberty to live like philosophers, so we must let it be known that we desire to live a life of devotion, that we may be left at liberty to live devoutly. If any one tell you you may live devoutly without the practice of these counsels and exercises, do not contradict him, but say mildly that you are so weak that you stand in need of more help and assistance than others.

In fine, my dearest Philothea, I conjure you by all that is sacred in heaven and on earth, by the baptism you have received, by the breasts which Jesus Christ sucked, by the charitable heart wherewith He loved you, and the bowels of that mercy in which you hope, continue to persevere in this blessed enterprise of a devout life. Our days glide away; death is at the gate: "the trumpet," says St. Gregory Nazianzen, "sounds the retreat, let every man be ready, for judgment is near." St. Symphorian's mother seeing him led to martyrdom, cried after him: "My son, my son, remember eternal life, look up to heaven, and think upon Him who reigns there; your approaching end will quickly terminate the short course of this life." My Philothea, shall I say the same to you? look up to heaven and do not forfeit it for this base earth; look down to hell, and do not cast yourself into it for transitory toys; look at Jesus Christ, and do not renounce Him for the world; and, when the labours of a devout life seem hard to you, say with St. Paul, "*I reckon that the sufferings of this present life are not worthy to be compared with the glory which shall be revealed to us.*[3]

Hail Jesus! to whom, with the Father and Holy Ghost, be all honour and glory, now and always, world without end. *Amen.*

[3] Rom. viii. 18.